9 April, 1948

Greetings on your Birthday with
best wishes for many more
from
Heather.
and
Lois

SWITZERLAND IN ENGLISH PROSE AND POETRY

THE ALPBACHFALL NEAR MEIRINGEN
(From an aquatint by Lory fils)

THE NEW ALPINE LIBRARY

SWITZERLAND IN ENGLISH PROSE AND POETRY

By

ARNOLD LUNN

EYRE & SPOTTISWOODE

LONDON

THIS BOOK, FIRST PUBLISHED IN 1947, IS PRODUCED IN COMPLETE
CONFORMITY WITH THE AUTHORIZED ECONOMY STANDARDS
AND IS MADE AND PRINTED IN GREAT BRITAIN FOR EYRE AND
SPOTTISWOODE (PUBLISHERS) LIMITED, 15 BEDFORD STREET,
LONDON, W.C.2. BY BILLING AND SONS LIMITED, GUILDFORD
AND ESHER

THE NEW ALPINE LIBRARY
GENERAL INTRODUCTION

IT is, I hope, not inappropriate that *The New Alpine Library*, a series of new books on Mountaineering, should be introduced by an Anthology selected from the mountaineering literature of the past. *Switzerland in English Prose and Poetry* is intended to serve as a link between the old and the new in Alpine literature.

The first new work in this series, *Mountain Paths*, by Mr. H. E. G. Tyndale, will be published either concurrently with this Anthology or shortly after it. Many years have passed since Mr. Tyndale and I founded the Oxford Mountaineering Club. He is today Editor of the *Alpine Journal* and Vice-President of the Alpine Club. A passage from his Alpine writing will be found in this Anthology.

I have read in typescript many of the chapters of Mr. G. Winthrop Young's new book of mountain reminiscences. Mr. Young lost a leg in the first world war, and his story of the last climb he made many years later, the ascent of the Zinal Rothorn, will rank with, if not above, the finest chapters in his established classic *On High Hills*.

Lord Schuster has also promised to contribute to the new Alpine Library.

ARNOLD LUNN.

TO
LIEUT.-COLONEL B. W. BOWDLER,
C.M.G., D.S.O.

INTRODUCTION

(1)

"NO historian," I wrote in my Introduction to *Switzerland and the English*, "seems to have commented on, much less attempted to explain, the unique character of Anglo-Swiss relations. Switzerland is the only European country which has never fought either as our ally or as our enemy, and with whom our relations have never been embittered by enmity, poisoned by alliance, or undermined by economic rivalry. . . . No historian and no critic of the contemporary theme has done justice to the fact that the English, who have to travel five hundred miles to find high mountains and good ski-ing country, should have played so great a rôle in the development of sports which are native to Switzerland."

The first contacts between the British and the Swiss originated in something more important than sport. The first British visitors to Switzerland arrived as missionaries not for the mountain cult, but for Christianity. Whether St. Luzius or St. Fridolin ever existed save in legend is doubtful, but the British mission of the sixth century belongs to history, and St. Gallus, born in West Leinster in 543, has given his name to a Swiss canton.

Throughout the Middle Ages Anglo-Swiss relations were mainly determined, directly or indirectly, by religious needs. Dr. Gustav Schirmer, in his erudite and fascinating book *Die Schweiz im Spiegel Englischer und Amerikanischer Literatur bis* 1848, has traced the links between English, Scottish and Irish ecclesiastics and Switzerland. In the same chapter he quotes from an earlier anthology of mine the lamentations of John de Bremble, who crossed the St. Bernard in the twelfth century. Of the thousands of English pilgrims who crossed the Alps on the way to Rome during the Middle Ages we have no record from any who enjoyed the experience or who admired the mountain scenery through which they passed.

The English literature of the Middle Ages is almost barren in reference to Switzerland. I found nothing worth quoting in this anthology other than a few bleak references to Switzerland in the *Morte d'Arthur*. This romance, which was published in the fourteenth century, describes King Arthur's campaign against Emperor Lucius Iberius of Rome. After defeating the Roman Emperor in France, King Arthur reached Lucerne, where he lingered "with liking enough" as many thousands of English have done since his day. "And on the Lammen-day to Lucerne he wendez, lengez thare at laysere with lykynge inowe." King Arthur mobilised a fleet on the lake and advanced towards "the strayte londez"—that is, the narrow Reuss valley—and after inflicting further defeat on the enemy endeavoured to halt them on the "Goddarde," and finally reached Italy "ouere mowntes so hye thase meruailes wayes." Dr. Ernst Brugger of Davos points out that no other Arthur romance mentions Lucerne and the Gotthard pass, and it is therefore possible that the poet, Huchown of the Awle Ryale, may have been writing from personal experience of Lucerne and the Gotthard.

(2)

The martial virtues of the Swiss were famous in England many centuries before the English discovered the beauty of the Swiss mountains. The successful resistance of the young Confederation to the attacks of Austria provoked as much astonishment in the fourteenth century as did the successful resistance of Great Britain in 1940 after the collapse of France.

As a result of these victories the military prestige of the Swiss stood so high that Henry VIII sent Sir Richard Pace to Zürich to negotiate an alliance with the Swiss League. Pace, who was a friend of Thomas More and Erasmus, wrote of the Swiss much as a modern diplomatist might write of an atom-bomb monopoly. He was convinced that a State which gained their active support would dominate Europe. His respect for their valour was balanced by his dislike for their business methods. He admitted that the Swiss kept their bargains, but he insisted that those who negotiated with the Swiss would need to be provided with ample wealth, for the greed of the Swiss was such that they threatened with death any foreign negotiator who was niggardly in his offers. The expenses of such negotiations were increased by the necessity to keep "open-house" and to entertain the Swiss on a lavish scale.

The results of Sir Richard Pace's experiences are seen in the writing of his great friend Sir Thomas More. More's disapproval of the Swiss emerges very clearly in the passage quoted from *Utopia* in the present anthology.

The English, indeed, found it difficult to disassociate the Swiss from their mercenaries, mercenaries whose martial virtues were admired and whose alleged brutality was condemned.

"Law, logicke, and the Switzers," wrote Thomas Nash in 1594, "may be hired to fight for anybody." The terror which the Switzers inspired emerges very clearly in Sir William Davenant's *News from Plymouth* (1645):

> If this Zwitz had but a two-handed sword,
> He would depopulate the island, leave none but
> His huntsman alive, the rest should be minc'd
> For his hounds.

Perhaps the peak of anti-Swiss invective is attained by Pope in his *Dunciad*:

> Around him wide a sable Army stand,
> A low-born, cell-bred, selfish, servile band,
> Prompt or to guard or stab, to saint or damn,
> Heav'n's Swiss, who fight for any God or Man.

On the other hand, many Englishmen realised that the most surprising thing about the Swiss was not their valour as soldiers, but the miracle of their survival. How did this mosaic of races avoid disintegration, surrounded as they were with powerful and often hostile neighbours? "We see the Switzers last well in spite of their diversity of religion and canton. For utility is their bond and not respect," writes Lord Bacon. Two hundred years later Boswell attributed the survival of the Swiss to their statesmanship. "Let those," he writes, "who despise the capacity of the Swiss, tell us by what wonderful policy, or by what happy conciliation of interests, it is brought to pass, that in a body made up of different communities and different religions, there should be no civil commotions, though the people are so warlike that, to nominate and raise an army is the same."

(3)

In the sixteenth and seventeenth centuries, as in the first six centuries, religion was the key to Anglo-Swiss relations.

Protestant cantons welcomed Protestants who had left England to avoid being burnt by Queen Mary, and the Catholic cantons were equally ready to receive Catholics who left England to avoid being racked and hanged by Queen Elizabeth. Such was the prestige of Protestant Swiss that the Protestant cantons intervened with good effect in the Anglo-Dutch Naval War. They drew the attention of both belligerents to the scandal provoked by this internecine struggle between two great Protestant powers, and they sent Johann Stockar, Town Clerk of Schaffhausen, to lay before Oliver Cromwell in London their proposals for mediating. Johann Stockar returned with a long letter written by Cromwell's Latin secretary, whose name, by the way, was Milton. In the peace treaty of 1654 the good offices of the Protestant cantons were recognised, and they were named as arbitrators for disputed points.

That Great Britain had a direct interest in the independence of the Protestant cantons gradually became accepted as an axiom of our foreign policy, an axiom which found practical expression as late as 1848, when Palmerston prevented Austria intervening in the civil war between the Protestant and Catholic cantons, a war which ended in the defeat of the Catholic cantons.

One of the most interesting chapters in Dr. Schirmer's book is the chapter in which he summarises the activities of British Ministers in Switzerland during the seventeenth and eighteenth centuries. In the sixteenth century England was not diplomatically represented in Switzerland, but the arguments advanced by Sir Isaac Wake, who visited Switzerland in 1589 and in 1632, proved decisive. Wake insisted that a British Ambassador could give powerful support to the Protestant cantons and could obtain first-hand information about the designs of hostile Catholic powers. His advice was accepted, and on September 29th, 1629, Sir Oliver Fleming was sent to Switzerland as British Minister. Fleming describes his reception. The senior Senator made a speech in his own language, because the Swiss considered it below their dignity to address foreign representatives in any language but their own. Great demands were made by the Swiss upon the hospitality of Ambassadors, with the result that Swiss friendship was expensive. In spite of this, Fleming returned to England with a real affection for Switzerland. He kept up his communications with the Swiss on his return home, and frequently added to his signature when writing to them "Suisse-Britannique." Dr. Schirmer quotes in this connection a charming letter which he wrote to a Swiss friend: "Sehr wurdiger Herr Gevatter, lacht mich nicht aus mit mein ungehobelt Teutsch, ich gestehe gern, dass Mundt und Fedder nicht gut Teutsch können, aber das Herz ist redlich eidgenössisch."

One of Fleming's successors, Abraham Stanyan, made an outstanding contribution to English understanding of the Swiss by his book *Account of Switzerland Written in the Year* 1714:

"The Switzers are a People equally brave in Arms, and faithful to their Engagements; who have more Esteem for the Military Virtues, than for the Civil Ones, yet are desirous to live in a perpetual Peace themselves, and to make War for others. They are perfectly able, when united, to defend themselves against any Invader, but not in a Condition to make Conquests upon their Neighbours. Their Country is crowded with People, which generally makes the Riches of other Nations, but for want of Trade, increase the Poverty of this. It produces none of the Superfluities of Life, and not enough of the Necessaries; yet by the Advantage of their Situation, both are supplied them by their Neighbours at reasonable Rates. It happens to be placed almost in the Center of Europe, without being thoroughly known, and they are courted for their Valour by some of their Neighbours, who scarce allow them any other good Quality. One may say of their Republicks, as of private Men: They are placed in a certain Mediocrity of Fortune, which puts them below Envy, and above Contempt. One finds among them none of the gaudy Pleasures of Courts, but a great deal of the Satisfaction which proceeds from a quiet easie Life. In short, they have more Wit, and perhaps less Sincerity, than the World allows them; and seem to conceal some of the Subtleties of the Italian, under the Frankness of the German. Their Virtues are natural to them; and their Vices chiefly owing to the Temptations, which Men struggling with Difficulties are apt to fall under."

(4)

The discovery of mountain beauty dates from about the middle of the eighteenth century, and was associated with a new fashion in literature and philosophy—"The Return to Nature."

Rousseau, high priest of this sect, was also one of the first and most influential prophets of the mountain cult. The contrast between the virtue of man in a primitive state of nature and man degraded by civilisation is the key to his philosophy. The idealisation of man in a state of nature led by a natural transition to the idealisation of the mountain peasant, but Rousseau's encounters with mountain peasants were as infrequent as those of Housman with Shropshire lads, and he did not expose his ideological admiration for mountains to the coarse test of mountain travel.

The English apostles of the "Return to Nature" were as uninterested as Rousseau in the real Switzerland, but they wrote with great eloquence about ideological Swiss peasants. The freedom-loving Swiss are the heroes of many eighteenth-century poems such as James Thomson's *Liberty*, Collins's *Ode to Liberty*, and George Keate's *Helevetiad*, poems which throw far more light on the eighteenth-century Englishman than on the eighteenth-century Swiss. Characteristic of this school is Goldsmith's *Traveller*:

> turn we to survey
> Where rougher climes a nobler race display,
> Where the bleak Swiss their stormy mansions tread
> And force a churlish soil for scanty bread.
> Though poor the peasant's hut, his feast though small,
> He sees his little lot the lot of all;
> Sees not contiguous palace rear its head,
> To shame the meanness of his humble shed;
> No costly lord his sumptuous banquet deal,
> To make him loathe his vegetable meal. . . .
> Dear is that shed to which his soul conforms,
> And dear that hill which lifts him to the storms;
> And as a child, when scaring sounds molest,
> Clings close and closer to the mother's breast,
> So the loud torrent, and the whirlwind's roar,
> But bind him to his native mountains more.

The British were the leading pioneers of the æsthetic revolution which discovered beauty in the Swiss mountains. In the latter half of the eighteenth century the majority of those who visited Switzerland for the sake of its scenery were British. Wäber indeed assures us that of twenty guests in a Swiss inn at this period it was usual to find that fourteen were British.

Whereas the earlier travellers and residents in Switzerland

often wrote with great affection of the Swiss people and ignored the scenery, some of the later travellers wrote with greater enthusiasm of the scenery than of the people. Maria Helen Williams, for instance, who dabbled in French revolutionary politics and who escaped to Switzerland in 1794, found it harder to say goodbye to Switzerland than to the Swiss.

"With sincere reluctance I bade Switzerland farewell. Who can leave such a country without regret? If we find its governments defective, or its societies dull, there is always a resource against every feeling of dislike, or of weariness, in the meditation of that glorious scenery, the view of which renders the mind insensible to human evils by lifting it beyond their reach. Switzerland has opened to me a new world of ideas; its landscapes are indelibly impressed upon my memory; whenever the delightful images of nature present themselves to my imagination, I find that I have been thinking only of Switzerland; and whenever I amuse myself in that sort of visionary architecture, called castle-building, my chateau is always seated at the foot of an Alpine hill, a torrent stream rolls invisibly past the dwelling, and an enormous glacier lifts its snows in the neighbourhood."

In the pages of Thomas Martyn's *Sketch of a Tour through Swisserland* (1787) we find many compliments to the Swiss for their cleanliness, honesty, and love of freedom, and also complaints of overcharging. To these complaints the Swiss hotel keepers seem to have replied with a candour unknown in modern times, for they answered with unrivalled composure that the summer was their hunting season, and the English the noblest game, or alternatively that the British were ten times as rich as other people, and should not therefore complain if they are expected to pay twice as much.

Most of the references to the Swiss in the English literature of the period are friendly and flattering. Byron's "Switzerland is a curst, selfish, swinish country of brutes, placed in the most romantic region of the world. I never could bear the inhabitants" is quite unrepresentative. That "the knowledge of a thing is the daughter of love" is a maxim of Leonardo da Vinci. The reverse is also true. Mountain people are often lacking in superficial charm and do not display their better qualities to the casual stranger. Love is the daughter of knowledge, and it is not in the least surprising that the more favourable verdicts on

B

the Swiss should have emanated from those Englishmen who had either lived for long periods in the country, or, like Coxe, a discerning and friendly critic, had travelled extensively in Switzerland.

(5)

Men perceived that the mountains were beautiful long before they discovered the joys of mountaineering. Indeed, though isolated ascents were made before the eighteenth century, it was the ascent of Mont Blanc in 1786 by Paccard and Balmat, both of Chamonix, that first turned men's minds to mountaineering. Many of the great Alpine peaks had been climbed before the British attacked the High Alps in earnest. Mont Vélan, the Gross Glockner, the Titlis, the Rheinwaldhorn, the Dent du Midi, the Wetterhorn, Jungfrau, Finsteraarhorn, the Piz Bernina, Pelvoux and Gross Venediger were all conquered by continental climbers before the Alpine Club was founded on December 22nd, 1857. None the less, the British were the first to popularise the sport. The Alpine Club is the mother of all Alpine clubs, *The Alpine Journal* is the oldest of mountaineering journals.

Most of the continental pioneers of mountaineering were content to climb a single mountain as a stunt, and though there were exceptions, such as Father Placidus a Spescha, who was in some sense the father of sporting mountaineering, we may fairly claim for the British the credit of transforming mountaineering from the pursuit of a few eccentrics into a worldwide sport.

Due credit must be given to the Swiss, French, Italian and Austrian guides whose assistance was in most cases an indispensable factor in success, but we must also concede that British enterprise was largely responsible for transforming the chamois hunter into a skilled Alpine guide. Certainly British mountaineers dominated the Alpine scene not only in the Golden Age which closed with the conquest of the Matterhorn by Hudson and Whymper and in the Silver Age associated with Mummery and the conquest of the Chamonix aiguilles, but also in the final phase before the First World War when Geoffrey Young and Ryan and Owen Glynne Jones were making Alpine history.

Some magnificent ascents were made by British climbers

during those years of uneasy armistice between the two world wars; but it must be admitted that the last and greatest of Alpine problems were solved in this period not by the British, but by Swiss, French, Italian, German and Austrian mountaineers. It was perhaps inevitable that climbers fortunate enough to live in or near Alpine country should eventually take our place as the leaders in Alpine exploration.

It is perhaps in the realm of literature that the British made the most notable contribution to the sport. I do not think that I shall be accused of undue nationalism by my friends abroad if I claim that it is to English writers that we owe the supreme classics of Alpine literature. It is not only in the interpretation of the romance of mountaineering that British writers have led the way. The great family of "Climbers' Guides," upon which guideless climbers depend, descends from Martin Conway's *Zermatt Pocket Book* and Coolidge's *Climbers' Guides*.

(6)

1865, the year which witnessed the conquest of the Matterhorn, and with that conquest the end of the golden age of mountaineering, also witnessed the beginning of the exploitation of the Alpine winter by foreign visitors. In that year a German political refugee, by name Alexander Spengler, persuaded two consumptives to spend the winter in Davos. Both recovered, and to this fact Mr. W. G. Lockett attributes "the beginning of the exploitation of the Alpine winter." Invalids were among the first sportsmen at Davos, and it was the British invalids who transformed tobogganing, a mere means of locomotion in the eyes of the native Swiss, into a sport. At Davos the moving spirit in this development was the distinguished author, John Addington Symonds. At St. Moritz, the foundation of the Cresta run was due to the initiative of three English visitors, George Robertson, Digby Jones and W. H. Bulpett.

In 1883 a passing Nowegian presented the Canons of St. Bernard with a pair of ski, but it was not until 1889 that the first expert Norwegian ski-runner appeared in Switzerland.

The English were among the first to introduce ski-ing to Switzerland. In 1888, a year before the Norwegian O. Kjelsberg introduced ski to Winterthur, Colonel Napier brought a pair of ski to Davos, and Katharine Symonds (now Dame Katharine Furse) made a few experiments with them.

In 1891 Gerald Fox introduced ski-ing to Grindelwald. On March 24th, 1894, Sir Arthur Conan Doyle, guided by the brothers Branger of Davos, crossed the Maienfelder Furka from Davos to Arosa, this being the first full day's tour on ski by an Englishman, little more than a year after the first real ski expedition in the Alps, the crossing of the Pragel Pass (1,544 metres) between Glarus and the Muotatal by a Swiss party led by Christoph Iselin. In December 1898 the present writer began to ski at Chamonix.

In the winter of 1901-1902 the brothers Richardson visited Davos. E. C. Richardson, by common consent the father of British ski-ing, was not only the founder of the Ski Club of Great Britain (1903), but is also regarded by the Swiss as a pioneer of ski-ing in Switzerland.

Though the British played a less prominent part in the pioneer phase of ski-mountaineering than in the golden age of mountaineering, many important first ski ascents were accomplished by a British skier, notably The Dom, the highest mountain wholly in Switzerland, ascended on ski to the actual summit, the Weisshorn, the Eiger from the Eigerjoch, etc. Two books by Englishmen, *Alpine Ski-ing* and Gerald Seligman's classic, *Snow Structure*, have been acclaimed by continental skiers as outstanding contributions to our knowledge of winter and spring snowcraft.

(7)

It was in competitive ski-ing rather than in ski-mountaineering that the British influence was most marked.

In Norway and Sweden the classic competitions were decided on the combined results of a long-distance race, in which short ascents and descents succeeded each other, and a jumping competition. The *langlauf* (long-distance race) developed as naturally out of the gentle terrain in Scandinavia as the downhill race out of the mountainous terrain in the Alps, but the Alpine people, instead of deciding their championships by racing down their magnificent mountains, ran their *langlauf* races along their valley floors. The first protest against this method of deciding championships and the first published defence of downhill racing (with the veto on stick-riding) as the logical method of deciding Alpine championships will be found in my book *Ski-ing*, published in 1913.

My first task was to convert our own people, for the Ski Club of Great Britain followed Norwegian precedents and awarded its championship on the "classic combination" (*langlauf* and jumping). Our next problem was to obtain support in Switzerland, where our first ally was Walter Amstutz, and the Anglo-Swiss Universities' ski race, which he and I organised together, was the first international event decided on the combined result of a pure downhill race and a slalom race. The slalom in its modern form is an invention of my own and has nothing but the name in common with the old slalom style competition, in which marks were given for style. A slalom is a race down a course defined by pairs of flags *through* which competitors are required to pass. The flags are arranged so as to test every variety of turn, long and sweeping, short and abrupt.

That there should be opposition to the slalom was inevitable, but the skiers of the future will find it difficult to understand how anybody could ever have opposed the official recognition of downhill racing. It was not until the Oslo congress of 1930 that I succeeded, as the delegate of the Ski Club of Great Britain, in obtaining international recognition for downhill and slalom races. The rules which were adopted at Oslo were, to all intents and purposes, the same as the British Ski Racing Rules. It is no exaggeration to say that the British completely revolutionised competitive ski-ing.

In the campaign for downhill racing, the Kandahar Ski Club, which was founded at Mürren on January 30th, 1924, played a decisive rôle. The Club takes its name from the world's senior challenge cup for downhill ski-racing, the Roberts of Kandahar.

Every Alpine valley was potentially capable of producing ten times as many first-class racers as Great Britain. The Alpine cracks skied for five months in the year, whereas many of our young racers could not spend more than three or four weeks on the snow. In spite of these handicaps we did very well. Our ladies won two world championships and in the last peace winter our University teams beat the Swiss and Italian Universities. Readhead won the Duke of Kent and Marion Steedman won the Ladies' Arlberg-Kandahar.

Finally Geoffrey Appleyard won the Anglo-Norwegian race

in Norway in 1938 and 1939. Appleyard was awarded the D.S.O., M.C. and Bar before his death in action.

(8)

Henry James, in his story *At Isella*, attributed to his hero regrets which do not trouble those undiscerning visitors for whom Switzerland is nothing more than an arena for athletic feats. Of the old Burgher mansions in the Swiss towns through which he is passing, the narrator writes: "I wondered of course who lived in them, and how they lived and what was society in Altdorf, longing plaintively, in the manner of roaming Americans, for a few stray crumbs from the native social board, with my fancy vainly beating its wings against the great blank wall, behind which, in travel-haunted Europe, all gentle private interests nestle away from intrusion. Here, as elsewhere, I was struck with the mere surface-relation of the Western tourist to the soil he treads. He filters and trickles through the dense social body in every possible direction, and issues forth at last the same virginal waterdrop. 'Go your way,' these antique houses seemed to say, from their quiet courts and gardens; 'the road is yours and welcome, but the land is ours. You may pass and stare and wonder, but you may never know us!' "

The Alpine clubmen invaded with success the privacy of the glacier world, but few of them passed the barrier of "the great blank wall behind which all gentle private interests nestle away from intrusion." They knew, of course, the great hotel-keeping dynasties, and they knew the guides, but there were very few contacts between the British and Swiss amateur mountaineers, or between the University mountaineering clubs in Switzerland and in Great Britain. Again, whereas it was the *assistance* of the great guides which rendered possible the triumphs of the Victorian mountaineers, it was *in competition* against the best guides that the Georgian ski-racers achieved their most prized successes.

The old affectionate but semi-feudal relationship between the "Herr" and a great guide gave way to a newer and more egalitarian relationship, divorced from the cash-nexus, between men who competed on equal terms. In *Die Schnee Hase* (1945) Dr. Herman Gurtner, one of the founders of the Swiss University Ski Club, pays a moving tribute to the British racers. After pointing out that at first the Swiss skied better than the British, he adds: "but they had some advantages over us. Their conception of sport was much more developed than our own, clarified through an age-old tradition. While they analysed our ski technique, we also profited from the mutual relationship. We learned to reinforce our balance on ski with a balance of the spirit. We learned to lose with a smile."

Many of those gallant boys who carried British colours to victory in races against the skiers of Alpine countries have since died in battles on which the fate of the world depended. Some of them fought as fighter pilots in the Battle of Britain under the command of a former President of the Ski Club of Great Britain, Lord Dowding. "The new sport," writes Lord Schuster, "has brought other changes. Ski-ing is a sport for the young. It is essentially gay and care-free; and its spirit is essentially unlike the somewhat serious outlook of the older mountaineers." Many of the Victorian mountaineers sought among the mountains for a substitute for religion. At its best this search for the ultimate reality beyond the temporal beauty of the mountains produced some noble and moving confessions of faith, one of which is quoted in the pages that follow. But the religion which has no surer foundation than mountain worship degenerates all too easily into religiosity. No ski-racer has equated high-speed ski-ing with religion, or the mountains with cathedrals, and it may well be that D'Egville's boisterous account of the "Inferno" race from the summit of the Schilthorn to Lauterbrunnen will distress those for whom "mountains are things to be reverenced and not treated as slides." As one who is equally happy in the esoteric world of mountain initiates and also in the less sacerdotal society of light-hearted skiers, I am grateful for the glorious variety of happiness which mountains and hills provide. "The ski-ing fraternity," to quote from *The Fell and Rock Climbing Journal*, "seem to move in a friendly and open-minded atmosphere. Isn't there too much of the feeling in some mountaineering circles that ski-racers are inferior beings?" Fortunately the old prejudices are dying, and I am sanguine enough to hope not only that skiers will read with interest the mountaineering parts of this anthology, but also that the less sectarian mountaineers will recognise in the passion for ski-racing a spirit not wholly alien to the mountaineering ethos, for the asceticism that prefers the happiness which is a by-product of danger, discomfort and pain, is common to ski-racing and to the noblest of all sports, mountaineering.

(9)

The two world wars have greatly increased our debt to the Swiss. Thousands owe their lives to this miniature mosaic of races in the heart of Europe. In the First World War prisoners suffering from consumption, serious illness or grave wounds were interned in Switzerland. Old men, women and children, repatriated from occupied France by arrangement with the German Government, passed through Switzerland on their journey home. They arrived in pitiable condition. They left well-clothed and well-shod. In Zürich, Basle, and Schaffhausen it was almost a disgrace for a well-to-do family to have more than one spare suit of clothes.

Major Lord Iddesleigh, who was specially concerned with prisoners of war, tells me that it is impossible to speak too highly of the courage with which the Swiss stood up to the Japanese in the uphill struggle to secure some amelioration of the conditions of the prison camps.

There has been a marked deterioration in the climate of Europe between the two world wars. In the First World War the English-speaking world was united in defence of the rights of small nations and oppressed nationalities, but today it is the fashion in progressive circles to sneer at the weak and to appease the strong. "The small weak State," writes the distinguished Socialist Sidney Dark, "is an international nuisance. It is generally misgoverned. It is nearly always jealous of its neighbours." To this Mr. Voigt replied in an editorial in *The Nineteenth Century* (April 1943): "The fashionable contempt for small countries is not reached by any process of reasoning, but belongs to the irrational cult which has been called 'the cult of the colossal,' and arises out of a certain coarseness of mind which is more impressed by some crude monstrosity in monumental granite than by the most exquisite cameo."

No juster tribute to the value of Swiss neutrality has ever been paid than the tribute from the same writer in a later issue (November 1944) of the same periodical:

"Apart from the issue of peace and war, there are reasons why it is necessary that there should always be neutrals, reasons that arise out of the very substance of our civilised heritage. Future generations will, perhaps, be grateful that in the Second World War, when Europe was being destroyed, there was a country called Switzerland, which remained neutral, not because she was inadequately conscious of wider and deeper issues, but because she was supremely conscious of them, and was, when disaster came upon the world, ready for the armed defence of a neutrality that meant not only the preservation of her own peace, but of the common heritage. Those who live in countries at war to-day will the better realise—perhaps with anguish— how that heritage has been stricken by the outer violence and increased decay, if they will consider the present state of Switzerland, glancing at Swiss books and periodicals, following an occasional discussion about art, letters, science, philosophy, politics, God, men, and Nature, as conducted in Switzerland, and marking the tone, the balance, the urbanity, the high level, the tolerance (though also the strong, mature conviction that will set a period upon tolerance and so preserve convictions content). They will then see that in Switzerland a light, which elsewhere burns with flickering or murky flame or has been extinguished altogether, burns clear, bright and steady. If it be said, a hundred years from now, perhaps, that despite the many years of destructive and murderous violence and inner disintegration, there was, after all, something imperishable in the European heritage, it shall be said, even if but by way of corollary, that Europe was saved, not only by the release of those who overthrew the armed might of Germany, but also by the Swiss, because they kept a light burning amid what, even with the approach of victory, indeed, even after victory had been won, threatened to become universal darkness."

(10)

The mountain lover who searches in vain for some favourite passage in this anthology should not unhesitatingly assume that I am blind to its merits, for the passage may be included either in the original edition (1913) of my anthology, *The Englishman in the Alps*, or in the revised and enlarged edition which will be republished before long.

As the present anthology is intended to be representative and complete, many passages inevitably appear in both anthologies, but I have made a special effort to include as much new reading matter as possible. I have, unless there was good reason for the contrary, quoted different passages from the same authors, with the result that the new material in this anthology exceeds in total the entire material in *The Englishman in the Alps*.

The scope of this anthology is far less restricted than that of previous Alpine anthologies. It includes not only ski-ing and winter sports, but also other aspects of Switzerland partially or wholly ignored in earlier anthologies, and therefore writers who are wholly uninterested in the Swiss mountains but very interested in the Swiss people are represented in this book. Ski-ing was not represented in my anthology or in any previous anthology.

On my travels I have often regretted my inadequate knowledge or failing memory when some brief reference in a guide book to a celebrity associated with the place I am visiting evokes the wish that I knew more about that celebrity or the circumstances of his sojourn in or visit to a place through which I was passing.

I hope that this book will be read among the scenes which it describes, and I believe that many readers will be glad, to quote only one example, not only to re-read the appropriate passages from Byron and Shelley beside the shores of Lac Leman, but also to be reminded of the circumstances which brought them together at Geneva during the summer of 1816. Again, the passages which I have quoted from Whymper's *Scrambles amongst the Alps* will gain in interest if those who are not mountaineers and who have no specialised knowledge of Alpine history will first read my introductory notes on the Matterhorn drama, and I believe that even mountaineers will find in those notes some facts which will be new to them, such as the passage quoted from an article by Leslie Stephen which has never been republished and a quotation from a hitherto unpublished letter of Whymper's.

In many cases I have drawn attention to the author's age at the time he wrote the passage quoted or made the ascent described. It is sometimes difficult to remember that famous men were once young. We tend to add a decade or two to their age. I find it difficult, for instance, to remember that Whymper was only twenty-five when he climbed the Matterhorn.

In this anthology, as in *Switzerland and the English*, I am restricted by my terms of reference to the English people, for these books are designed, among other things, to illustrate the influence which the British have exercised in the discovery of the cultural, æsthetic and sporting possibilities of the Swiss mountains; but in the new edition of *The Englishman in the Alps* "Englishman" will be deemed to include all the English-speaking people, an interpretation which is legitimate, for nobody could possibly publish an anthology under the title "The English Speaker in the Alps," however anxious he might be to include, as I intend to include, quotations from American writers who have loved Switzerland.

And now all that remains is to express once again my most sincere thanks to Lieut.-Colonel B. W. Bowdler, C.M.G., D.S.O., to whom this book is dedicated, and to Lieut.-Colonel G. R. de Beer, F.R.S., both of whom have read these proofs, and of course to all the authors and publishers and photographers who have allowed me to use copyright material.

I am indebted to my friend Herr G. Michel of Interlaken for the loan of the block from which the frontispiece is reproduced. Gabriel Lory fils was producing his charming coloured prints in the first decade of the present century.

Finally, I should like to express my thanks to Miss Dorothy Cast, who has seen this book through the press.

ACKNOWLEDGMENTS

My thanks are due for permission to quote copyright material from the following books:

For the Heathen are Wrong, by Eugene Bagger (Eyre and Spottiswoode); *The Path to Rome,* by Hilaire Belloc (George Allen and Unwin); *The Alps from End to End,* by Lord Conway (Constable); *Mountain Memoirs,* by Lord Conway (Cassels); *Monte Leone in May,* by Lord Dowding, *The British Ski Year Book; The Inferno Race,* by A. H. D'Egville; *The Making of a Mountaineer,* by George Finch, F.R.S. (Arrowsmith); *Rainbow Mountains,* by Miss Mary FitzGibbon, *Journal of the Fell and Rock Climbing Club; Hearts and Pomegranates,* by Dame Katharine Furse, C.B.E.; *Casting Rosemary on the Graves,* by Squadron Leader K. D. Foster, R.A.F., *British Ski Year Book; L.S.,* by Thomas Hardy; *The Romance of Mountaineering,* by R. L. G. Irving (J. M. Dent and Sons); *Autobiography* (unpublished), by Hugh Kingsmill; *An Atheist in Heaven,* by Anthony Viscount Knebworth, *Kandahar Review,* 1933; *Switchback,* by Brian Lunn (Eyre and Spottiswoode); *Through a Glass Darkly,* by Captain Peter Lunn, *The British Ski Year Book,* 1944; *Climbing Days,* by Dorothy Pilley (Bell); *Early Days,* by E. C. Richardson, *The British Ski Year Book; St. Gervais,* by Michael Roberts (Jonathan Cape); *Men, Women and Mountains,* by Lord Schuster (Ivor Nicholson and Watson); *Snow Structure and Ski Fields,* by Gerald Seligman (Macmillan); *The Treasures of the Snow,* by Gerald Seligman, *The British Ski Year Book; Climbs and Ski Runs,* by Frank Smythe (W. Blackwood and Sons); *Over Tyrolese Hills,* by Frank Smythe (Hodder and Stoughton); *The Playground of Europe,* by Leslie Stephen (Longmans); *First Affections,* by H. E. G. Tyndale, *The Alpine Journal,* 1942; *Scrambles Amongst the Alps,* by Edward Whymper (John Murray and Sons); *Tour on the Continent,* by Dorothy Wordsworth (Dove Cottage Trustees: *On High Hills,* by G. W. Young (Methuen); *Wind and Hill,* by G. W. Young (Smith, Elder and Co.).

LIST OF ILLUSTRATIONS

SWITZERLAND IN ENGLISH
PROSE AND POETRY

JOHN DE BREMBLE

De Bremble was a monk of Canterbury who crossed the Alps in February,
1188.

The Mountain Terror

PARDON me for not writing. I have been on the Mount of
Jove; on the one hand looking up to the heavens of the
mountains, on the other shuddering at the hell of the valleys;
feeling myself so much nearer to heaven that I was more sure
that my prayer would be heard. "Lord," I said, "restore me to
my brethren, that I may tell them, that they come not into this
place of torment." Place of torment, indeed, where the marble
pavement of the stony ground is ice alone, and you cannot set
down a foot safely; where, strange to say, although it is so
slippery that you cannot stand, the death, into which there is
every facility for a fall, is certain death. I put my hand in my
scrip, that I might scratch out a syllable or two to your sincerity;
lo, I found my ink-bottle filled with a dry mass of ice: my fingers,
too, refused to write: my beard was stiff with frost, and my
breath congealed into a long icicle. I could not write the news
I wished.

ST. THOMAS MORE
(1477-1535)

According to J. H. Lupton the word "Zapoletes" is derived from the Greek
Ζαπωλῆται or Ζαπωλητοί—i.e., "those who sell themselves freely." Mr.
Lupton points out that More's contemporaries would rightly interpret this as
a reference to the Swiss even without the marginal note in the first edition,
"Gens haud ita dissimilis Elvetiis."

"They be borne onelye to warre"

THEREFORE they hiere soldiours oute of all countreis
and sende them to battayle, but cheifly of the Zapoletes.
This people is 500 myles from Utopia eastewarde. They be

hideous, savage and fyerce, dwellynge in wild woodes and high mountaines, where they were bredde and brought up. They be of an harde nature, hable to abide and susteine heate, colde, and labour, abhorrynge from all delicate deintyes, occupyenge no husbandrye nor tyllage of the ground, homelye and rude both in buildinge of their houses and in their apparel, geven unto no goodnes, but onely to the breedinge and bringynge up of cattel. The moste parte of their lyvinge is by huntynge and stealynge. They be borne onelye to warre, whyche they diligently and earnestelye seek for. And when they have gotten it, they be wonders glad thereof. They goo furthe of theire countreye in greate companyes together, and whosoever lackethe souldyours, there they proffer theire service for small wages. This is onelye the crafte they have to gette theire livyinge by. They maynteyne theire lyfe by sekinge theire deathe. For them whomesyth they be in wayges they fyghte hardelye, fyerslye, and faytherfullye. But they bynde themselfes for no certeyne tyme. But upon this condition they entre into bondes, that the nexte daye they wyll take parte with the other syde for greatter wayges, and the nexte daye after that, they wyll be readye to come backe agayne for a lytle more moneye. There be fewe warres thereawaye, wherein is not a greate numbre of them in bothe partyes. Therefore it dayelye chauncethe that nye kynsefolke whyche were hiered together on one parte, and there verye frendelye and familiarlye used themselfes one wyth another, shortely after being separate in contrarye partes, runne one againste another envyouslye and fyercelye: and forgettinge bothe kindred and frendeshype, thruste theire swordes one in another. And that for none other cause, but that they be hyered of contrarye prynces for a lytle moneye. Whyche they doo so hyghlye regarde and esteame, that they will easelye be provoked to chaunge partes for a halfepenye more wayges by the daye. So quyckelye they have taken a smacke in covetesenes. Whyche for all that is to them no proffyte. For that they gette by fyghtynge, immedyatelye they spende unthryftelye and wretchedlye in ryotte. This people fighteth for the Utopians agaynste all nations, bycause they geve them greatter wayges, then annye other nation wyll. For the Utopians lyke as they seke good men to use wel, so they seke these evell and vicious men to abuse. Whome, when neade requirethe, with promisses of greate rewardes they putte forthe

into great jeopardyes. From whens the mooste parte of them
never cummeth againe to aske their rewardes. But to them that
remaine alive they paye that which they promissed faithfully,
that they maye be the more willinge to put themselfes in like
daunger another time. Nor the Utopianes passe not how many
of them they bring to destruction. For they beleve that they
should doo a verye good deade for all mankind, if they could
ridde out of the worlde all that fowle stinking denne of that
most wicked and cursed people.

HERMANN KIRCHNER OF MARBURG
(*Circa* 1580)
The Height of Hills

WHO is so crabbed, austere, & angry, whom the humanity, affability, gentleness, & placability of our consorts
and companions, that communicate with vs in our iourneys
and Innes, wil not change? Who is so tender, effeminate, &
cowardly, whom the heat of the sun, cold, snow, raine, hard
seats, stony pillows, and such infinite inconueniences of trauels,
so many wailayings, & dangers of theeus, wil not make more
couragious & valiant? Who is so simple, improuident and
incontinent, whom the subtilty of spies, the wonderful cunning
of Inkeepers and baudes, and the great danger of his life
will not stirre vp to vigilancy, prudence and temperance? . . .
What I pray you is more pleasant, more delectable, and more
acceptable vnto a man then to behold the heighth of hilles, as it
were the very Atlantes themselues of heauen? to admire *Hercules*
his pillers? to see the mountaines Taurus and Caucasus? to view
the hill Olympus, the seat of *Iupiter*? to passe ouer the Alpes
that were broken by *Annibals* Vineger? to climbe vp the
Apennine promontory of Italy? from the hill Ida to behold the
rising of the Sunne before the Sunne appeares? to visite
Pernassus and Helicon, the most celebrated seates of the Muses?
Neither indeed is there any hill or hillocke, which doth not
containe in it the most sweete memory of worthy matters.

From *Coryats Crudities*, 1611. (An Oration
in praise of Trauell in generall.)

JOHN EVELYN
(1620-1706)
The Simplon Pass

THE first day we got as far as Castellanza, by which runs a considerable river into Lago Maggiore; here, at dinner, were two or three Jesuits, who were very pragmatical and inquisitive, whom we declined conversation with as decently as we could: so we pursued our journey through a most fruitful plain, but the weather was wet and uncomfortable. At night, we lay at Sesto.

The next morning, leaving our coach, we embarked in a boat to carry us over the lake (being one of the largest in Europe), and whence we could see the towering Alps, and amongst them the great San Bernardo, esteemed the highest mountain in Europe, appearing to be some miles above the clouds. Through this vast water passes the river Ticinus, which discharges itself into the Po, by which means Helvetia transports her merchandizes into Italy, which we now begin to leave behind us. . . .

The next morning, we mounted again through strange, horrid, and fearful crags and tracts, abounding in pine-trees, and only inhabited by bears, wolves, and wild goats; nor could we anywhere see above a pistol-shot before us, the horizon being terminated with rocks and mountains, whose tops, covered with snow, seemed to touch the skies, and in many places pierced the clouds. Some of these vast mountains were but one entire stone, betwixt whose clefts now and then precipitated great cataracts of melted snow, and other waters, which made a terrible roaring, echoing from the rocks and cavities; and these waters in some places breaking in the fall, wet us as if we had passed through a mist, so as we could neither see nor hear one another, but, trusting to our honest mules, we jogged on our way. The narrow bridges, in some places made only by felling huge fir-trees, and laying them athwart from mountain to mountain, over cataracts of stupendous depth, are very dangerous, and so are the passages and edges made by cutting away the main rock; others in steps; and in some places we pass between mountains that have been broken and fallen on one another; which is very terrible, and one had need of a sure foot and steady head to climb some of these precipices, besides that they are harbours for bears and wolves, who have sometimes assaulted travellers. In these straits, we frequently alighted, now freezing in the snow, and anon frying by the reverberation of the sun against the cliffs as we descend lower, when we meet now and then a few miserable cottages so built upon the declining of the rocks, as one would expect their sliding down. Amongst these, inhabit a goodly sort of people, having monstrous gullets, or wens of flesh, growing to their throats, some of which I have seen as big as an hundred pound bag of silver hanging under their chins; among the women especially, and that so ponderous, as that to ease them, many wear linen cloth bound about their head, and coming under the chin to support it; but *quis tumidum guttur miratur in Alpibus?* Their drinking so much snow-water is thought to be the cause of it; the men, using more wine, are not so strumous as the women. The truth is, they are a peculiar race of people, and many great water-drinkers here have not these prodigious tumours; it runs, as we say, in the blood, and is a vice in the race, and renders them so ugly, shrivelled and deformed, by its drawing the skin of the face down, that nothing can be more frightful; to this add a strange puffing dress, furs, and that barbarous language, being a mixture of corrupt High German, French, and Italian. The people are of great stature, extremely rude and fierce, yet very honest and trusty.

This night, through almost inaccessible heights, we came in prospect of Mons Sempronius, now Mount Sampion, which has on its summit a few huts and a chapel. . . .

From this uncomfortable place we prepared to hasten away the next morning; but, as we were getting on our mules, comes a huge young fellow demanding money for a goat which he affirmed that Captain Wray's dog had killed; expostulating the matter, and impatient of staying in the cold, we set spurs and endeavoured to ride away, when a multitude of people being by this time gotten together about us (for it being Sunday morning and attending for the priest to say mass), they stopped our mules, beat us off our saddles, and, disarming us of our carbines, drew us into one of the rooms of our lodging, and set a guard upon us. Thus we continued prisoners till mass was ended, and then came half a score grim Swiss, who, taking on them to be magistrates, sate down on the table, and condemned us to pay a pistole for the goat, and ten more for attempting to ride away, threatening that if we did not pay it speedily, they would send us to prison, and keep us to a day of public justice, where, as they perhaps would have exaggerated the crime, for they pretended we had primed our carbines and would have shot some of them (as indeed the Captain was about to do), we might have had our heads cut off, as we were told afterwards, for that amongst these rude people a very small misdemeanour does often meet that sentence. Though the proceedings appeared highly unjust, on consultation among ourselves we thought it safer to rid ourselves out of their hands, and the trouble we were brought into; and therefore we patiently laid down the money, and with fierce countenances had our mules and arms delivered to us, and glad we were to escape as we did. This was cold entertainment, but our journey after was colder, the rest of the way having been (as they told us) covered with snow since the Creation; no man remembered it to be without; and because, by the frequent snowing, the tracts are continually filled up, we passed by several tall masts set up to guide travellers, so as for many miles they stand in ken of one another, like to our beacons. In some places, where there is a cleft between two mountains, the snow fills it up, whilst the bottom, being thawed, leaves as it were a frozen arch of snow, and that so hard as to bear the greatest weight; for as it snows often, so it perpetually freezes, of which I was so sensible that it flawed the very skin of my face. . . .

Late at night, we got to a town called Briga, at the foot of the Alps, in the Valteline. Almost every door had nailed on the outside and next the street a bear's, wolf's, or fox's head, and divers of them all three; a savage kind of sight, but, as the Alps are full of the beasts, the people often kill them. The next morning, we returned to our guide, and took fresh mules, and another to conduct us to the Lake of Geneva, passing through as pleasant a country as that we had just travelled was melancholy and troublesome. . . .

Passing through the same pleasant valley between the horrid mountains on either hand, like a gallery many miles in length, we got to Martigni, where also we were well entertained. The houses in this country are all built of fir boards, planed within, low, and seldom above one story. The people very clownish and rusticly clad, after a very odd fashion, for the most part in blue cloth, very whole and warm, with little variety of distinction betwixt the gentleman and common sort, by a law of their country being exceedingly frugal. Add to this their great honesty and fidelity, though exacting enough for what they part with. I saw not one beggar. We paid the value of twenty shillings English for a day's hire of one horse. Every man goes with a sword by his side, the whole country well-disciplined, and indeed impregnable, which made the Romans have such ill success against them; one lusty Swiss at their narrow passages is sufficient to repel a legion. . . .

Proceeding on our journey, we passed this afternoon through the gate which divides the Valais from the Duchy of Savoy, into which we were now entering, and so, through Montei, we arrived that evening at Beveretta. Being extremely weary and complaining of my head, and finding little accommodation in the house, I caused one of our hostess's daughters to be removed out of her bed, and went immediately into it whilst it was yet warm, being so heavy with pain and drowsiness that I would not stay to have the sheets changed; but I shortly after paid dearly for my impatience, falling sick of the small-pox so soon as I came to Geneva, for by the smell of frankincense, and the tale the good woman told me of her daughter having had an ague, I afterwards concluded she had been newly recovered of the small-pox. Notwithstanding this, I went with my company the next day, hiring a bark to carry us over the lake; and indeed sick as I was, the weather was so serene and bright, the water so calm, and air so temperate, that never had travellers a sweeter passage. Thus, we sailed the whole length of the lake, about thirty miles, the countries bordering on it (Savoy and Berne) affording one of the most delightful prospects in the world, the Alps covered with snow, though at a great distance, yet showing their aspiring tops. Through this lake, the river Rhodanus passes with that velocity as not to mingle with its exceeding deep waters, which are very clear, and breed the most celebrated trout for largeness and goodness of any in Europe.

(1646 in the *Diary*.)

THOMAS BURNET
(1635-1715)

Thomas Burnet's book "The Sacred Theory of the Earth" (1684) was used as a textbook for geological students at Cambridge at the beginning of the eighteenth century. Burnet wrote in an age in which, as Leslie Stephen remarks, it was believed that geological problems could be solved "with the Book of Genesis for their authority, a happy faculty of guessing to eke out any deficiencies of information, and a few inferences from the Newtonian theories to produce a scientific tinge." Burnet tells us that when he crossed the Alps and Apennines "the sight of those vast undigested heaps of stone did so strike my fancy that I was not easy till I could give myself some tolerable account of how that confusion arose in nature." His "tolerable account" is of no interest to-day except in so far as it reflects the prevalent suspicion that it was none too easy to reconcile the existence of these monstrosities with a belief in a beneficent Creator.

"Neither Form nor Beauty"

'TIS prodigious to see and to consider of what Extent these Heaps of Stones and Rubbish are! . . . in what Confusion do they lie? They have neither Form nor Beauty, nor Shape, nor Order, no more than the Clouds in the Air. Then how barren, how desolate, how naked are they? How they stand neglected by Nature? Neither the Rains can soften them, nor the dews from Heaven make them fruitful. . . . These Mountains are placed in no Order one with another, that can either respect Use or Beauty; and if you consider them singly, they do not consist of any Proportion of Parts that is referable to any Design, or that hath the least Footsteps of Art or Counsel. There is nothing in Nature more shapeless and ill-figured than an old Rock or a Mountain, and all that Variety that is among them, is but the various Modes of Irregularity. . . . 'Tis true, they cannot look so ill now as they did at first; a Ruin that is fresh, looks much worse than afterwards, when the Earth grows discoloured and skinn'd over. But I fancy, if we had seen the Mountains, when they were new born and raw, when the Earth was fresh broken, and the Waters of the Deluge newly retired, the Fractions and Confusions of them would have appeared very ghastly and frightful.

BISHOP BURNET
(1643-1715)

Gilbert Burnet, a Whig in politics, a latitudinarian in religion, left England on the accession of James II, who detested him, and "Some Letters Containing an Account of what seem'd most remarkable in travelling thro' Switzerland, Italy, Some Parts of Germany, etc. In the Years 1685 and 1686" were written in exile. He returned to England with William of Orange (he was responsible for the choice of Torbay as a landing place for the invasion) and composed the text of his Declaration to the British people. As Bishop of Salisbury he was an outstanding success. "His episcopate," writes the D.N.B., "stands alone in that age as a record of able and conscientious government."

Burnet is the theme and victim of some famous lines in Dryden's "The Hind and the Panther."

> Broad-back'd and brawny-built for love's delight,
> A prophet form'd to make a female proselyte
> Loud praises to prepare his path he sent,
> And then himself pursued his compliment . . .
> So fond of loud report, that not to miss
> Of being known (his last and utmost bliss)
> He rather would be known for what he is.

One does not turn to political satire for a just appraisal of those who do not share the author's political beliefs, and in the case of Dryden's attack on Burnet the Tory-Whig feud was still further envenomed by religious differences, for Dryden was a convert to the Church of Rome.

All parsons who owe their Alpine holidays to the institution of continental chaplaincies should remember the good Bishop in their prayers, for he was, as we shall see, the first to introduce "the way of the Church of England" to the Alps.

Burnet's lack of interest in the mountains is only equalled by the tendency of modern Alpine writers to ignore the political and religious views of the Alpine peoples.

Burnett was a shrewd observer of people and of politics, though his critical faculty would seem to have been in abeyance during his visit to Berne. "The people of Berne," he tells us, "were apt to swallow anything, and not disposed to make severe Enquiries into extraordinary Matters," but if any Bernese citizens subsequently read the Bishop's comments on the ladies of Berne, alleged to be allergic to "Amours," they might well have doubted whether the Bishop had made "severe Enquiries" before accepting this "extraordinary Matter."

Switzerland in 1685

SWITZERLAND lies between France and Italy, that are both of them Countries incomparably more rich, and better furnished with all the pleasures and Conveniences of

Life than it is; and yet *Italy* is almost quite dispeopled, and the People in it are reduced to a Misery that can scarce be imagined by those who have not seen it: And *France* is in a great measure dispeopled, and the Inhabitants are reduced to a Poverty that appears in all the Marks in which it can shew itself, both in their Houses, Furniture, Clothes, and Looks.

On the contrary, Switzerland is extreme full of People, and in several Places, in the Villages as well as in their Towns, one sees all the Marks he can look for of Plenty and Wealth; their Houses and Windows are in good Case, the Highways are well maintained, all People are well clothed, and every one lives at his Ease.

"*Nor did they know what Amours were*"

THE Men (of Bern) are generally sincere, but heavy: They think it necessary to correct the Moisture of the Air with liberal Entertainments; and they are well furnished with all necessary Ingredients; for as their Soil produces good Cattle, so their Lakes abound in Fish, and their Woods in Fowl; the Wine is also light and good. The Women (of Bern) are generally employ'd in their domestick Affairs; and the Wives even of the chief Magistrates of *Bern*, look into all the Concerns of the House and Kitchen, as much as the Wives of the meanest Peasants. Men and Women do not converse promiscuously together; and the Women are so much amused with the Management at Home, and enter so little into Intrigues, that among them, as an eminent Physician there told me, *they know not what Vapours are*, which he imputed to the Idleness and the Intrigues that abound elsewhere; where-as, he said, among them the Blood was cleansed by their Labour; and as that made them sleep well, so they did not amuse themselves with much thinking, nor did they know what Amours were. The third Adultery is punished with Death; which is also the Punishment of the fifth Act of Fornication, of which I saw an Instance while I was in Bern.

Popish Cantons. Their Heat and Bigotry

IN my Way from *Bern* to this Place I passed by *Solothurn*, and I came thro' *Fribourg* in my Way from *Lausanne* to *Bern*. These are two of the chief of the Popish *Cantons* after *Lucern*;

and one sees in them a Heat and Bigotry beyond what appears either in *France* or *Italy*. Long before they come within the Church Doors they kneel down in the Streets when Mass is saying in it. The Images are also extreme gross. In the chief Church of *Solothurn* there is an Image of God the Father, as an old Man with a great black Beard, having our Saviour on his Knees, and a Pigeon over his Head. Here also begins a Devotion at the *Ave-Mary* Bell, which is scarce known in *France*, but is practised all *Italy* over: At Noon and at Sun-set the Bell rings, and all say the *Ave-Mary* and a short Prayer to the Virgin. But whereas in *Italy* they content themselves with putting off their Hats, in *Switzerland* they do for the most part kneel down in the Streets; which I saw no where practised in Italy, except at Venice, and there it is not commonly done. But notwithstanding this extreme Bigotry, all the *Switzers* see their common Interest so well, that they live in a very good Understanding one with another. This is indeed chiefly owing to the *Canton* of *Lucern*, where there is a Spirit in the Government very different from what is in most of the other Popish Cantons. The Residence of the *Spanish* Ambassador, and of the *Nuncio* in that Town, contributes also much to the preserving it in so good a Temper, it being their Interest to unite Switzerland; and by this means the Heat and Indiscretion of the rest is often moderated.

"Worship in our own Language"

BEFORE I left *Geneva*, the Number of the *English* there was such, that I found we could make a small Congregation, for we were twelve or fourteen; so I addressed myself to the Council of *Twenty-five*, for Liberty to have our own Worship in our own Language, according to the *English* Liturgy. This was immediately granted in so obliging a manner, that as there was not one Person that made any Exception to it, so they sent one of their Body to me, to let me know, that in case our Number should grow to be so great that it were fit for us to assemble in a Church, they would grant us one which had been done in Queen Mary's Reign; but till then, we might hold our Assemblies as we thought fit: So after that time, during the rest of my Stay there, we had every *Sunday* our Devotions according to the Common Prayer Morning and Evening; and at the Evening-

Prayer I preach'd in a Room that was indeed too large for our small Company: But there being a considerable Number in *Geneva* that understand *English*, and in particular some of the Professors and Ministers, we had a great many Strangers that met with us; and the last *Sunday* I gave the Sacrament according to the Way of the Church of *England*; and upon this Occasion I found a general Joy in the Town for this, that I had given them an Opportunity of expressing the Respect they had for our Church.

WILLIAM BURNET

William Burnet, the son of the Bishop, visited Grindelwald in 1708.

The Glaciers of Grindelwald

SIR,—After I had been at *Zurich*, I resolved to go myself and see the Mountains of Ice in Switzerland. Accordingly I went to the *Grindelwald*, a Mountain two Days' Journey from Bern. There I saw, between two mountains, like a River of Ice, which divides itself in two Branches, and in its way from the top of the Mountains to the bottom swells in vast Heaps, some bigger than St. *Paul's* Church, the Original of which seems to have been this. These Mountains are covered all the Year with Snow on their Tops; this Snow has been melted in the Summer, and has fallen to the Bottom which the Sun never reaches. There it has Frozen, which everybody knows happens more easily to melted Snow than ordinary Water. Thus every year it has increased, till it has touched the very Top. The reason why the Water has always frozen, tho' the Sun in the middle of the Mountain, and higher, shines upon it some part of the Day, is that the melted Water goes under the Ice already formed and there Freezes, and so expanding itself raises the Ice above it, and sometimes makes Cracks in it, that frighten the whole Neighbourhood: the reason appears plainly, because the upper Surface being solid, cannot be dilated without making great Chinks, and that with a terrible noise. They told me, upon the Place, that every seven Years the Mountain increases and the next seven decreases; but I doubt this Observation is not exact, and I suspect that they say it, to seem to know something singular. Besides there are none there that have themselves observed it long enough, to affirm anything of that kind certainly. If there is any Ground in that Observation, it seems to be, that in the hottest Summers it increases, and the more moderate ones it decreases, there being then less melted Snow; in which case it is at present, as we know of late the Summers have been moderate.

JOSEPH ADDISON
(1672-1719)

Addison visited Switzerland in 1701, and his rare allusions to mountain scenery suggest that the disgust which mountains provoked in the mind of a man of taste might be coloured by a faint element of pleasure. "At one sight of the walks," he writes of Tonon, "you have a near prospect of the Alps, which are broken into so many steps and precipices, that they fill the mind with an agreeable kind of horror."

There is a more modern note in his tribute to the view from the terrace at Berne, and we may forgive him his erratic geography ("country of the Grisons") for his praise of the "noblest summer prospect in the world."

The Terrace at Berne

WHAT pleased me most at Berne was, their public walks by the great church. They are raised extremely high, and that their weight might not break down the walls and pilasters which surround them, they are built upon arches and vaults. Though they are, I believe, as high as most steeples in England from the streets and gardens that lie at the foot of them, yet about forty years ago a person in his drink fell down from the very top to the bottom, without doing himself any other hurt than the breaking of an arm. He died about four years ago. There is the noblest summer-prospect in the world from this walk, for you have a full view of a huge range of mountains that lie in the country of the Grisons, and are buried in snow. They are about twenty-five leagues' distance from the town, though by reason of their height and their colour they seem much nearer. The cathedral church stands on one side of these walks, and is, perhaps, the most magnificent of any Protestant church in Europe out of England. It is a very bold work, and a master-piece in Gothic architecture.

Benefits of a Phlegmatic Temper

I HAVE often considered, with a great deal of pleasure, the
profound peace and tranquillity that reigns in Switzerland
and its alliances. It is very wonderful to see such a knot of
governments, which are so divided among themselves in matters
of religion, maintain so uninterrupted an union and corre-
spondence, that no one of them is for invading the rights of
another, but remains content within the bounds of its first
establishment. This, I think, must be chiefly ascribed to the
nature of the people, and the constitution of their governments. Were the Swiss animated by zeal or ambition, some or
other of their states would immediately break in upon the rest;
or were the states so many principalities, they might often have
an ambitious sovereign at the head of them, that would
embroil his neighbours, and sacrifice the respose of his subjects
to his own glory. But as the inhabitants of these countries
are naturally of a heavy, phlegmatic temper, if any of their
leading members have more fire and spirit than comes to their
share, it is quickly tempered by the coldness and moderation of
the rest who sit at the helm with them.

PIERRE MARTEL

The Glaciers of Savoy

I HAVE already said, that the Thickness of the Ice is very
considerable, and I will now say something upon its
Consistence. We found it generally much lighter, and much
thinner towards the Edges of the Valley than in the Middle:
For although both the one and the other swim upon the Water,
yet that in the Middle sinks the deepest. I observed before that
the Mountains or Points, which we saw from the Mountain
which we went up, are very high, and that there are many of
them. I particularly mentioned three of the principal of them,
namely, one towards the South and two towards the West.
That which is towards the South, and which we first discovered
before us, is called *L'Eguille du Dru*; this Point looks very like an
Obelisk, the Top of which is lost in the Clouds, making a very

acute Angle at the Summit, and not much unlike a great Gothic Tower, built of white and brown Stone, the Parts of which are very rough. For we must observe, that the Pieces which fall off break in a perpendicular Direction, leaving here and there little Parts by themselves, which make the Mountain look as if it was composed of an infinite Number of little Towers. The Effect of this is very beautiful when the Sun shines on them, by reason of the agreeable Mixture of *Clair Obscur*, which is prodigiously varied; this Mountain is too steep to have any Ice upon it; or indeed much Snow. The two other Points on the West Side are *L'Eguille de Montmallet*, which is covered always with Ice and is the nearest the *L'Eguille du Dru*; and Mont Blanc, which is the farthest to the West. 'Tis this Point of *Mont Blanc* which is supposed to be the Highest in all the *Glacieres*, and perhaps of all the Alps. Many persons of the Country who have travelled assured me, that they had seen it from *Dijon*, and others from *Langres*, which is 135 Miles distance. For the Top of it is easy to be distinguished, because it is blunt, and quite steep on the North-side; if the Sides were prolonged, so as to make an Angle at the Top, I imagine it would be of 25 or 30 Degrees. This Mountain is entirely covered with Ice, quite from the Top down to the Bottom. The Mountain which we went up in order to see the Valley of Ice has three Names, the East-side is called *Montanvert*, and that towards the West *Blaitiere*, and that in the Middle the *Charmaux*. Upon this Mountain there rise four Points something like the *L'Eguille du Dru*, which are called the Points of *Charmaux*. All these Points are absolutely inaccessible, some by reason of the Ice, which covers their Surface almost entirely, as *Montmallet* and *Mont Blanc*, and others on account of their Steepness. 'Tis at the Foot of these Mountains, and along the Valley of the *Glacieres*, that they find Crystal, and not under the Ice, as some have pretended. The Crystal is found in the very Substance of the Rock, after this Manner: Those who go in search of it know where to find it by certain white and blue Veins, which they see upon the Rock. These Veins are either alone, or many of them together, which unite in one Point; they strike upon the Extremity of the Veins, and when they hear a hollow Sound they break the Rock, and find the Crystal in Cavities, which are sometimes many Feet deep, which they call Ovens. Crystal is a Stone which, in my Opinion, is produced by a gentle Vegetation, and

not by Congelation; every one knows that they are Shoots, all
of the Figure of a Hexagon, joined one to another, almost like
the Cells in Honey Combs. These Shoots are sometimes
unequal in Thickness and Length, but all terminate in a Point,
as if they had been cut Diamond Fashion; they all stick to a
kind of Stone of an irregular Shape, which is a kind of Root to
them, partaking of the Nature both of Rock and Crystal, of a
blue, white, black, and brown Colour, extremely hard and
heavy; this Stone is called the *Matrix*. We must observe that
when once the Crystal is taken away, there never comes any
other, although the *Matrix* be left in the same Place where it
was found: And this has made some People think that Crystal
was formed from the Beginning of the World. It happens
sometimes that Pieces of Rocks fall down with the Ovens of
Crystal contained in them, and roll upon the Ice. 'Tis for this
Reason that the Countrymen often find Pieces of Crystal on the
Surface of the Ice, and sometimes adhering to it, and even in
the Current of the Water, which forces itself up through the
Clefts of the Ice. There are some Places where the Cattle cross
over the Ice to go and feed at the Bottom of the Mountains, on
the other Side of the Valley, in Places where the Sun can come,
and where there is some Pasture, and they do it the more easily,
because the Surface of the Ice is sprinkled over with Gravel, or
small Particles of Rock, which the Wind probably brings from
the neighbouring Mountains. We found also upon the Ice
many large Stones, which in my Opinion had fallen down from
the Tops of the Mountains, altho' the People of the Place pretend that they were raised from the Bottom of the *Glacieres*.

(*An Account of the Glacieres in Savoy*, 1744.)

WILLIAM WINDHAM

Chamounix

WE set out about Noon, the 22nd of June, and crossed
the *Arve* over a wooden Bridge. Most Maps place the
Glacieres on the same Side with *Chamoigny*, but this is a Mistake.
We were quickly at the Foot of the Mountain, and began to
ascend by a very steep Path through a Wood of Firs and Larche
Trees. We made many Halts to refresh ourselves, and take

breath, but we kept on at a good Rate. After we had passed
the Wood, we came to a kind of Meadow, full of large Stones,
and Pieces of Rocks, that were broke off, and fallen down from
the Mountain; the Ascent was so steep that we were obliged
sometimes to cling to them with our Hands, and make use of
Sticks, with sharp Irons at the End, to support ourselves. Our
Road lay slantways, and we had several Places to cross where
the *Avalanches* of Snow were fallen, and had made terrible
Havock; there was nothing to be seen but Trees torn up by the
Roots, and large Stones, which seemed to lie without any
Support; every step we set, the Ground gave way, the Snow
which was mixed with it made us slip, and had it not been for
Staffs, and our Hands, we must many times have gone down
the Precipice. We had an uninterrupted View quite to the
Bottom of the Mountain, and the Steepness of the Descent,
join'd to the Height where we were, made a View terrible
enough to make most People's Heads turn. In short, after
climbing with great Labour for four Hours and three Quarters,
we got to the Top of the Mountain, from whence we had the
Pleasure of beholding Objects of an extraordinary Nature.
We were on the Top of a Mountain, which, as well as we could
judge, was at least twice as high as Mount *Saleve*, from thence
we had a full View of the *Glacieres*. I own to you that I am
extremely at a Loss how to give a right Idea of it, as I know no
one thing which I have ever seen that has the least Resemblance
to it.

The Description which Travellers give of the Seas of *Greenland* seems to come the nearest to it. You must imagine your
Lake put in Agitation by a strong Wind, and frozen all at
once, perhaps even that would not produce the same Appearance.

The *Glacieres* consist of three large Valleys, that form a kind
of Y, the Tail reaches into the *Val d'Aoste*, and the two Horns
into the Valley of *Chamoigny*, the Place where we ascended was
between them, from whence we saw plainly the Valley, which
forms one of these Horns.

I had unluckily left at *Chamoigny* a pocket Compass, which I
had carried with me, so that I could not well tell the Bearings
as to its Situation; but I believe it to be pretty nearly from North
to South. These Valleys, although at the Top of a high
Mountain, are surrounded with other Mountains; the Tops of

which, being naked and craggy Rocks, shoot up immensely high; something resembling old Gothic Buildings or Ruines, nothing grows upon them, they are all the Year round covered with Snow; and our Guides assured us, that neither the *Chamois*, or any Birds, ever went so high as the Top of them.

Those who search after Crystal, go in the Month of *August* to the Foot of these Rocks, and strike against them with Pick-axes; if they hear them resound as if they were hollow, they work there, and opening the Rock, they find Caverns full of Crystalisations. We should have been very glad to have gone there, but the Season was not enough advanced, the Snow not being yet sufficiently melted. As far as our Eye-sight could reach, we saw nothing but this Valley; the Height of the Rocks, which surrounded it, made it impossible for the Eye to judge exactly how wide it was; but I imagine it must be near three Quarters of a League. Our Curiosity did not stop here, we were resolved to go down upon the Ice; we had about four hundred Yards to go down, the Descent was excessively steep, and all of a dry crumbling Earth, mixt with Gravel, and little loose Stones, which afforded us no firm footing; so that we went down partly falling, and partly sliding on our Hands and Knees. At length we got upon the Ice, where our Difficulty ceased, for that was extremely rough, and afforded us good footing; we found in it an infinite Number of Cracks, some we could step over, others were several Feet wide. These Cracks were so deep, that we could not even see to the Bottom; those who go in search of Crystal are often lost in them, but their Bodies are generally found again after some Days, perfectly well pre-served. All our Guides assured us, that these Cracks change continually, and that the whole *Glaciere* has a kind of Motion. In going up the Mountain we often heard something like a Clap of Thunder, which, as we were informed by our Guides, was caused by fresh Cracks then making; but as there were none made while we were upon the Ice, we could not determine whether it was that, or *Avalanches* of Snows, or perhaps Rocks falling; though since Travellers observe, that in *Greenland* the Ice cracks with a Noise that resembles Thunder, it might very well be what our Guides told us. As in all Countries of Ignorance People are extremely superstitious, they told us many strange stories of Witches, etc., who came to play their Pranks upon the *Glacieres*, and dance to the Sound of Instruments. We should have been surprised if we had not been entertained in these Parts, with some such idle Legends. The *Bouquetins* go in Herds often to the Number of fifteen or sixteen upon the Ice, we saw none of them; there were some *Chamois* which we shot at, but at too great a Distance to do any Execution.

There is Water continually issuing out of the *Glacieres*, which the People look on as so very wholesome, that they say it may be drank of in any Quantities without Danger, even when one is hot with Exercise.

The Sun shone very hot, and the Reverberation of the Ice, and circumjacent Rocks, caused a great deal of thaw'd Water to lie in all the Cavities of the Ice; but I fancy it freezes there constantly as soon as Night comes on.

Our Guides assured us, that, in the time of their Fathers, the *Glaciere* was but small, and that there was even a Passage thro' these Valleys, by which they could go into the *Val d'Aoste* in six Hours; But that the *Glaciere* was so much increased, that the Passage was then quite stopped up, and that it went on increasing every Year.

We found on the Edge of the *Glaciere* several Pieces of Ice, which we took at first for Rocks, being as big as a House; these were pieces quite separate from the *Glaciere*. It is difficult to conceive how they came to be formed there.

Having remained about half an Hour upon the *Glaciere*, and having drank there in Ceremony Admiral *Vernon's* Health, and Success to the *British* Arms, we climb'd to the Summit, from whence we came, with incredible Difficulty, the Earth giving way at every step we set. From thence, after having rested ourselves a few Minutes, we began to descend and arrived at *Chamouny* just about Sun-set, to the great Astonishment of all the People of the Place, and even of our Guides, who owned to us they thought we should not have gone through with our Undertaking.

Our Curiosity being fully satisfied, we left *Chamouny* the next Day, and lying at *Salanches*, we got the 23ᵈ to *Bonneville*. The Nearness of this Place to the *Maule* raised in us an Inclination to go up it. We set about this Task the next Day early in the Morning; we fancied that after the *Glacieres* every Mountain would be easy to us, however, it took us more than five Hours' hard labour in getting up; the Ascent being extremely steep;

though, after two-thirds of the Way, there is a fine green Turf quite up to the Top, which ends in a Point, the Mountain being like a Sugar-Loaf on one Side, and quite perpendicular on that Part which lies farthest from *Geneva*. From this Point there is a most delightful View, on one Side, upon the Lake, *Geneva*, and the adjacent Parts; on the other, upon High Mountains cover'd with Snow, which rise around, in form of an Amphitheatre, and make a most Picturesque Prospect. After having stay'd some time here, we returned back, and went on to *Annecy*, where we lay, from whence the next Day we got to *Geneva*.

(*An Account of the Glacieres of Savoy*, 1744.)

ARCHDEACON COXE
(1747-1828)

William Coxe paid four long visits to Switzerland between 1776 and 1786. In his approach to his subject he is midway between Burnet, who was only interested in Swiss institutions, and Mountaineers such as Mummery, who was only interested in the Swiss mountains. He had a very genuine love for mountain scenery, and he was also deeply interested in Swiss institutions. Politically he was a Whig—that is to say, he was equally hostile to despotism and to democracy, and had a firm faith in the merits of oligarchy. Representative government and a franchise restricted to men of property was the key, so he believed, to prosperity. He makes the proper observations about Romish superstition, but none the less found the Abbot of the Benedictine Abbey at Engelberg more congenial than the Swiss pietists whom he met at St. Moritz, and who pleased him as little as they pleased Addison. "They employ," he writes, "so much time in prayer as to neglect their ordinary business." The Archdeacon, one feels, was never guilty of such foolishness.

Coxe's Memoirs of the Duke of Marlborough and of Horace Walpole are of great historical value. No historian until recent times had access to a greater range of unpublished documents and family archives.

"*Notwithstanding the natural defects of a democratical constitution*"

IF I had never seen these little democratical states, I could have formed no idea of the general equality and indistinction that prevails among the inhabitants. All the houses, like those of Appenzel, are built of wood; large, solid, and compact, with great penthouse roofs that hang very low, and extend beyond the area of the foundation. This peculiar structure is of use to keep off the snow; and, from its singularity, accords surprisingly with the beautiful wilderness of the country. The houses of the richer inhabitants in the principal burghs are of the same materials: the only difference consists in their being larger.

If that sort of government be confessedly the best, which constitutes the greatest good of the greatest number in the community, these little states, notwithstanding the natural defects of a democratical constitution, may justly claim a large share of our approbation. General liberty, general independence, and an exemption from arbitrary taxes, are blessings which amply compensate for a want of those refinements that are introduced by opulence and luxury. However, it is only in these small republics, and in such a state of society, that this kind of general democracy can have place. And although the machine of government is considerably clogged by that variety of wheels required to put it into motion; yet it is not necessary that its decisions should be sudden and expeditious; for, as there is no fear of an invasion, and as the people have no conquests either to make or to defend, their principal policy consists in maintaining their independence, and in preserving the public tranquillity.

The police is well regulated throughout Switzerland; and even in these democratical states, liberty does not often degenerate into licentiousness: we may except, perhaps, the day of their general assemblies, when it is impossible to prevent some degree of confusion in a meeting where there is scarcely any distinction of persons; and where every peasant considers himself as equal to the first magistrate.

Our host is an open-hearted, honest Swiss: he brings his pint of wine, sits down to table with us, and chats without the least ceremony. There is a certain forwardness of this kind which is insupportable when it apparently is the effect of impertinent curiosity, or fawning officiousness; but the present instance of frank familiarity, arising from a mind conscious of its natural equality, and unconstrained by arbitrary distinctions, is highly pleasing; as the simple demeanour of unsophisticated nature is far preferable to the false refinements of artificial manners.

Theory and Practice

THOSE theorists, who are so anxious to reform the English House of Commons by transferring to *the people at large* the election of their representatives in parliament, might, examining with attention the features of the Grison diet, fondly imagine that an *annual* assembly, in the choice of whose members every male of the state should have a vote, and which, in all material occurrences should be liable to *be directed by its constituents*, must *necessarily* be the purest sanctuary of general freedom. In this instance, however, their conjectures are by no means consonant to fact and experience; as corruption and influence are not in any national parliament more conspicuous than in the diet of the Grisons.

The delegation of deliberative authority to the people at large unavoidably tends to introduce an actual, though not an acknowledged aristocracy. For a *numerous* populace summoned to determine upon political, legislative, and judicial questions, *far above their comprehensions*, must necessarily resign themselves to the direction of more informed men, especially when aided by the recommendation of superior wealth. As the deputies are generally the chiefs of those communities which they represent, they must of course have the principal influence, and easily find means to incline the opinion of the people to the side which they have espoused. In fact, without this aristocratical influence the excess of freedom would often degenerate into anarchy, and public deliberations would be attended with endless disputes and factions.

If therefore corruption and aristocratical influence alone diminish factions and prevent anarchy in so poor a country as that of the Grisons, and in a republic scarcely known among the nations of Europe; to what a dreadful excess must the same evils prevail, if the *same* mode of electing, and giving instructions to, members of parliament, subsisted in a kingdom like England; where riches and luxury are continually advancing with such rapid strides; where the most important political and commercial debates are agitated without restraint; and where the decisions of public affairs frequently affect the peace and interests of all Europe.

The Blessings of Freedom

FROM Porto the traveller may observe, with satisfaction mingled with compassion, the strong contrasts effected by the influence of a free and of an arbitrary government: the borders of the lake subject to Switzerland studded with a succession of villages, houses, and gardens; this part of the Milanese desolate, and almost unpeopled.

Passage of the Scheidegg

AFTER having ascended about three hours from the time of our quitting Meyringen, we refreshed ourselves and our horses in a delightful vale strewed with hamlets; a sloping hill, adorned with variegated verdure and wood, on one side; on the other, the Rosenlavir and Schwartz-wald . . . and before us the highest point of the Wetterhorn lifting its pyramidical top capped with eternal snow. As we were taking our repast, we were suddenly startled by a noise, like the sound of thunder, occasioned by a large body of snow falling from the top of the mountain, which, in its precipitate descent, had the appearance of a torrent of water reduced almost into spray.

We continued our course at the foot of the Wetterhorn, which in this part is so extremely perpendicular and tapering as to appear like half of an immense pyramid. Here we conceived it impossible, that any scenes could be more rude and majestic than those before us; but on reaching the top of the Scheidegg, we burst upon a view which so far exceeded them in wildness and horror, that we unanimously exclaimed, "There is the *Schreckhorn,* or the *Peak of Terror.*"

The descent from hence to Grindelwald is gentle but tedious: that village consisting of numerous cottages, dispersed over the plain and upon the rising hills, exhibits an agreeable and picturesque scene, heightened at the same time by a view of the vallies of ice; which stretch along the steep tides of the mountains in a regular curve, and are beautifully skirted with wood.

EDWARD GIBBON
(1737-1794)

Gibbon was converted to Catholicism as an undergraduate. His indignant father removed him from Oxford and sent him to Lausanne, where he was entrusted to the care of Monsieur Pavilliard, a Calvinistic Minister. The results were all that his father could have desired. "The various articles of the Romish creed disappeared like a dream, and after a full conviction, on Christmas Day 1754, I received the sacrament in the Church of Lausanne."

He was no sooner cured of his unfortunate attachment to the Catholic Church than he fell in love with a lady, equally unsuccessful in securing his father's approval, Susanne Curchod, the daughter of the Minister at Crassy.

Susanne's guardian angel had destined her to be the bride of a famous man, and after being jilted by the future historian she married Necker, Louis XIV's Minister of Finance. She forgave her timid wooer, and in later years often entertained him. "She was very fond of me," writes Gibbon of Madame Necker, "and her husband particularly civil. Could they have insulted me more cruelly? Ask me every evening to supper; go to bed, and leave me alone with his wife—what an impertinent security! It is making an old lover of mighty little consequence."

Gibbon's life had a rounded quality of neat perfection within a framework of achievable ambition. He described himself as "a fervent admirer of opulence," and though he was never as rich as he could have wished, he records with satisfaction that he was "seldom mortified by the denial of any reasonable gratification" and that "the annual deficiencies of my revenue were readily provided by some accidental resource or some extraordinary supply," as for instance that pleasant little sinecure, the appointment as "one of the Lords Commissioners of trade and plantations," by means of which his private income was "enlarged by a clear addition of between seven and eight hundred pounds a year," an appointment which did not interfere with the writing of his history. "It must be allowed that our duty was not intolerably severe, and that I enjoyed many days and weeks of repose without being called away from my library to my office."

Gibbon returned to Lausanne at the age of forty-six, and made Lausanne his home for the rest of his life.

Gibbon left six separate sketches of his life which in part supplement each other and which also contain different versions of the same episodes.

The synthesis of these six sketches, prepared under the skilful and discreet editorship of Lord Sheffield, held the field until 1894 when the original memoirs were first published. Sheffield performed his task with considerable dexterity, but though he can hardly be blamed for omitting passages which would have given great offence to the orthodox, and should be commended for leaving unprinted personal attacks upon individuals such as Madame Pavilliard, he had no right to manipulate the text. He was entitled for instance to suppress Gibbon's "I was too bashful to enjoy like a manly Oxonian the taverns and bagnios of London," but not to substitute "the pleasures" for "the taverns and bagnios," and it is impossible to understand the obscure mental processes which led him to substitute "the boarders" (at a Lausanne pension) "were select" for "the boarders were numerous."

It is interesting to compare the versions of his love affair in Memoir B and Memoir C. Both versions are given below. The passages which Sheffield omitted are indicated by brackets. The latter version places the author in a slightly more dignified light. In Memoir B, Gibbon writes "without his consent I was myself destitute and helpless." In Memoir C, the jilting of Susan is ascribed "to the prejudice or prudence" of his Father.

An Anglo-Swiss Romance

I HESITATE, from the apprehension of ridicule, when I approach the delicate subject of my early love. By this word I do not mean the polite attention of the gallantry, without hope or design, which has originated from the spirit of chivalry, and is interwoven with the texture of French manners. (I do not confine myself to the grosser appetite which our pride may affect to disdain, because it has been implanted by Nature in the whole animal creation, "Amor omnibus idem." The discovery of a sixth sense, the first consciousness of manhood, is a very interesting moment of our lives; but it less properly belongs to the memoirs of an individual, than to the natural history of the species.) I understand by this passion the union of desire, friendship, and tenderness, which is inflamed by a single female, which prefers her to the rest of her sex, and which seeks her possession as the supreme or the sole happiness of our being. I need not blush at recollecting the object of my choice; and though my love was disappointed of success, I am rather proud that I was once capable of feeling such a pure and exalted sentiment. The personal attractions of Mademoiselle Susanne Curchod were embellished by the virtues and talents of the mind. Her fortune was humble, but her family was respectable: her mother, a native of France, had preferred her religion to her country; the profession of her father did not extinguish the moderation and philosophy of his temper, and he lived content with a small salary and laborious duty in the obscure lot of Minister of Crassy, in the mountains that separate the Pays de Vaud from the County of Burgundy. In the solitude of a sequestered village he bestowed a liberal, and even learned, education on his only daughter; she surpassed his hopes by her proficiency in the sciences and languages; and in her short visits to some relations at Lausanne, the wit and beauty and erudition of Mademoiselle Curchod were the theme of universal applause. The report of such a prodigy awakened my curiosity; I saw and loved. I found her learned without pedantry, lively in conversation, pure in sentiment, and elegant in manners; and the first sudden emotion was fortified by the habits and knowledge of a more familiar acquaintance. She permitted me to make her two or three visits at her father's house: I passed some happy days in the mountains of Burgundy; and her parents honourably encouraged a connection (which might raise their daughter above want and dependence). In a calm retirement the gay vanity of youth no longer fluttered in her bosom; she listened to the voice of truth and passion, and I might presume to hope that I had made some impression on a virtuous heart. At Crassy and Lausanne I indulged my dream of felicity; but, on my return to England, I soon discovered that my father would not hear of this strange alliance, and that, without his consent, I was myself destitute and helpless. After a painful struggle I yielded to my fate; the remedies of absence and time were at length effectual, and my love subsided in friendship and esteem.

Revised Version of the Above

THE beauty of Mademoiselle Curchod, the daughter of a country clergyman, was adorned with science and virtue: she listened to the tenderness which she had inspired; but the romantic hopes of youth and passion were crushed, on my return, by the prejudice or prudence of an English parent. I sighed as a lover, I obeyed as a son; my wound was insensibly healed by time, absence, and the habits of a new life; and my cure was accelerated by a faithful report of the tranquillity and cheerfulness of the Lady herself.

The Charm of Lausanne

SINCE my establishment at Lausanne more than seven years have elapsed, and if every day has not been equally soft and serene, not a day, not a moment has occurred in which

I have repented of my choice. During my absence, a long portion of human life, many changes had happened; my elder acquaintance had left the stage; virgins were ripened into matrons, and children were grown to the age of manhood. But the same manners were transmitted from one generation to another: my friend alone was an inestimable treasure; my name was not totally forgotten, and all were ambitious to welcome the arrival of a stranger, and the return of a fellow-citizen. The first winter was given to a general embrace, without any nice discrimination of persons and characters. . . . Our importance in society is less a positive than a relative weight: in London I was lost in the crowd; I ranked with the first families of Lausanne, and my style of prudent expence enabled me to maintain a fair balance of reciprocal civilities. . . .

Lausanne is peopled by a numerous gentry, whose companionable idleness is seldom disturbed by the pursuits of avarice or ambition; the women, though confined to a domestic education, are endowed for the most part with more taste and knowledge than their husbands or brothers; but the decent freedom of both sexes is equally remote from the extremes of simplicity and refinement. I shall add, as a misfortune rather than a merit, that the situation and beauty of the Pays de Vaud, the long habits of the English, the medical reputation of Dr. Tissot, and the fashion of viewing the mountains and *glaciers*, have opened us on all sides to the incursions of foreigners.

Rome, 1761—*Lausanne*, 1787

I MUST not forget the day, the hour, the most interesting in my literary life. It was on the fifteenth of October, in the gloom of evening, as I sat musing on the Capitol, while the barefooted fryars were chanting their litanies in the temple of Jupiter, that I conceived the first thought of my history. My original plan was confined to the decay of the City; my reading and reflection pointed to that aim; but several years elapsed, and several avocations intervened, before I grappled with the decline and fall of the Roman Empire.

I have presumed to mark the moment of conception; I shall now commemorate the hour of my final deliverance. It was on the day, or rather the night, of the 27th of June, 1787, between the hours of eleven and twelve, that I wrote the last lines of the last page in a summer-house in my garden. After laying down my pen I took several turns in a *berceau,* or covered walk of Acacias, which commands a prospect of the country, the lake, and the mountains. The air was temperate, the sky was serene, the silver orb of the moon was reflected from the waters, and all Nature was silent. I will not dissemble the first emotions of joy on the recovery of my freedom, and perhaps the establishment of my fame. But my pride was soon humbled, and a sober melancholy was spread over my mind by the idea that I had taken my everlasting leave of an old and agreable companion, and that, whatsoever might be the future date of my history, the life of the historian must be short and precarious.

"I despise the French much less than I did"

The following extracts are from letters written by Gibbon to Lord Sheffield during the French Revolution:

LAUSANNE, April 4th, 1792.

It is the opinion of the master-movers in France, (I know it most certainly,) that their troops will not fight, that the people have lost all sense of patriotism, and that on the first discharge of an Austrian cannon the game is up.

LAUSANNE, May 30th, 1792.

The late events in Flanders seem to have diffused a general contempt, as well as abhorrence, for the lawless savages, who fly before the enemy, hang their prisoners, and murder their officers.

LAUSANNE, August 23rd, 1792.

The last revolution of Paris appears to have convinced almost every body of the fatal consequences of Democratical principles, which lead by a path of flowers into the Abyss of Hell. I may therefore wait with patience and tranquillity till the Duke of Brunswick shall have opened the French road.

LAUSANNE, October 13th, 1792.

Should Geneva yield to fear or force, this country is open to an invasion; and though our men are brave, we want Generals; and I despise the French much less than I did two months ago.

It should seem from Trevor's letters, who is indeed low-spirited, that our hopes from the King of Sardinia and the Austrians of Milan are faint and distant; Spain sleeps, and the Duke of Brunswick (amazement!) seems to have failed in his great project. For my part, till Geneva falls, I do not think of a retreat; but, at all events, I am provided with two strong horses, and a hundred Louis in gold.

"I am not nervous, but I will not be rash"

LAUSANNE, October 5th, 1792.

AS our English newspapers must have informed you of the invasion of Savoy by the French, and as it is possible that you may have some trifling apprehensions of my being killed and eaten by those Cannibals, it has appeared to me that a short extraordinary dispatch might not be unacceptable on this occasion. It is indeed true, that about ten days ago the French army of the south, under the command of de Mountesquiou, (if any French army can be said to be under any command,) has entered Savoy, and possessed themselves of Chamberry, Montmelian, & several other places. . . .

In this situation, you may suppose that we have some fears. I have great dependence, however, on the many chances in our favour, the valour of the Swiss, the return of the Piedmontese with their Austrian Allies, 8 or 10 thousand men from the Milanese, a diversion from Spain, the great events (how slowly they proceed) on the side of Paris, the inconstancy and want of discipline of the French, and the near approach of the winter season. I am not nervous, but I will not be rash. It will be painful to abandon my house and library; but if the danger should approach, I will retreat before it, first to Bern, and gradually to the North. Should I even be forced to take refuge in England (a violent measure so late in the year) you would perhaps receive me as kindly as you do the French priests—a noble act of hospitality! Could I have foreseen this storm, I would have been there six months ago; but who can foresee the wild measures of the Savages of Gaul? We thought ourselves perfectly out of the Hurricane latitudes. Adieu. I am going to bed, and must rise early to visit the Neckers at Rolle, whither they have retired, from the frontier situation of Copet.

"The democratical aspect of the opposite coast"

LAUSANNE, January 1st, 1793.

THE revolution of Geneva has already taken place, as I announced, but sooner than I expected. The Swiss troops had no sooner evacuated the place, than the *Egaliseurs*, as they are called, assembled in arms; and as no resistance was made, no blood was shed on the occasion. They seized the gates, disarmed the garrison, imprisoned the magistrates, imparted the rights of citizens to all the rabble of the town and country, and proclaimed a *national* convention, which has not yet met. They are all for a pure and absolute Democracy; but wish to remain a small independent state, whilst others aspire to become a part of the republic of France; and as the latter, though less numerous, are more violent and absurd than their adversaries, it is highly probable that they will succeed. The Citizens of the best families and fortunes have retired from Geneva into the Pays de Vaud, but the French methods of recalling or proscribing emigrants will soon be adopted. You must have observed, that Savoy has now become *le Départment du Mont Blanc*. I cannot satisfy myself whether the mass of the people is pleased or displeased with the change; but my noble scenery is clouded by the democratical aspect of twelve leagues of the opposite coast, which every morning obtrude themselves on my view.

WILLIAM WORDSWORTH
(1770-1850)

Wordsworth's first visit to the Alps was in 1790, and a letter which he wrote on the road between Grindelwald and Lauterbrunnen is quoted in "Switzerland and the English." He had travelled to Switzerland through France, which was "mad with joy in consequence of the Revolution."

Wordsworth's strong sympathies with the Jacobins survived the Terror, but were finally extinguished when the Revolutionary armies invaded Switzerland on January 28th, 1798. Switzerland was the symbol of freedom, the country in which a primitive democracy had obtained its first victories against reactionary feudalism. The attack upon Switzerland by a power claiming to be in the vanguard of progress produced much the same effect as the attack on democratic Finland by Soviet Russia in 1939. Wordsworth wrote the famous sonnet "Thought of a Briton on the Subjugation of Switzerland."

In 1820 Wordsworth returned to Switzerland with his sister Dorothy.

Wordsworth's noblest mountain poetry was inspired, not by the Alps, but by the Cumberland mountains. His Swiss sonnets are, with one exception, commonplace and uninteresting, but his superb lines on the Simplon Pass cannot be omitted from any representative anthology of mountain literature.

Thoughts of a Briton on the Subjugation of Switzerland

TWO Voices are there; one is of the sea,
   One of the mountains; each a mighty Voice:
In both from age to age thou didst rejoice,
They were thy chosen music, Liberty!
There came a Tyrant, and with holy glee
Thou fought'st against him; but hast vainly striven:
Thou from thy Alpine holds at length art driven,
Where not a torrent murmurs heard by thee.
Of one deep bliss thine ear hath been bereft:
Then cleave, O cleave to that which still is left;
For, high-souled Maid, what sorrow would it be
That Mountain floods should thunder as before,
And Ocean bellow from his rocky shore,
And neither awful Voice be heard by thee!

The Simplon Pass

———BROOK and road
Were fellow-travellers in this gloomy Pass,
And with them did we journey several hours
At a slow step. The immeasurable height
Of woods decaying, never to be decayed,
The stationary blasts of waterfalls,
And in the narrow rent, at every turn,
Winds thwarting winds bewildered and forlorn,
The torrents shooting from the clear blue sky,
The rocks that muttered close upon our ears,
Black drizzling crags that spake by the wayside
As if a voice were in them, the sick sight
And giddy prospect of the raving stream,
The unfettered clouds and region of the heavens,
Tumult and peace, the darkness and the light—
Were all like workings of one mind, the features

Of the same face, blossoms upon one tree,
Characters of the great Apocalypse,
The types and symbols of Eternity
Of first, and last, and midst, and without end.

DOROTHY WORDSWORTH
(1771-1855)

*In 1820 Wordsworth returned to Switzerland with his sister Dorothy. The
most complete version of Dorothy Wordsworth's "A Tour on the Continent in
1820" is that which we owe to the editorship of the late E. de Selincourt
(Journals of Dorothy Wordsworth. Macmillan).*

*Dorothy Wordsworth's descriptions of mountain scenery are incomparably
better than anything to be found in the works of Wordsworth, Shelley or Byron.*

A Hill above Berne

WE ascended a hill till we came in view of as magnificent
a prospect as can be conceived—the Jungfrau, the
Finster-aar-horn, the Shreck-horn, the Wetter-horn, and many
other famous mountains—their summits covered with snow. I
sate upon one of the seats placed under shade of trees beside the
broad high-way; and the party went further. I should have
been ungrateful could I have felt a regret at parting from
them, with such a spectacle before me; indeed it seemed almost
a privilege that my weakness removed all temptation to go
further. Seeing only one side of the peninsula from my resting-
place, the city appeared to hang upon the half of a semi-circle
of the near bank, crowned by the cathedral, and adorned by
spires and towers; yet they are not numerous, as in the Roman
Catholic countries. The green-tinted river flows below—wide,
full, and impetuous. I saw the snows of the Alps burnished by
the sun about half an hour before his setting. After that, they
were left to their wintry, marble coldness, without a farewell
gleam, yet suddenly the city, and the cathedral tower and trees,
were singled out for favour by the sun among his glittering
clouds, and gilded with the richest light—a few minutes and
that glory vanished. I stayed till evening gloom was gathering
over the city, and over hill and dale, while the snowy tops of the
Alps were still visible. Before I reached the city gates, the stars

THE RIGI IN 1850
From an old print

EVENING ON LAKE BRIENZ
(Looking towards Meiringen)

Photo: Albert Steiner, St. Moritz

were beginning to appear, and, taking my solitary way through the streets I overpassed the Inn, it being only indicated by a small golden crown over the door within the cloistral foot-way. I was tired; and truly thankful when a woman, who undertook to be my guide, landed me in the court of the Inn.

Storm at Meiringen

WE reached the Inn at a little after seven o'clock. The sky became very gloomy; frequent claps of thunder with vivid lightning; and in the night, heavy rain. While I lay on my bed, the terrible solitudes of the Wetterhorn were revealed to me by fits—its black chasms, and snowy, dark grey summits. All night, and all day, and for ever, the Vale of Meiringen is sounding with torrents.

August 13th, Sunday, Meiringen. Rain over and the storm past away. Long before the sunshine had touched the top of any other mountain, the snow upon the Wetterhorn shone like silver, and its grey adamantine towers appeared in a soft splendour all their own. I looked in vain for the rosy tints of morning of which I had so often heard; but they could not have been more beautiful than the silvery brightness.

Grindelwald

Dorothy Wordsworth crossed the Little Scheidegg to Grindelwald.

THE first notice we had of our actual approach to Grindelwald (long seen as I have described it) was a flowergarden beside a large comfortable wooden house, upon a slope at a little distance from the road. A girl came tripping over the grass with a dish of starveling cherries and a bunch of flowers in one hand, and in the other a wooden bowl of handsome fir apples—merchandise to be paid for according to the generosity or humour of the traveller. Soon the vale lay before us with its two glaciers, and as it might seem, its *thousand* cabins sown upon the steeps. The descent became so precipitous that all were obliged to walk: deep we go into the broad cradle valley; every cottage we passed had its small garden, and cherry-trees sprinkled with leaves, bearing half-grown, half-ripe fruit. In plunging into this vale I was overcome with a sense of melancholy pervading the whole scene—not desolation, or dreariness: it is not the melancholy of the Scotch Highlands; but connected with social life in loneliness, not less than with the strife of all the seasons. When near the bottom of the declivity we were almost stunned by the roaring of the stream—under our feet (as it seemed); and from the centre of the wooden bridge, we beheld it issuing from its icy cavern beneath the snow-like roof of the larger Glacier. A cold blast, following the river, blew upon us while we passed over the bridge. I shall never forget the wintery sensation. The blast seemed as if its birthplace was in the icy cavern, and thence issuing, it would be fed with indestructible power. As I have said, when I first saw this vale from a point sufficiently near to distinguish the objects, the impressions were very melancholy;—the greeting of the river strengthened those impressions;—and our ascent from the bridge to the village (distant about half a mile) did not abate the feeling. The church stands upon an eminence towards the head of the vale: the most distinguished of several large houses near it, was our Inn. The sunshine had long deserted the valley, and was quitting the summits of the mountains behind the village; but red hues, dark as the red of rubies settled in the clouds, and lingered there after the mountains had lost all but their cold whiteness and the black hue of the crags. The gloomy grandeur of this spectacle harmonised with the melancholy of the vale; yet it was *heavenly* glory that hung over those cold mountains.

The Rigi

AS rapidly, that vapour broke beneath our feet hurrying on till it turned the hill of Rigi; and then dropped down to join a solid mass, condensed, and as white as snow, which was resting on the Lake of Zug. Again fresh volumes rushed on beneath us. It was a wonderful spectacle. Thick masses of clouds, and light smoky mists alike drove away with inconceivable rapidity, while, in the stiller air, the condensed vapour lay on the hills of Zug, as motionless as the snow on the far distant mountains. What would not the exhibition-contrivers of London or Paris give for such power of rapid transformation! The change from earth to ocean, or rather to a resemblance of moving sky, was instantaneous. Lake, houses, woods, fields, lost in the twinkling of an eye,—again appearing in full view, and yet again concealed! Meanwhile, we were assailed by ruffling breezes, and gusty rain-drops—yet I cannot express the quietness of the valley sounds of matin bells, alike descending to our ears through dense or light vapours—or in their partial clearing away, when houses and churches were descried, how far below! The rain was over before the sun was above the mountain line of our horizon. A part of the orb appeared below a canopy of rosy clouds into which it passed in the moment of ascent. Some of the distant Pikes were touched by glowing hues; but only *touched*; and the hues were gone. Again the vapours gathered in our neighbourhood, soon pierced by transient beams from the sun; and a rainbow spanned the mountain.

PERCY BYSSHE SHELLEY
(1792-1822)

On July 29th, 1814, Shelley crossed the Straits of Dover and landed in France. He was eloping with Mary Godwin, who was accompanied by her stepsister, Jane Clairemont. They drove to Paris and decided to walk from Paris to Switzerland through a country with which Britain had been at war for twenty years, and which was then overrun with a recently demobilised army after a demoralising defeat. Shelley bought an ass to carry the luggage, but the ass revolted and was disposed of at Charenton, where they bought a mule for ten napoleons. "About nine o'clock," writes Mary, "we departed. We were clad in black silk. I rode on the mule, which carried also our portmanteau, Shelley and Claire followed."

From Troyes Shelley wrote a letter to the wife he had left in England, and invited her to join the coalition. "I write to show you that I do not forget you; I write to urge you to come to Switzerland, where you will at least find one firm and constant friend, to whom your interests will always be dear—by whom your feelings will never be wilfully injured. From none can you expect this but me—all others are either unfeeling or selfish, or have beloved friends of their own." The fascinating thing about this letter is its shattering sincerity.

The mule that had been bought in exchange for the ass was sold at Troyes and replaced by an open voiture, and three weeks after landing at Calais, Shelley, Mary and Claire crossed the Swiss frontier near Pontarlier. Shelley had just turned twenty-two and Mary was within a few weeks of her seventeenth birthday. They travelled via St. Sulpice and Neuchâtel, near which they had their first view of the High Alps, to Lucerne, whence they went by boat to Brunnen.

It had cost them £60 to cross France, and the discovery that they had only £28 left compelled them to return home as quickly as possible and by the cheapest possible route. They cut things pretty fine, but fortunately Shelley's first wife Harriet was able to pay the cab which delivered Shelley at her doors. The following passage is from Mary Shelley's "History of a Six Weeks' Tour." I have retained her erratic spelling of place-names.

The Distant Alps

TWO leagues from Neufchâtel we saw the Alps: range after range of black mountains are seen extending one before the other, and far behind all, towering above every feature of the scene, the snowy Alps. They were a hundred miles distant, but reach so high in the heavens that they look like those accumulated clouds of dazzling white that arrange themselves on the horizon during summer. Their immensity staggers the imagination, and so far surpasses all conception, that it requires an effort of imagination to believe that they indeed form a part of the earth.

Brunnen

BRUNNEN is situated on the northern side of the angle which the lake makes, forming the extremity of the lake of Lucerne. Here we rested for the night, and dismissed our boatmen. Nothing could be more magnificent than the view from this spot. The high mountains encompassed us, darkening the waters; at a distance on the shores of Uri, we could perceive the chapel of Tell, and this was the village where he matured the conspiracy which was to overthrow the tyrant of his country; and, indeed, this lovely lake, these sublime mountains, and wild forests, seemed a fit cradle for a mind aspiring to high adventure and heroic deeds. Yet we saw no glimpse of his spirit in his present countrymen. The Swiss appeared to us then, and experience has confirmed our opinion, a people slow of comprehension and of action; but habit has made them unfit for slavery, and they would, I have little doubt, make a brave defence against any invader of their freedom.

Such were our reflections, and we remained until late in the evening on the shores of the lake, conversing, enjoying the rising breeze, and contemplating with feelings of exquisite delight the divine objects that surrounded us.

The following day was spent in a consideration of our circumstances, and in contemplation of the scene around us. A furious *vent d'Italie* (south wind) tore up the lake, making immense waves, and carrying the water in a whirlwind high in the air, when it fell like heavy rain into the lake. The waves broke with a tremendous noise on the rocky shores. This conflict continued during the whole day, but it became calmer towards the evening. S . . . and I walked on the banks, and sitting on a rude pier, S . . . read aloud the account of the Siege of Jerusalem from Tacitus.

(History of a Six Weeks' Tour.)

Early in May 1816, *Shelley and Mary, whom he was to marry after the suicide of Harriet, on December* 30th, 1816, *returned to Switzerland. They were accompanied once again by the indefatigable Claire, who was anxious to renew her acquaintance with the Alps and also her liaison with Lord Byron, a liaison which she had forced on him in London. She had written him a letter signed "E. Trefusis," in which she invited him to state what would be his reactions if a "woman whose reputation remained unstained . . . should throw herself on your mercy."*

Byron left her letter unanswered and her problem unsolved, but a lady tired of an "unstained reputation" is not easily baulked, and the reluctant stainer finally succumbed to her siege. "I was not in love," wrote Byron to his half-sister Augusta Leigh, "nor have any love left for any, but I could not exactly play the Stoic with a woman who had scrambled eight hundred miles to un-philosophise me."

Lord Byron had left England for ever on April 25th, 1816. *"The howl of contumely," wrote Macaulay, "followed him across the sea, up the Rhone, over the Alps."*

Byron, who might be described as a parlour Jacobin, had affected keen admiration for Napoleon, who, like Stalin in our time, continued to be regarded as a revolutionary long after he had liquidated revolutionaries. He declared that he was "damned sorry" that Napoleon had been defeated at Waterloo. His Jacobin sympathies were well known in France and he was accordingly refused permission to cross the country to Switzerland. After travelling through Belgium and the Rhineland he arrived in Lucerne on May 17th, *and at the Hotel Secheron near Geneva on May* 25th. *He was twenty-eight years of age, not one hundred as he stated in the hotel register. On the following morning, just as he was getting into a rowing boat, he was informed that the boat belonged to a "Monsieur Anglais." The boat was Shelley's, for the Shelley party had arrived on May* 16th.

The British colony at Geneva were agreeably scandalised by the relations between Shelley and Mary, Byron and Claire, and by the backwash of rumours which had followed Byron from England, rumours of which his relations with his half-sister were the theme. An English novelist, Mrs. Hervey, of sixty-five virtuous summers, fainted when confronted by the notorious reprobate.

Byron and the Shelleys soon tired of the curiosity of their fellow-guests and left the hotel only to discover that the villa which they had leased was over-looked by the hotel, the obliging landlord of which provided his guests with a telescope in order that they might continue their researches into the habits of the Byron-Shelley ménage. Byron and Shelley escaped their attentions by transferring themselves to Cologny on the opposite side of the lake.

Byron leased the Villa Diodatti, still in existence, and the Shelleys moved into the diminutive Maison Chapuis within a few minutes' walk of the Diodatti. During the weeks that followed Mary Shelley wrote the famous novel "Frankenstein," and Claire made herself useful copying out parts of the third Canto of "Childe Harold." Mary Shelley has described their early days beside the Lake in a letter dated May 17th.

Lake Geneva

WE have not yet found out any very agreeable walks, but you know our attachment to water excursions. We have hired a boat, and every evening, at about six o'clock, we sail on the lake, which is delightful, whether we glide over a glassy surface or are speeded along by a strong wind. The waves of this lake never afflict me with that sickness that deprives me of all enjoyment in a sea voyage; on the contrary, the tossing of our boat raises my spirits and inspires me with unusual hilarity. Twilight here is of short duration, but we at present enjoy the benefit of an increasing moon, and seldom return until ten o'clock, when, as we approach the shore, we are saluted by the delightful scent of flowers and new-mown grass, and the chirp of grasshoppers, and the song of the evening birds.

We do not enter into society here, yet our time passes swiftly and delightfully. We read Latin and Italian during the heats of noon, and when the sun declines we walk in the garden of the hotel, looking at the rabbits, relieving fallen cockchafers, and watching the motions of a myriad of lizards, who inhabit a southern wall of the garden. You know that we have just escaped from the gloom of winter and of London; and coming to this delightful spot during this divine weather, I feel as happy as a new-fledged bird, and hardly care what twig I fly to, so that I may try my new-found wings. A more experienced bird may be more difficult in its choice of a bower; but, in my present temper of mind, the budding flowers, the fresh grass of spring, and the happy creatures about me that live and enjoy these pleasures, are quite enough to afford me exquisite delight, even though clouds should shut out Mont Blanc from my sight. Adieu!

(Mary Shelley's Letters.)

On June 22nd Byron and Shelley left for a tour of Lake Léman, in the course of which they were nearly wrecked between Meillerie and St. Gingolph. Byron told Shelley, who could not swim, that he thought he could save him, but "Shelley answered me with the greatest coolness that 'he had no notion of being saved, and that I would have enough to do to save myself and begged 'not to trouble me.' " It is interesting to contrast Shelley's and Wordsworth's reactions to the danger of shipwreck. In 1820, when Wordsworth was returning to England, the ship struck upon the sands. "My brother," writes Dorothy Wordsworth, "thinking it would be impossible to save his wife and me, stripped off his coat to be ready to swim."

Shelley was a fervent admirer of Rousseau, who is often credited with initiating the mountain cult, but Rousseau's mountain worship was only an ideological deduction from his political philosophy. The idealisation of man in a state of nature led by natural transition to the idealisation of the Alpine peasant and thence to the idealisation of the peasant's Alpine environment, but Rousseau had no genuine interest in mountains. He was born in Geneva but never mentions Mont Blanc. He spent a great deal of time at Vevey but never refers to the Dent du Midi.

No pilgrim to Mecca was more devout than Shelley on his pilgrimage to the scenes immortalised by Rousseau in the "Nouvelle Héloïse."

A Storm on Lake Geneva

THE lake appeared somewhat calmer as we left Meillerie, sailing close to the banks, whose magnificence augmented with the turn of every promontory. But we congratulated ourselves too soon: the wind gradually increased in violence, until it blew tremendously; and, as it came from the remotest extremity of the lake, produced waves of a frightful height, and covered the whole surface with a chaos of foam. One of our boatmen, who was a dreadfully stupid fellow, persisted in holding the sail at a time when the boat was on the point of being driven under water by the hurricane. On discovering his error, he let it entirely go, and the boat for a moment refused to obey the helm; in addition, the rudder was so broken as to render the management of it very difficult; one wave fell in, and then another. My companion, an excellent swimmer, took off his coat, I did the same, and we sat with our arms crossed, every instant expecting to be swamped. The sail was, however, again held, the boat obeyed the helm, and still in imminent peril from the immensity of the waves, we arrived in a few minutes at a sheltered port, in the village of St. Gingoux.

I felt in this near prospect of death a mixture of sensations, among which terror entered, though but subordinately. My feelings would have been less painful had I been alone; but I knew that my companion would have attempted to save me, and I was overcome with humiliation, when I thought that his life might have been risked to preserve mine.

(Shelley's Letters.)

The Sentimental Pilgrim

WE proceeded with a contrary wind to Clarens against a heavy swell. I never felt more strongly than on landing at Clarens, that the spirit of old times had deserted its once cherished habitation. A thousand times, thought I, have Julia and St. Preux walked on this terraced road, looking towards these mountains which I now behold; nay, treading on the ground where I now tread. From the window of our lodging our landlady pointed out "le bosquet de Julie." At least the inhabitants of this village are impressed with an idea, that the persons of that romance had actual existence. In the evening we walked thither. It is, indeed, Julia's wood. The hay was making under the trees; the trees themselves were aged, but vigorous, and interspersed with younger ones, which are destined to be their successors, and in future years, when we are dead, to afford a shade to future worshippers of nature, who love the memory of that tenderness and peace of which this was the imaginary abode. We walked forward among the vineyards, whose narrow terraces overlook this affecting scene. Why did the cold maxims of the world compel me at this moment to repress the tears of melancholy transport which it would have been so sweet to indulge, immeasurably, even until the darkness of night had swallowed up the objects which excited them?

I forgot to remark, what indeed my companion remarked to me, that our danger from the storm took place precisely in the spot where Julie and her lover were nearly overset, and where St. Preux was tempted to plunge with her into the lake. . . .

We, however, visited Lausanne, and saw Gibbon's house. We were shown the decayed summer-house where he finished his History, and the old acacias on the terrace, from which he saw Mont Blanc, after having written the last sentence. There is something grand and even touching in the regret which he expresses at the completion of his task. It was conceived amid the ruins of the Capitol. The sudden departure of his cherished and accustomed toil must have left him, like the death of a dear friend, sad and solitary.

My companion gathered some acacia leaves to preserve in remembrance of him. I refrained from doing so, fearing to outrage the greater and more sacred name of Rousseau; the contemplation of whose imperishable creations had left no vacancy in my heart for mortal things. Gibbon had a cold and unimpassioned spirit. I never felt more inclination to rail at the prejudices which cling to such a thing, than now that Julie and Clarens, Lausanne and the Roman Empire, compelled me to a contrast between Rousseau and Gibbon.

When we returned, in the only intervals of sunshine during the day, I walked on the pier which the lake was lashing with its waves. A rainbow spanned the lake, or rather rested one extremity of its arch upon the water, and the other at the foot of the mountains of Savoy. Some white houses, I know not if they were those of Meillerie, shone through the yellow fire.

(Shelley's Letters.)

In July Shelley, Mary and Claire spent four days at Chamonix. In the hotel registers in which other travellers had recorded their impressions of the scenery Shelley described himself as an atheist, democrat and philanthropist, but the first glorious impact of Mont Blanc provoked a reaction which dispelled, if only for the moment, the fumes of Rousseauesque philosophy. "I never knew," he wrote to Peacock, "I never imagined what mountains were before. The immensity of these aerial summits excited, when they suddenly burst upon the sight, a sentiment of ecstatic wonder, not unallied to madness. . . . There is more in all these scenes than mere magnitude of proportion: there is a majesty of outline; there is an awful grace in the very colours which invest these wonderful shapes—a charm which is peculiar to them, quite distinct even from the reality of their unutterable greatness," but few and far between are the evocative phrases which suggest a picture, phrases such as his reference to the glacier pinnacles "covered with a network of frosted silver." The "snowy pinnacles which shot into the bright blue sky" stimulated him like a powerful drug. The poet who remained to the last a stranger on this earth had a natural affinity with peaks which "pierce the clouds like things not belonging to this earth."

There is something inhuman about Shelley, as if he were an elemental incarnate in human form. Mr. Sydney Scott's Trilogy of hitherto unpublished letters ("The Athenians," "Harriet and Mary," "Shelley at Oxford," The Golden Cockerel Press) confirms me in my belief that Shelley was not wholly sane. He had the serene, untroubled conscience of a small child even when he was behaving most outrageously. Surely there is a touch of genuine insanity in the letter which he wrote to the wife he was deserting and in his enthusiastic invitation to his friend, Jefferson Hogg, to take full advantage of Mary Shelley's affectionate advances, for the sentence quoted from Shelley's letter to Hogg on page 51 of this book is difficult to interpret in any other sense. And no sane man could, in the same letter, write: "Let this horrid Galilean rule the canaille then," and "I took the Sacrament with her on Sunday." Mr. Scott tells me that Shelley covered his letters with doodles of trees and clouds, particularly clouds. He had no roots in this earth, and though the mountains might excite him to a "sentiment of ecstatic wonder, not unallied with madness," they did not excite him to love and worship. Their grandeur might provoke him to awe but their beauty left him unmoved. There are fewer lovelier views than that of Mont Blanc mirrored and reversed in the blue waters of Lake Geneva, but the distant snows of Mont Blanc, though beautiful, are not as overpowering in their impact of mountain grandeur as the closer view of rugged mountains obtainable from the eastern end of the lake, and it is the former which Shelley accordingly preferred. "The eastern boundary, or head of this lake, is exceedingly grand. Geneva is far from interesting and is a place which for the sake of the scenery I should never have made my habitation."

There is no hint in Shelley's poems of genuine affection for any spot on earth. He never showed the least desire to return to any particular place. He never seems to have suffered from any nostalgia for England when he was abroad nor for Switzerland when he was in England. Shelley would never have written anything in the least like the passage, quoted below, in which Mary Shelley recorded her sentiments on returning many years later to the scene of this memorable summer at Geneva.

Shelley's "Mont Blanc" tells us very little about Mont Blanc and a great deal about Shelley:

> . . . and when I gaze on thee
> I seem as in a trance sublime and strange
> To muse on my own separate fantasy. . . .

Mont Blanc, like Shelley and like Rousseau, holds strong views about the inequality of the existing social system:

> Thou hast a voice, great Mountain, to repeal
> Large codes of fraud and woe. . . .

Shelley discovered in Mont Blanc not only his sociology but also his philosophy, a confused blend of pantheism rather than atheism pervaded by the idealistic scepticism which denies reality to anything but thought:

> . . . The secret Strength of things
> Which governs thought, and to the infinite dome
> Of Heaven is as a law, inhabits thee!
> And what were thou, and earth, and stars, and sea,
> If to the human mind's imaginings
> Silence and solitude were vacancy?

Mont Blanc is the inspiration of Shelley's poem in the same sense that opium was the inspiration of Kubla Khan. Shelley was in "a trance sublime and strange" when he wrote a poem the scenery of which has less in common with the valley of Chamonix than with the dream scenery of Xanadu:

> Where Alph, the sacred river, ran
> Through caverns measureless to man
> Down to a sunless sea.

Is it fanciful to detect Coleridge's influence in the following passage, particularly in its concluding lines?

> Thy giant brood of pines around thee clinging,
> Children of elder time, in whose devotion
> The chainless winds still come and ever came
> To drink their odours, and their mighty swinging
> To hear—an old and solemn harmony;
> Thine earthly rainbows stretched across the sweep
> Of the æthereal waterfall, whose veil
> Robes some unsculptured image; the strange sleep
> Which when the voices of the desert fall
> Wraps all in its own deep eternity;
> Thy caverns echoing to the Arve's commotion,
> A loud, lone sound no other sound can tame;
> Thou art the path of that unresting sound. . . .

The majesty and the terror of the mountains you will find in Shelley:

> Mont Blanc appears—still, snowy, and serene—
> Its subject mountains their unearthly forms
> Pile around it, ice and rock; broad vales between. . . .

A desert peopled by the storms alone,
Save when the eagle brings some hunter's bone,
And the wolf tracks her there—how hideously
Its shapes are heaped around! rude, bare, and high,
Ghastly, and scarred, and riven. . . .

Even the glaciers seem sinister and evil:

The glaciers creep like snakes that watch their prey.

Shelley and Rousseau have often been acclaimed as high-priests of the mountain cult, but Dr. Engel's verdict on Rousseau is equally true of Shelley: "He neither knew nor loved the Alps."

LORD BYRON
(1788-1824)

Many critics prefer Byron's letters to his poetry. As a letter writer he was in the front rank.

The stanzas of "Childe Harold," nominally inspired by Lake Léman, are, for the most part, autobiographical material for the Byron legend, but the loveliness of the lake breaks through in the exquisite stanza, quoted below, a stanza which should be compared with Mary Shelley's letter on page 38.

"The Prisoner of Chillon" is one of my favourite Swiss poems, for reasons which I have tried (and failed) to explain in "Switzerland and the English."

Evening on Lake Geneva

IT is the hush of night, and all between
Thy margin and the mountains, dusk, yet clear,
Mellow'd and mingling, yet distinctly seen,
Save darken'd Jura, whose capt heights appear
Precipitously steep; and drawing near,
There breathes a living fragrance from the shore,
Of flowers yet fresh with childhood; on the ear
Drops the light drip of the suspended oar,
Or chirps the grasshopper one good-night carol more.

(*Childe Harold's Pilgrimage.*)

From "*The Prisoner of Chillon*"

LAKE Leman lies by Chillon's walls:
A thousand feet in depth below
Its massy waters meet and flow;
Thus much the fathom-line was sent
From Chillon's snow-white battlement,
  Which round about the wave inthrals:
A double dungeon wall and wave
Have made—and like a living grave
Below the surface of the lake
The dark vault lies wherein we lay,
We heard it ripple night and day;
  Sounding o'er our heads it knock'd;
And I have felt the winter's spray
Wash through the bars when winds were high
And wanton in the happy sky;
  And then the very rock hath rock'd,
  And I have felt it shake, unshock'd,
Because I could have smiled to see
The death that would have set me free. . . .
I made a footing in the wall,
  It was not therefrom to escape, . . .
But I was curious to ascend
To my barr'd windows, and to bend
Once more, upon the mountains high,
The quiet of a loving eye.
I saw them, and they were the same,
They were not changed like me in frame;
I saw their thousand years of snow
On high—their wide long lake below,
And the blue Rhone in fullest flow;
I heard the torrents leap and gush
O'er channell'd rock and broken bush;
I saw the white-wall'd distant town,
And whiter sails go skimming down;
And then there was a little isle,
Which in my very face did smile,
  The only one in view;
A small green isle, it seem'd no more,
Scarce broader than my dungeon floor,

But in it there were three tall trees,
And o'er it blew the mountain breeze,
And by it there were waters flowing,
And on it there were young flowers growing,
   Of gentle breath and hue.
The fish swam by the castle wall,
And they seem'd joyous each and all;
The eagle rode the rising blast,
Methought he never flew so fast
As then to me he seem'd to fly;
And then new tears came in my eye,
And I felt troubled—and would fain
I had not left my recent chain.

On September 17th, 1816, Byron and his lifelong friend, John Cam Hobhouse, left Clarens for a tour of the Bernese Oberland, the scenery of which is introduced into his dramatic poem "Manfred."

Byron's descriptions of mountain scenery are more effective in his letters and more evocative when fresh from the mind than in the more polished form in which they appear in "Manfred." The only mountain lines in "Manfred" which remain in my memory are the following:

   . . . yon red cloud, which rests
On Eigher's pinnacle, so rested then
So like that it might be the same; the wind
  As faint and gusty, and the mountain snows
Began to glitter with the climbing moon.

The only interest of "Manfred," the third act of which even Byron admitted to be "damned bad," is pathological. The theme is Manfred's forbidden love. "No avowal," wrote Mrs. Villiers, "can be more complete. It is too barefaced for her (Augusta's) friends to attempt to deny the allusion." Byron enjoyed expelling a reluctant cat from the bag. On October 6th, 1816, Byron left Geneva and never again crossed the Swiss frontier.

Byron's Tour of the Oberland

YESTERDAY, September 17th, I set out with Mr. Hobhouse on an excursion of some days to the mountains. . . .
Went to Chillon through scenery worthy of I know not whom; went over the Castle of Chillon again. On our return met an

English party in a carriage; a lady in it fast asleep—fast asleep in the most anti-narcotic spot in the world—excellent! I remember at Chamouni, in the very eyes of Mont Blanc, hearing another woman, English also, exclaim to her party, "Did you ever see anything more *rural?*"—as if it was Highgate, or Hampstead, or Brompton, or Hayes—"Rural"!—Rocks, pines, torrents, glaciers, clouds, and summits of eternal snow far above them—and "rural"! . . .

September 19th. Rose at five. Crossed the mountains to Montbovon on horseback, and on mules, and, by dint of scrambling, on foot also; the whole route beautiful as a dream, and now to me almost as indistinct. . . .

Hobhouse climbed the Dent de Jaman; Byron loitered below the summit.

The whole of the mountain's superb. A shepherd on a very steep and high cliff playing upon his *pipe*; very different from *Arcadia*, where I saw the pastors with a long musket instead of a crook, and pistols in their girdles. Our Swiss shepherd's pipe was sweet, and his tune agreeable. . . .

The music of the cow's bells (for their wealth, like the patriarchs', is cattle) in the pastures, which reach to a height far above any mountains in Britain, and the shepherds shouting to us from crag to crag, and playing on their reeds where the steeps appeared almost inaccessible, with the surrounding scenery, realised all that I have ever heard or imagined of a pastoral existence: much more so than Greece or Asia Minor, for there we are a little too much of the sabre and musket order, and if there is a crook in one hand, you are sure to see a gun in the other: but this was pure and unmixed—solitary, savage, and patriarchal. As we went, they played the "Rans des Vaches" and other airs, by way of farewell. I have lately repeopled my mind with nature. . . .

Byron and Hobhouse reached Thun via the Simmenthal and took the boat to Interlaken. On September 22nd they lodged with the curate at Lauterbrunnen, and visited the Staubbach.

The torrent is in shape curving over the rock, like the *tail* of a white horse streaming in the wind, such as it might be conceived would be that of the "pale horse" on which Death is mounted in the Apocalypse. It is neither mist nor water, but a something between both; its immense height (nine hundred feet) gives it a wave or curve, a spreading here, or condensation there, wonderful and indescribable. . . .

This seems to me more effective than the "Manfred" version which reads:

> It is not noon—the sunbow's rays still arch
> The torrent with the many hues of heaven,
> And roll the sheeted silver's waving column
> O'er the crag's headlong perpendicular,
> And fling its lines of foaming light along,
> And to and fro, like the pale courser's tail,
> The Giant steed, to be bestrode by Death,
> As told in the Apocalypse.

On September 23rd they crossed the Scheidegg.

Before ascending the mountain, went to the torrent (seven in the morning) again; the sun upon it, forming a *rainbow* of the lower part of all colours, but principally purple and gold; the bow moving as you move; I never saw any thing like this; it is only in the sunshine. Ascended the Wengen mountain; at noon reached a valley on the summit; left the horses, took off my coat, and went to the summit, seven thousand feet (English feet) above the level of the *sea*, and about five thousand above the valley we left in the morning. On one side, our view comprised the Jungfrau, with all her glaciers; then the Dent d'Argent, shining like truth; then the Little Giant (the Kleine Eigher); and the Great Giant (the Grosse Eigher), and last, not least, the Wetterhorn. The height of the Jungfrau is 13,000 feet above the sea, 11,000 above the valley: she is the highest of this range. Heard the avalanches falling every five minutes nearly. From whence we stood, on the Wengen Alp, we had all these in view on one side; on the other, the clouds rose from the opposite valley, curling up perpendicular precipices like the foam of the ocean of hell, during a spring tide—it was white, and sulphury, and immeasurably deep in appearance. The side we ascended was (of course) not of so precipitous a nature; but on arriving at the summit, we looked down upon the other side upon a boiling sea of cloud, dashing against the crags on which we stood (these crags on one side quite perpendicular). Staid a quarter of an hour; begun to

WENGERNALP AND JUNGFRAU

Photo: Franz Roth, Interlaken

THE CASTLE OF CHILLON
(The Dent du Midi in the background)

descend; quite clear from cloud on that side of the mountain. In passing the masses of snow, I made a snowball and pelted Hobhouse with it.

Got down to our horses again; eat something; remounted; heard the avalanches still; came to a morass; Hobhouse dismounted to get over well; I tried to pass my horse over; the horse sunk up to the chin, and of course he and I were in the mud together; bemired, but not hurt; laughed, and rode on. Arrived at the Grindelwald; dined, mounted again, and rode to the higher glacier—like *a frozen hurricane*. Starlight, beautiful, but a devil of a path! Never mind, got safe in; a little lightning, but the whole of the day as fine in point of weather as the day on which Paradise was made. Passed *whole woods of withered pines, all withered;* trunks stripped and barkless, branches lifeless; done by a single winter,—their appearance reminded me of me and my family. . . .

Once again Byron's prose is better than his poetry. "Frozen hurricane," a perfect simile, says more effectively in two words what Byron takes thirty words to say in "Manfred":

> O'er the savage sea,
> The glassy ocean of the mountain ice,
> We skim its rugged breakers, which put on
> The aspect of a tumbling tempest's foam,
> Frozen in a moment.

After crossing the Great Scheidegg to Meiringen, they embarked on the lake of Brienz and reached Interlaken after three hours of rowing.

Dined at Interlachen. Girl gave me some flowers, and made me a speech in German, of which I know nothing; I do not know whether the speech was pretty, but as the woman was, I hope so. . . .

Moore does not mention that this letter-journal was intended for Augusta and suppresses the concluding words, which are:

"To you dearest Augusta, I send, and for you I have kept, this record of what I have seen and felt. Love me as you are beloved by me."

4

MARY SHELLEY
(1797-1851)

Shelley was drowned on July 8th, 1822. Byron died two years later. On October 10th, 1840, Mary Shelley, who was then forty-two years of age, revisited the scenes of the memorable summer of 1816.

"Living after that"

IT was not a pleasant day for my voyage, as I have said. The far Alps were hid; the wide lake looked drear. At length, I caught a glimpse of the scenes among which I had lived, when first I stepped out from childhood into life. There, on the shores of Bellerive, stood Diodati; and our humble dwelling, Maison Chapuis, nestled close to the lake below. There were the terraces, the vineyards, the upward path threading them, the little port where our boat lay moored; I could mark and recognise a thousand slight peculiarities, familiar objects then —forgotten since—now replete with recollections and associations. Was I the same person who had lived there, the companion of the dead? For all were gone: even my young child, whom I had looked upon as the joy of future years, had died in infancy—not one hope, then in fair bud, had opened into maturity; storm and blight, and death, had passed over, and destroyed all. While very young, I had reached the position of an aged person, driven back on memory for companionship with the beloved; and now I looked on the inanimate objects that had surrounded me, which survived, the same in aspect as then, to feel that all my life since was but an unreal phantasmagoria—the shades that gathered round that scene were the realities—the substance and truth of the soul's life, which I shall, I trust, hereafter rejoin."

(Rambles in Germany and Italy.)

THOMAS JEFFERSON HOGG
(1800-1869)

Thomas Jefferson Hogg, the friend and biographer of Shelley, cordially disliked travel in general and Switzerland in particular, and he would never have undertaken the journey described in "Two Hundred and Nine Days" but *for Jane Williams' insistence. Hogg could not resist making love to any woman who attracted Shelley's fancy. "I attach little value to exclusive cohabitation," wrote Shelley to Hogg apropos of Hogg's advances to Shelley's first wife, Harriet. Mr. W. S. Scott has recently published the letters which were exchanged between Shelley, Mary Shelley (the poet's second wife) and Hogg. Even the most censorious of critics will find it difficult not to make allowances for a man who was being urged by his best friend to take full advantage of the passionate advances of his friend's wife. "I shall be very happy," writes Shelley, "to see you again, and to give you your share of our common treasure, of which you have been cheated for several days. . . . We will not again be deprived of this participated pleasure."* One of Shelley's loveliest poems, "To Jane—the Recollection," was written to Jane Williams, with whom Shelley was in love at the time of his death. Her first husband, a Mr. Jones, to whom she had been unhappily married in the West Indies, had deserted her, and she took the name of Edward Williams, drowned with Shelley, and later of Jefferson Hogg, though she was never legally married to anybody but Jones. Hogg, deprived of "participated pleasure" by Shelley's death, resigned himself to the prospect of a posthumous triangle, and resolved to marry Jane. Now Jane knew that Hogg was one of those Englishmen for whom "black men begin at Calais," and she therefore insisted on Hogg undertaking a continental journey as an exacting test of his devotion. Hogg sadly missed the "three things which daily habit has taught me to consider a prime necessity of life—law, Greek, or an English newspaper." He resented the fact that the lower races of humanity were not always resigned to being treated as such. "We were obliged," he writes of Venice under the Austrians, "to go personally to the police for our passports; they told us to take off our hats, with which order we sulkily complied."*

Hogg seems in retrospect to have been more jealous of Shelley, who had loved and been loved by Jane, than the living Shelley had ever been of Hogg, for nothing else can satisfactorily explain the fact that Hogg devotes twenty-eight pages of his book to Geneva without ever mentioning Shelley or without ever recording a single visit to the Maison Chapuis where Shelley had lived in the summer of 1816.

Bern in 1825

I APPROACHED this city with great expectation because I had seen a beautiful panorama—because I had been told, that it is the abode of Swiss beauty, its focus and very centre— and because I had heard all who visited it repeat, one after another, the most lavish and exaggerated praise. I was disappointed in all respects: the panorama was flattering to an

---

* *Harriet and Mary.* Golden Cockerel Press.

excess—the women were in the streets in their Sunday attire, yet they appeared hard-featured, stern and rusticated; and the strangers who visit the place repeat, like parrots, the laud that has originally been bestowed by some innkepeer, or interested inhabitant. The stone arcades which line the streets on both sides, are solid; they are good against sun and rain; but being low, have a gloomy aspect, especially on a Sunday, when the shops are shut. . . .

We visited the only public amusement in the place, the fosses, in which the bears are kept; there were two young bears and two old ones in separate places, open courts, as in the *Jardin des Plantes* at Paris. Persons of all ages and of all ranks, from the counsellor, or M.P., to the beggar, are never weary of gazing at the animals, and hang over the wall in fond delight; the opulent sometimes spend a halfpenny in pears or ginger-bread to throw to the bears. They watch them eating; and if the bears catch a piece of gingerbread in their paws, the happiness of the spectator is complete. This is the only notion a Bernois can form of pleasure: when he reads that we soon become tired of pleasure, he understands of feeding bears; a man of pleasure, or a woman of pleasure, is a person who is occupied all day long in throwing gingerbread to bears. . . . In the evening we visited a sort of raree-show of Swiss views and costumes; when we travel, we go to see persons and things that we would not tolerate at home.

"One great Waterloo bridge"

THE eternal granite is remarkable, all is granite, the solidity of which has a noble appearance: the whole country is one great Waterloo Bridge.

*Kantonligeist**

SWITZERLAND is the Scotland of Europe; a land that supplies servants—a land to be boasted of by its inhabitants, and quitted. The Swiss, like the Scotch, are all of good families, and of old families; I should like much to see a person from either nation of a bad family.

The quarrels amongst the different cantons are very ridicu-

* A Swiss expression for excessive cantonal patriotism.

lous; each petty state will have its separate coinage, to the unspeakable inconvenience of travellers: they cannot agree to have one general money, so cordially do they hate each other. The mutual dislike of the neighbouring inhabitants of Geneva and the Pays de Vaud is extremely strong: a good Vaudois, of an old family, complained to me most bitterly of the Genevese, and lamented that they had been turned into Swiss, and their country made one of the cantons; he insisted, in a great rage, that the wretches ought to have been handed over to the king of Sardinia, if he would have accepted of them. It should seem that they endeavoured to prove themselves to be not unworthy of his contempt by requiring a passport at the gate, before they would permit their fellow-countrymen to enter their old town.

The Pfarrer of Gadmen

I WAS civilly received at a wooden house; I asked for supper immediately, and was told that in a short time they would give me what they had for themselves, and I was conducted to a good clean bedroom. After a short toilette I came downstairs, and found the person who received me, conversing with a German traveller of the mercantile class. I was dying with thirst; I asked for wine, a bottle was given me, which was good, and for water; a bottle was brought from the opposite side of the table; I remarked that it was not fresh, and I was answered that he had just fetched it himself from the fountain. I thought that my host talked well for an innkeeper, or waiter, and in the corner of the room I saw many books. When he went out of the room I examined them; I found many German works, and to my great surprise, the Elzevir Scapula, a Virgil, some other Latin classics, and a Homer, Tauchnitzii. I admired such volumes in a valley of goatherds, and I learned of the traveller that I was not at an inn, but in the house of M. le Curé. When he returned I did all in my power to repair, by respect, the injustice I had unwittingly done to the proprietor of a Scapula by taking him for a landlord. . . . I asked in what language the mass was said in his church: he told me that I was in the canton of Bern, where they are Protestants. Soon afterwards the loud crying of a child in the next room showed that all questions about the mysterious sacrifice of mass would be out of place.

Advocatus Diaboli

The following passage occurs in a letter, dated November 29th, 1825, which was written by T. J. Hogg to Peacock, and first published in "The Athenians" by W. S. Scott (Golden Cockerell Press). I am indebted to Mr. Scott and his publishers for permission to reproduce this extract.

I WAS much pleased with Germany and with the Germans; the banks of the Rhine satisfy my ideas of Paradise and Rhenish of Nectar. With respect to Switzerland I was rather foreign than English in my feelings: the English admire that scenery very extravagantly; foreigners, and T.J.H., look upon it as a frightful wilderness: parts are certainly lovely, but the greater portion deserves no better name; some places had an extraordinary effect on my nerves and imagination, and it seems to be a strange insensibility, which is not affected in a like manner. I expected a dread and dismay, of which I could have had no notion, when I was in those horrible regions, where vegetation has ceased, and where there is nothing but bare unchanging rock, perpetual snow and everlasting ice; I cannot describe the satisfaction I used to feel, when I descended to flowers and vines and fruit trees and felt a genial air, and saw the clouds in their proper places, above my head and not beneath my feet. The fatigue of ascending to these abodes of the damned is beyond all conception, and the recollection of it adds to my dislike of the Alpine passes: the Simplon is bad enough, but St. Bernard, and especially St. Gotthard, will always be remembered with pain and terror. I used to think of you when I was on the mountains and to wonder, if you also would be a worshipper of Switzerland.

JOHN HOGG

By way of contrast to the disgruntled traveller, let me quote a tribute to Switzerland from John Hogg, brother of T. J. Hogg. The quotation is from "Letters from Abroad," published in 1844. I was delighted to discover that one at least of the early travellers had discovered the exceptional beauty of Lungern.

Lungern

PASSING through the lovely valley, and by the lake of Sarnen, I saw that *bijou*—the small, but most enchanting of lakes—the Lake of Lungern—of which the water is of an exquisite blue, transparent, and truly "splendidior vitro"; it is surrounded by, or as I will rather call it, set in, mountains of the loveliest and most pleasing forms, clothed with delicious verdure, and at its southern extremity is seen that snow covered Alp—the Wetterhorn, erecting its lofty pinnacle in vivid contrast with the rich green of the mountains below it, and the deep and azure sky above it. This scene, though less sublime than some I had witnessed, yet perhaps exceeded all I had experienced in extreme beauty. . . .

Being again fairly in Italy, I must say that I felt great regret on quitting that beautiful and pastoral district of Switzerland— a country, which, I may safely state, for its extent cannot yield to any in the world, in interest and in varied and stupendous scenes, that present themselves on all sides to the traveller. The kindness and simplicity too of the inhabitants I always found added much to the delights of the country.

DANIEL WALL

I borrow from Hugh Kingsmill's anthology "What They Said at the Time" the following extracts from an early guidebook:

General Remarks

IF Italy be deservedly styled the first country in the world for monuments of the arts, Switzerland is unquestionably entitled to claim a distinguished rank, being enriched with sublime monuments, and the most extraordinary phenomena of nature that can be found on the face of the globe.

Grindelwald

THERE is only one inn at Grindelwald; but, when it happens to be full, travellers are treated with hospitality at the parsonage-house. . . . Above the upper extremity of the little glacier rise on the S. the Viescherhorns, which are known by the dazzling whiteness that characterises the eternal snows with which they are covered. From those mountains issue a long range of pointed peaks, of a whimsical appearance, that descend towards the Eigher interieur.

The Lake of Lucerne

NOTWITHSTANDING all that has been said to the contrary, the navigation is not dangerous, provided the steersman and rowers be not intoxicated.

Mont Blanc

THE distance from the plains of Chamouny is only six miles and a half in a straight line; but, owing to the bad roads, the windings, and the great perpendicular height, the summit cannot be gained in less than eighteen hours. It is 15,662 feet above the level of the sea.

(NOTE.—"*There is,*" writes Mr. Kingsmill, "*no other authority than Mr. Wall for the existence of a road up Mont Blanc in* 1820.")

(From *The Traveller's Guide through Switzerland,* by Daniel Wall, London, 1819.)

THOMAS ARNOLD
(1795-1842)

My early prejudice against Thomas Arnold, provoked by the fact that I was called after him, was reinforced by reading Lytton Strachey's delicate dénigrement of the great Rugby headmaster in "Eminent Victorians." I have since discovered that Strachey's "fundamental fault was a moral one, in the last resort he did not care enough for truth." The verdict is that of the great historian of the Second Empire, Mr. F. A. Simpson. A writer who cared for truth could not have failed to draw attention to a passage in Stanley's "Life" which gives us a very different aspect of the headmaster from that portrayed by Strachey. "A mere plodding boy was above all others encouraged by him. At Laleham he had once got out of patience, and spoken

*sharply to a pupil of this kind, when the pupil looked up in his face and said,
'Why do you speak angrily, sir?—indeed, I am doing the best that I can.'
Years afterwards he used to tell the story to his children, and said, 'I never
felt so much ashamed in my life—that look and that speech I have never forgotten.' " Arnold was not a consistent character. He was a great liberal and
yet he opposed the granting of the franchise to the Jews and was the only
member of the Senate of London University who opposed the granting of
degrees to Jews. He despised the Italians, but loved Rome and found it
difficult to resist the Circe-like charm of the Italian lakes. He anticipated
Carlyle in his Gospel of the noble Teuton, and even Carlyle found it difficult to
improve on the vigour with which Arnold contrasts the nobility of German
Protestantism and the decadence of Latin Catholicism. "Far before us," he
writes on approaching Germany, "lay the land of our Saxon and Teutonic
forefathers—the land uncorrupted, by Roman or any other mixture; the birthplace of the most moral races of men that the world has yet seen . . . the
regenerating element in modern Europe." He hated the ages of chivalry, and
the ideals of feudal aristocracy, and the beliefs and culture of the Middle Ages.
When he was appointed Regius Professor of Modern History he shrank from
writing about the Middle Ages. "I could not bear to plunge myself into the
very depths of that noisome cavern, and have to toil through centuries of dirt and
darkness"; but his uncivilised attitude to the great centuries may be forgiven to a
man who loved mountains as Arnold loved them, and who could write of his
own beloved Westmoreland mountains: "Our residence in Westmoreland
attaches us all to it more and more; the refreshment which it affords me is
wonderful; and it is especially so in the winter, when the country is quieter, and
actually, as I think, more beautiful than in summer. I was often reminded, as I
used to come home to Grasmere of an evening, and seemed to be quite shut in by
the surrounding mountains, of the comparison of the hills standing about
Jerusalem, with God standing about His people. The impression, which the
mountains gave me, was never one of bleakness or wildness, but of a sort of
paternal shelter and protection to the valley." St. Bernard of Clairvaux, who
rode from dawn to sunset beside Lake Geneva so engrossed in prayer that he
replied "What lake?" when one of his companions commented on its beauty,
would perhaps have approved Arnold's misgivings about his own reactions to
the beauty of Como. The similar note of faint distrust can be detected in
Belloc's praise of the Italian lakes, quoted later in this volume. But then St.
Bernard, Dr. Arnold and Hilaire Belloc believed in original sin, and their
deep sense of moral evil accompanied them to the mountains. Fortunately,
thanks to modern progress, no such incongruous note disturbs the modern
prophets of the mountain cult.*

Arnold was thirty-four when he wrote the first of the letters quoted below.

St. Cergues and Lake Geneva

July 16th, 1829.

HOW completely is the Jura like Cithæron, with its νάπαι and λειμῶνες, and all that scenery which Euripides has given to the life in the Bacchæ. Immediately beyond the post-house, at St. Cergues, her view opens,—one that I never saw surpassed, nor can I ever; for if America should afford scenes of greater natural beauty, yet the associations cannot be the same. No time, to civilised man, can make the Andes like the Alps; another Deluge alone could place them on a level. There was the Lake of Geneva, with its inimitable and indescribable blue,—the whole range of the mountains which bound its southern shore,—the towns that edge its banks,—the rich plain between us and its waters,—and immediately around us, the pines and oaks of the Jura, and its deep glens, and its thousand flowers,—out of which we looked on this Paradise.

"England has other destinies"

On the Lake of Como, August 3rd, 1829.

I FANCY how delightful it would be to bring one's family and live here; but then, happily, I think and feel how little such voluptuous enjoyment would repay for abandoning the line of usefulness and activity which I have in England, and how the feeling myself helpless and useless, living merely to look about me, and training up my children in the same way, would soon make all this beauty pall, and appear even wearisome. But to see it as we are doing, in our moments of recreation, to strengthen us for work to come, and to gild with beautiful recollections our daily life of home duties,—this, indeed, is delightful, and is a pleasure which I think we may enjoy without restraint. England has other destinies than these countries,—I use the word in no foolish or unchristian sense,—but she has other destinies; her people have more required of them; with her full intelligence, her restless activity, her enormous means, and enormous difficulties; her pure religion and unchecked freedom; her form of society, with so much of evil, yet so much of good in it, and such immense power conferred by it;—her citizens, least of all men, should think of their own rest or enjoyment, but should cherish every faculty and improve every opportunity to the uttermost, to do good to themselves and to the world. Therefore these lovely valleys, and this surpassing beauty of lake and mountain, and garden and wood, are least, of all men, for us to covet; and our country, so entirely subdued as it is to man's uses, with its gentle hills and valleys, its innumerable canals and coaches, is best suited as an instrument of usefulness.

S. Maria del Monte

AT the foot of the mountain we began to walk, the road being a sort of paved way round the mountain in great zig-zags, and passing by in the ascent about twenty chapels or arches, introductory to the one at the summit. Over the first of these was written, "Her foundations are upon the holy hills"; and other passages of Scripture were written over the succeeding ones. In one of these chapels, looking in through the window, we saw that it was full of waxen figures as large as life, representing the Apostles on the day of Pentecost; and in another there was the sepulchre hewn out of the rock, and the Apostles coming, as on the morning of the Resurrection, "to see the place where Jesus lay." I confess, these waxen figures seemed to me anything but absurd; from the solemnity of the place altogether, and from the goodness of the execution, I looked on them with no disposition to laugh or to criticise. But what I did not expect was the exceeding depth and richness of the chestnut shade, through which the road partially ran, only coming out at every turning to the extreme edge of the mountain, and so commanding the view on every side. But when we got to the summit we saw a path leading up to the green edge of a cliff on the mountain above, and we thought if we could get there we should probably see Lugano. Accordingly, on we walked; till just at sunset we got out to the crown of the ridge, the brow of an almost precipitous cliff, looking down on the whole mountain of S. Maria del Monte, which on this side presented nothing but a large mass of rock and cliff, a perfect contrast to the rich wood of its other side. But neither S. Maria del Monte, nor the magnificent view of the plain of Lombardy, one mass of rich verdure, enlivened with its thousand white houses and church towers, were the objects which we most gazed upon. We looked westward full upon the whole range of mountains behind which, in a cloudless sky, the sun had just descended. It is utterly idle to attempt a description of such a scene. I counted twelve successive mountain outlines between us and the farthest horizon; and the most remote of all, the high peaks of the Alps, were brought out strong and dark in the glowing sky behind them, so that their edge seemed actually to cut it. Immediately below our eyes, plunged into a depth of chestnut forest, varied as usual with meadows and villages, and beyond, embosomed amidst the nearer mountains, lay the lake of Lugano. . . . If anyone wishes for the perfection of earthly beauty, he should see such a sunset as we saw this evening from the mountain above S. Maria del Monte.

"*To ordinary Christians there is something unnatural in this beauty*" (Belloc)

Mule track above the Lake of Como, under the chestnuts.
July 25th, 1830. (Third visit.)

ONCE more, dearest M——, for the third time, seated under these delicious chestnuts, and above this delicious lake, with the blue sky above, and the green lake beneath, and Monte Rosa and the S. Gothard, and the Simplon rearing their snowy heads in the distance. . . . It is almost awful to look at the overwhelming beauty around me, and then think of moral evil; it seems as if heaven and hell, instead of being separated by a great gulph from one another, were absolutely on each other's confines, and indeed not far from everyone of us. Might the sense of moral evil be as strong in me as my delight in external beauty, for in a deep sense of moral evil, more perhaps than in anything else, abides a saving knowledge of God!

Luzern and Windermere

July 29th, 1840.

WE arrived at Fluelen about half-past eight, and having had some food, and most commendable food it was, we are embarked on the Lake of Luzern, and have already passed Brunnen, and are outside the region of the high Alps.

It would be difficult certainly for a Swiss to admire our lakes, because he would ask, what is there here which we have not, and which we have not on a larger scale? I cannot deny that the meadows here are as green as ours, the valleys richer, the woods thicker, the cliffs grander, the mountains by measurement twice or three times higher. And if Switzerland were my home and country, the English lakes and mountains would certainly never tempt me to travel to see them, destitute as they are of all historical interest. In fact, Switzerland is to Europe, what Cumberland and Westmoreland are to Lancashire and Yorkshire; the general summer touring place. But all country that is actually beautiful, is capable of affording to those who live in it the highest pleasure of scenery, which no country, however beautiful, can do to those who merely travel in it; and thus while I do not dispute the higher interest of Switzerland to a Swiss, (no Englishman ought to make another country his home, and therefore I do not speak of Englishmen,) I must still maintain that to me Fairfield is a hundred times more beautiful than the Righi, and Windermere than the Lake of the Four Cantons. Not that I think this is overvalued by travellers, it cannot be so; but most people undervalue greatly what mountains are when they form a part of our daily life, and combine not with our hours of leisure, of wandering, and of enjoyment, but with those of home life, of work and of duty. *Luzern, July* 29.—We accomplished the passage of the lake in about three hours, and most beautiful it was all the way. And now, as in 1827, I recognise the forms of our common English country, and should be bidding adieu to mountains, and preparing merely for our Rugby lanes and banks, and Rugby work, were it not for the delightful excrescence of a tour which we hope to make to Fox How, and three or four days' enjoyment of our own mountains, hallowed by our English Church, and hallowed scarcely less by our English Law. Alas, the difference between Church and Law, and clergy and lawyers; but so in human things the concrete ever adds unworthiness to the abstract. I have been sure for many years that the subsiding of a tour, if I may so speak, is quite as delightful as its swelling; I call it its subsiding, when one passes by common things indifferently, and even great things with a fainter interest, because one is so strongly thinking of home and the returning to ordinary relations and duties.

MATTHEW ARNOLD
(1822-1888)

Matthew Arnold cannot be classified either with the Victorians who climbed or with the Victorians who only admired the mountains from below. He was elected to the Alpine Club in 1859, two years after its foundation, but in the early phase of the club the qualifications were not exacting, and Arnold's one Alpine Expedition, the Théodule, is the easiest of glacier passes.

It was in '46 that he first visited Switzerland. He fell in love at Thun with a woman who has never been identified. Hugh Kingsmill in his entertaining biography of the poet surmises that "Marguerite" was French, a governess or a companion in a family living in Thun. He quotes Arnold's

> Again I spring to make my choice,
> Again in tones of ire
> I hear a God's tremendous voice:
> "Be counselled and retire."

And Kingsmill adds:

"A lover who advances with one eye on his line of retreat is likely to have the retreat he contemplates imposed on him before he feels quite ready for it. This was Arnold's experience."

According to the tradition of the Arnold family, Marguerite was a creature of Arnold's fancy, but the recent publication of Arnold's letters to Clough have given the quietus to pious legend. Arnold writes to Clough (from Leuk on September 29th, '48):

"Tomorrow I repass the Gemmi and get to Thun, linger for one day at the hotel Bellevue for the sake of the blue eyes of one of its inmates . . . we know beforehand all they (women) can teach us, yet we are obliged to learn it directly from them."

Two years after parting from Marguerite, Arnold wrote "Obermann."

The last two stanzas of "Obermann Once More" are among the loveliest lines inspired by the mountains. These poems are in commemoration of a Frenchman who has published a collection of letters, written from Switzerland, under the title "Obermann."

De Senancour, the author of "Obermann," spent some years in Switzerland before returning with his wife to France. He writes with a certain charm of mountain scenery, and there are passages in his writings which would merit a place in this anthology if my choice was not restricted to English writers, but as a philosopher he is merely a dehydrated Rousseau, and it is not easy to understand Arnold's enthusiasm for him excepting on the hypothesis that he found in Obermann some echo of his own ineffective passion for Marguerite. The sudden crescendo of emotional feeling in the exquisite stanzas beginning

How often where the slopes are green

may be due, as Kingsmill suggests, to the memory of Marguerite penetrating "the vision of the incomparable lake along whose shores Arnold had first passed to meet her." And surely it is of Marguerite and not of Obermann that Arnold is thinking in the lines:

> I go, fate drives me; but I leave
> Half of my life with you.

Obermann

IN front the awful Alpine track
Crawls up its rocky stair;
The autumn storm-winds drive the rack,
Close o'er it, in the air.

Behind are the abandon'd baths
Mute in their meadows lone;
The leaves are on the valley paths,
The mists are on the Rhone—

The white mists rolling like a sea.
I hear the torrents roar.
—Yes, Obermann, all speaks of thee;
I feel thee near once more! . . .

How often, where the slopes are green
On Jaman, hast thou sate
By some high chalet-door, and seen
The summer day grow late,

And darkness steal o'er the wet grass
With the pale crocus starr'd,
And reach that glimmering sheet of glass
Beneath the piny sward,

Lake Leman's waters, far below!
And watch'd the rosy light
Fade from the distant peaks of snow;
And on the air of night

Heard accents of the eternal tongue
Through the pine branches play!
Listen'd, and felt thyself grow young!
Listen'd, and wept—Away! . . .

Farewell!—Whether thou now liest near
That much-lov'd inland sea,
The ripples of whose blue waves cheer
Vevey and Meillerie;

And in that gracious region bland,
Where with clear-rustling wave
The scented pines of Switzerland
Stand dark round thy green grave,

Between the dusty vineyard-walls
Issuing on that green place
The early peasant still recalls
The pensive stranger's face,

And stoops to clear thy moss-grown date
Ere he plods on again;—
Or whether, by maligner fate,
Among the swarms of men,

Where between granite terraces
The blue Seine rolls her wave,
The Capital of Pleasure sees
Thy hardly-heard-of grave—

Farewell! Under the sky we part,
In this stern Alpine dell.
O unstrung will! O broken heart!
A last, a last farewell!

Obermann Once More

(Composed many years after the preceding)

GLION?—Ah, twenty years, it cuts
 All meaning from a name!
White houses prank where once were huts;
Glion, but not the same!

And yet I know not! All unchanged
The turf, the pines, the sky!
The hills in their old order ranged;
The lake, with Chillon by!

And 'neath those chestnut-trees, where stiff
And stony mounts the way,
Their crackling husk-heaps burn, as if
I left them yesterday.

Across the valley, on the slope,
The huts of Avant shine!
Its pines under their branches ope
Ways for the tinkling kine.

Full-foaming milk-pails, Alpine fare,
Sweet heaps of fresh-cut grass,
Invite to rest the traveller there
Before he climb the pass—

The gentian-flower'd pass, its crown
With yellow spires aflame;
Whence drops the path to Allière down,
And walls where Byron came,

By their green river who doth change
His birth-name just below—
Orchard, and croft, and full-stored grange
Nursed by his pastoral flow.

But stop!—to fetch back thoughts that stray
Beyond this gracious bound,
The cone of Jaman, pale and grey;
See, in the blue profound!

Ah, Jaman! delicately tall
Above his sun-warm'd firs—
What thoughts to me his rocks recall!
What memories he stirs! . . .

The vision ended! I awoke
As out of sleep, and no
Voice moved—only the torrent broke
The silence, far below.

Soft darkness on the turf did lie;
Solemn, o'er hut and wood,
In the yet star-sown nightly sky,
The peak of Jaman stood.

Still in my soul the voice I heard
Of Obermann!—away
I turn'd; by some vague impulse stirr'd,
Along the rocks of Naye

And Sonchaud's piny flanks I gaze
And the blanch'd summit bare
Of Malatrait, to where in haze
The Valais opens fair,

And the domed Velan, with his snows,
Behind the upcrowding hills,
Doth all the heavenly opening close
Which the Rhone's murmur fills;

And glorious there, without a sound,
Across the glimmering lake,
High in the Valais-depth profound,
I saw the morning break.

The Terrace at Berne

TEN years!—and to my waking eye
Once more the roofs of Berne appear;
The rocky banks, the terrace high,
The stream!—and do I linger here?

The clouds are on the Oberland,
The Jungfrau snows look faint and far;
But bright are those green fields at hand,
And through those fields comes down the Aar;

And from the blue twin-lakes it comes,
Flows by the town, the church-yard fair;
And 'neath the garden-walk it hums,
The house!—and is my Marguerite there?

Switzerland Revisited
(1858)

An interval of nine years separates the Marguerite romance and Arnold's next visit to Switzerland. From Vevey he writes to his wife describing his journey to Switzerland.

FINALLY, it cleared up as we approached Geneva; at eleven the moon came out, and we saw the tall white houses, with their lights, scattered about the valley of the Rhône, and the high line of the Jura in the distance, beautifully soft and clear. . . .

I sat for a little while by my open window, and then went to bed. Next morning we were up at seven—a beautiful morning, —and there was the exquisite lake before us, with the Rhône issuing out of it, and the sun on the rocky summits of the Jura— all that one thinks of so often when one cannot see them with one's eyes. After breakfast we strolled about the town and by the lake.

(Letters of Matthew Arnold, vol. 1.)

Arnold had a gift for the evocative phrase which conjures up a picture of the scenes described, as, for instance:

ON looking back, was Mont Blanc in all his glory, with a few clouds playing about the middle of him, but his head and all his long line of Aiguilles cutting the blue sky sharp and bright, without a speck of mist.

Or again:

. . . the Chateau de Blonay, an old castellated house standing among those exquisite hills of park and lawn which are interposed between the high mountains and Vevey, and which make Vevey so soft and beautiful.

Lucerne in the Autumn
(1865)

WE have been at Lucerne, as the schools here are only just reopened, and I wanted to see something of those in a Catholic canton. At Lucerne we had good weather, the first time I have ever had good weather at Lucerne, and certainly there is no more beautiful place in the whole world. And the blaze of colour now that the rain had brought the purple that was wanted, the bright green still of the pastures, the black green of the firs, the yellow gold of the poplars, walnuts, chestnuts, and wych elms, and the red gold of the beeches, and at the foot of it all the lake, and at the head of it all the snowy line with Titlis, a mountain for whom Obermann has always given me a peculiar interest; then Lucerne itself with its curtain of old wall and trees and bridges, and the broad blue-green Reuss going through it. It required a day of mist and rain and penetrating damp, showing what the late autumn and winter at Lucerne are, to make it possible for one to depart. Tommy and I took the steamer on Sunday afternoon to Alpnach; the Alpnach arm of the lake goes among the recesses of the mountains as the Kussnacht arm goes among the opener pastoral country; and I have never seen anything more impressive than Pilatus as we gradually half-rounded him, and more solemn than the whole folding-in of the hills, at this autumnal season.

(Letters of Matthew Arnold, vol. 1.)

Pontresina
(1880)

MR. AYRE* is quite a power here, and it pleases me to see how the quality of Anglican chaplain gives a man a sort of natural headship among the English visitors, and quite the status of an agent of Government, yet without any officialdom, when he is like Ayre—a man who, by manners, conduct, and sense, is capable of filling such a position. His departure was quite the sensation of the day. The carriage in which he and his nieces went off was surrounded by people from all the hotels,

* The Rev. J. W. Ayre, Vicar of St. Mark's, North Audley Street.

who came to say good-bye and to thank him, and the innkeeper the night before sent in a bottle of champagne, that he and his nieces might drink success to their journey, though none of them drank wine. But on this occasion they had to drink it, and I helped them. . . .

. . . the valley I took led me to the Morteratsch glacier, which is perhaps the most beautiful thing here—a grand glacier, folded in by the Bernina and his great compeers; lovely names they have, but you would not know them. But nowhere even in the Oberland have I seen a more beautiful line than they make. I lunched at the restaurant by the glacier, and then wandered on by a path along the mountain side to a hut from which the ascent of the Bernina and the great peaks near him begins. I have seldom enjoyed anything more, and I did a good deal of botanising, as at that height the flowers linger on much later than down here. I did not see a soul. The moon rose, the black shadows stole gradually up the sparkling snow-sides of the mountains, and I could hardly tear myself away. . . .

The hotel is excellent and the *table d'hôte* all that can be desired. It is a much better class of English people here than in the other parts of Switzerland, because the fifteen hours' journey from the railway keeps off the mass of the "personally conducted."

What you would greatly like is the sight of the Bergamesque herdsmen, who have been feeding their herds on the pastures here for the summer, collecting them to drive them back to Italy. The men are picturesque objects, tall, swarthy Italians, with their civilised speech instead of the rough guttural German. And their cattle are too lovely. I could have stayed till night yesterday to see a herd driven through the swollen torrent of the Roseg which lay between their Alp and the road to Italy. In one place they had to swim, poor things, but it was beautiful to see how well they managed, greatly as they disliked it. At luncheon a gigantic St. Bernard seated himself between Miss Mundella and me. He entirely refused bread, and would eat nothing but beef-steak.

(*Letters of Matthew Arnold.*)

JOHN RUSKIN
(1819-1900)

No Victorian writer had more influence on contemporary taste than John Ruskin. He opened the eyes of the blind to the glory not only of Gothic architecture but also of Byzantine architecture, for until he wrote "The Stones of Venice," St. Mark's was invariably cited as an example of atrocious taste.

More than any other man he was responsible for transforming the trickle of English visitors to Switzerland into a mighty flood. Ruskin, who was the only son of a prosperous wine merchant with a taste for foreign travel, was fourteen when he first saw the Alps.

Ruskin is very fully represented in "The Englishman in the Alps," but at the time I compiled that anthology I had never read "Præterita" or "The Stones of Venice," and the passages quoted below, which are in my opinion as good as anything Ruskin ever wrote, are not to be found in any of the Alpine anthologies which have come my way.

The second passage quoted from the famous chapter in praise of Gothic ("The Stones of Venice") is unsurpassed in Ruskin's writings, and helps us to understand his mountain philosophy, for his mountain doctrine is unintelligible if divorced from that theocentric context which it has been the convention among the Alpine critics resolutely to ignore. Those who have attempted to separate Ruskin the mountain lover from Ruskin the art critic or Ruskin the sociologist have contributed little of value to our understanding of the greatest of mountain prophets.

In "Switzerland and the English" I have given my reasons for supposing that Ruskin narrowly escaped being a pioneer of mountaineering, and have quoted passages which show his understanding of the thing that makes men climb. His famous attack on the Alpine Club—"The Alps themselves, which your own poets used to love so reverently, you look upon as soaped poles in a bear-garden, which you set yourselves to climb and slide down again with 'shrieks of delight' "—was inspired partly by the alleged indifference of mountaineers to the historic associations of Switzerland, but still more by the feeling which finds expression in the following passage:

"*That question of the moral effect of danger is a very curious one; but this I know and find, practically, that if you come to a dangerous place, and turn back from it, though it may have been perfectly wise to do so, still your* character *has suffered some slight deterioration; you are to that extent weaker, more lifeless, more effeminate, more liable to passion and error in the future; whereas if you go through with the danger, though it may have been apparently wrong and foolish to encounter it, you come out of the encounter a stronger and better man, fitter for every sort of work and trial, and* nothing but danger *produces this effect.*"

The Journey to the Alps in 1833

THE poor modern slaves and simpletons who let themselves be dragged like cattle, or felled timber, through the countries they imagine themselves visiting, can have no conception whatever of the complex joys, and ingenious hopes, connected with the choice and arrangement of the travelling carriage in old times. The mechanical questions first, of strength—easy rolling, steady and safe poise of persons and luggage; the general stateliness of effect to be obtained for the abashing of plebeian beholders; the cunning design and distribution of store-cellars under the seats, secret drawers under front windows, invisible pockets under padded lining, safe from dust, and accessible only by insidious slits, or necromantic valves like Aladdin's trap-door; the fitting of cushions where they would not slip, the rounding of corners for more delicate repose; the prudent attachments and springs of blinds; the perfect fitting of windows, on which one-half the comfort of a travelling carriage really depends; and the adaptation of all these concentrated luxuries to the probabilities of who would sit where, in the little apartment which was to be virtually one's home for five or six months;—all this was an imaginary journey in itself, with every pleasure, and none of the discomfort, of practical travelling.

On the grand occasion of our first continental journey—which was meant to be half a year long—the carriage was chosen with, or in addition fitted with, a front seat outside for my father and Mary, a dickey, unusually large, for Anne and the courier, and four inside seats, though those in front very small, that papa and Mary might be received inside in stress of weather. I recollect, when we had finally settled which carriage we would have, the polite Mr. Hopkinson, advised of my dawning literary reputation, asking me (to the joy of my father) if I could translate the motto of the former possessor, under his painted arms, "Vix ea nostra voco,"—which I accomplishing successfully, father wittily observed that however by right belonging to the former possessor, the motto was with greater propriety applicable to us. . . .

Scarcely less official, for a travelling carriage of good class than its postillions, was the courier, or, properly, avant courier, whose primary office it was to ride in advance at a steady gallop, and order the horses at each post-house to be harnessed and ready waiting, so that no time might be lost between stages. His higher function was to make all bargains and pay all bills, so as to save the family unbecoming cares and mean anxieties, besides the trouble and disgrace of trying to speak French or any other foreign language. He, farther, knew the good inns in each town, and all the good rooms in each inn, so that he could write beforehand to secure those suited to his family. He was also, if an intelligent man and high-class courier, well acquainted with the proper sights to be seen in each town, and with all the occult means to be used for getting sight of those that weren't to be seen by the vulgar. Murray, the reader will remember, did not exist in those days; the courier was a private Murray, who knew, if he had any wit, not the things to be seen only, but those you would yourself best like to see, and gave instructions to your valet-de-place accordingly, interfering only as a higher power in cases of difficulty needing to be overcome by money or tact. He invariably attended the ladies in their shopping expeditions, took them to the fashionable shops, and arranged as he thought proper the prices of articles. Lastly, he knew, of course, all the other high-class couriers on the road, and told you, if you wished to know, all the people of consideration who chanced to be with you in the inn. . . .

Though my father never went into society, he all the more enjoyed getting a glimpse, reverentially, of fashionable people— I mean, people of rank,—he scorned fashion, and it was a great thing to him to feel that Lord and Lady —— were on the opposite landing, and that, at any moment, he might conceivably meet and pass them on the stairs. Salvador, duly advised, or penetratively perceptive of these dispositions of my father, entirely pleasing and admirable to the courier mind, had carte-blanche in all administrative functions and bargains. We found our pleasant rooms always ready, our good horses always waiting, everybody took their hats off when we arrived and departed. Salvador presented his accounts weekly, and they were settled without a word of demur.

To all these conditions of luxury and felicity, can the modern steam-puffed tourist conceive the added ruling and culminating one—that we were never in a hurry? coupled with the correlative power of always starting at the hour we chose, and that if we weren't ready, the horses would wait? As a rule, we breakfasted at our own home time—eight; the horses were pawing and neighing at the door (under the archway, I should have said) by nine. Between nine and three,—reckoning seven miles an hour, including stoppages, for minimum pace,—we had done our forty to fifty miles of journey, sate down to dinner at four,—and I had two hours of delicious exploring by myself in the evening; ordered in punctually at seven to tea, and finishing my sketches till half-past nine,—bed-time. . . .

And so, we reached the base of the Schwartzwald, and entered an ascending dingle; and scarcely, I think, a quarter of an hour after entering, saw our first "Swiss cottage." How much it meant to all of us,—how much prophesied to me, no modern traveller could the least conceive, if I spent days in trying to tell him. A sort of triumphant shriek—like all the railway whistles going off at once at Clapham Junction—has gone up from the Fooldom of Europe at the destruction of the myth of William Tell. To us, every word of it was true—but mythically luminous with more than mortal truth; and here, under the black woods, glowed the visible, beautiful, tangible testimony to it in the purple larch timber, carved to exquisiteness by the joy of peasant life, continuous, motionless there in the pine shadow on its ancestral turf,—unassailed and unassailing, in the blessedness of righteous poverty, of religious peace.

The myth of William Tell is destroyed forsooth? and you have tunnelled Gothard, and filled, it may be, the Bay of Uri; —and it was all for you and your sake that the grapes dropped blood from the press of St. Jacob, and the pine club struck down horse and helm in Morgarten Glen?

Difficult enough for you to imagine, that old travellers' time when Switzerland was yet the land of the Swiss, and the Alps had never been trod by foot of man. Steam, never heard of yet, but for short fair weather crossing at sea (were there paddle-packets across Atlantic? I forget). Any way, the roads by land were safe; and entered once into this mountain Paradise, we wound on through its balmy glens, past cottage after cottage on their lawns, still glistering in the dew.

The road got into more barren heights by the mid-day, the hills arduous; once or twice we had to wait for horses, and we were still twenty miles from Schaffhausen at sunset; it was past midnight when we reached her closed gates. The disturbed porter had the grace to open them—not quite wide enough; we carried away one of our lamps in collision with the slanting bar as we drove through the arch. How much happier the privilege of dreamily entering a mediæval city, though with the loss of a lamp, than the free ingress of being jammed between a dray and a tram-car at a railroad station!

It is strange that I but dimly recollect the following morning; I fancy we must have gone to some sort of church or other; and certainly, part of the day went in admiring the bow-windows projecting into the clean streets. None of us seem to have thought the Alps would be visible without profane exertion in climbing hills. We dined at four, as usual, and the evening being entirely fine, went out to walk, all of us,—my father and mother and Mary and I.

We must have still spent some time in town-seeing, for it was drawing towards sunset when we got up to some sort of garden promenade—west of the town, I believe; and high above the Rhine, so as to command the open country across it to the south and west. At which open country of low undulation, far into blue,—gazing as at one of our own distances from Malvern of Worcestershire, or Dorking of Kent,—suddenly—behold—beyond.

There was no thought in any of us for a moment of their being clouds. They were clear as crystal, sharp on the pure horizon sky, and already tinged with rose by the sinking sun. Infinitely beyond all that we had ever thought or dreamed,—the seen walls of lost Eden could not have been more beautiful to us; not more awful, round heaven, the walls of sacred Death.

(*Præterita.*)

The Mountain Brotherhood between the Cathedral and the Alp

THE charts of the world which have been drawn up by modern science have thrown into a narrow space the expression of a vast amount of knowledge, but I have never yet seen any one pictorial enough to enable the spectator to imagine the kind of contrast in physical character which exists between Northern and Southern countries. We know the differences in detail, but we have not that broad glance and grasp which would enable us to feel them in their fulness. We know that gentians grow on the Alps, and olives on the Apennines; but we do not enough conceive for ourselves that variegated mosaic of the world's surface which a bird sees in its migration, that difference between the district of the gentian and of the olive which the stork and the swallow see far off, as they lean upon the sirocco wind. Let us, for a moment, try to raise ourselves even above the level of their flight, and imagine the Mediterranean lying beneath us like an irregular lake, and all its ancient promontories sleeping in the sun: here and there an angry spot of thunder, a grey stain of storm, moving upon the burning field; and here and there a fixed wreath of white volcano smoke, surrounded by its circle of ashes; but for the most part a great peacefulness of light, Syria and Greece, Italy and Spain, laid like pieces of a golden pavement into the sea-blue, chased, as we stoop nearer to them, with bossy beaten work of mountain chains, and glowing softly with terraced gardens, and flowers heavy with frankincense, mixed among masses of laurel, and orange, and plumy palm, that abate with their grey-green shadows the burning of the marble rocks, and of the ledges of porphyry sloping under lucent sand. Then let us pass farther towards the north, until we see the orient colours change gradually into a vast belt of rainy green, where the pastures of Switzerland, and poplar valleys of France, and dark forests of the Danube and Carpathians stretch from the mouths of the Loire to those of the Volga, seen through clefts in grey swirls of rain-cloud and flaky veils of the mist of the brooks, spreading low along the pasture lands: and then, farther north still, to see the earth heave into mighty masses of leaden rock and heathy moor, bordering with a broad waste of gloomy purple that belt of field and wood, and splintering into irregular and grisly islands amidst the northern seas, beaten by storm, and chilled by ice-drift, and tormented by furious pulses of contending tide, until the roots of the last forests fail from among the hill ravines, and the hunger of the north wind bites their peaks into barrenness; and, at last, the wall of ice, durable like iron, sets, deathlike, its white teeth against us out of the polar twilight. And, having once traversed in thought this gradation of the zoned iris of the earth in all its material vastness, let us go down nearer to it, and watch the parallel change in the belt of animal life; the multitudes of swift and brilliant creatures that glance in the air and sea, or tread the sands of the southern zone; striped zebras and spotted leopards, glistening serpents, and birds arrayed in purple and scarlet. Let us contrast their delicacy and brilliancy of colour, and swiftness of motion, with the frost-cramped strength, and shaggy covering, and dusky plumage of the northern tribes; contrast the Arabian horse with the Shetland, the tiger and leopard with the wolf and bear, the antelope with the elk, the bird of paradise with the osprey; and then, submissively acknowledging the great laws by which the earth and all that it bears are ruled throughout their being, let us not condemn, but rejoice in the expression by man of his own rest in the statutes of the lands that gave him birth. Let us watch him with reverence as he sets side by side the burning gems, and smooths with soft sculpture the jasper pillars, that are to reflect a ceaseless sunshine, and rise into a cloudless sky: but not with less reverence let us stand by him, when, with rough strength and hurried stroke, he smites an uncouth animation out of the rocks which he has torn from among the moss of the moorland, and heaves into the darkened air the pile of iron buttress and rugged wall, instinct with work of an imagination as wild and wayward as the northern sea; creatures of ungainly shape and rigid limb, but full of wolfish life; fierce as the winds that beat, and changeful as the clouds that shade them.

There is, I repeat, no degradation, no reproach in this, but all dignity and honourableness: and we should err grievously in refusing either to recognise as an essential character of the existing architecture of the North, or to admit as a desirable character in that which it yet may be, this wildness of thought, and roughness of work; this look of mountain brotherhood between the cathedral and the Alp; this magnificence of sturdy power, put forth only the more energetically because the fine finger-touch was chilled away by the frosty wind, and the eye dimmed by the moor-mist, or blinded by the hail; this out-speaking of the strong spirit of men who may not gather redundant fruitage from the earth, nor bask in dreamy be-nignity of sunshine, but must break the rock for bread, and cleave the forest for fire, and show, even in what they did for their delight, some of the hard habits of the arm and heart that grew on them as they swung the axe or pressed the plough.

(*The Stones of Venice.*)

The Alps from the South

YOU see, then, from this spot, the plain of Piedmont, on the north and south, literally as far as the eye can reach; so that the plain terminates as the sea does, with a level blue line, only tufted with woods instead of waves, and crowded with towers of cities instead of ships. Then, in the luminous air beyond and behind this blue horizon-line, stand, as it were, the shadows of mountains, they themselves dark, for the southern slopes of the Alps of the Lago Maggiore and Bellinzona are all without snow; but the light of the unseen snowfields, lying level behind the visible peaks, is sent up with strange reflection upon the clouds; an everlasting light of calm Aurora in the north. Then, higher and higher around the approaching darkness of the plain, rise the central chains, not as on the Switzer's side, a recognisable group and following of successive and separate hills, but a wilderness of jagged peaks, cast in passionate and fierce profusion along the circumference of heaven; precipice behind precipice, and gulph beyond gulph, filled with the flaming of the sunset, and forming mighty channels for the flowings of the clouds, which roll up against them out of the vast Italian plain, forced together by the narrowing crescent, and breaking up at last against the Alpine wall in towers of spectral spray; or sweeping up its ravines with long moans of complaining thunder. Out from between the cloudy pillars, as they pass, emerge for ever the great battlements of the memorable and perpetual hills: Viso, with her shepherd witnesses to ancient faith; Rocca-Melone, the highest place of Alpine pilgrimage; Iseran, who shed her burial sheets of snow about the march of Hannibal; Cenis, who shone with her glacier light on the descent of Charlemain; Paradiso, who watched with her opposite crest the stoop of the French eagle to Marengo; and underneath all these, lying in her soft languor, this tender Italy, lapped in dews of sleep, or more than sleep—one knows not if it is trance, from which morning shall yet roll the blinding mists away, or if the fair shadows of her quietude are indeed the shades of purple death.

(*Inaugural Address*, Cambridge, October 29th, 1858.)

JAMES D. FORBES
(1809-1868)

*Forbes, a distinguished Scottish scientist, was the father of British mountain-
eering. He began to explore the Alps in 1832, and in 1841 made the fourth
ascent of the Jungfrau and the first ascent of the Stockhorn (11,796 ft.), this
being the first occasion on which a British mountaineer had made the first
ascent of a virgin peak.*

The History of a Glacier

POETS and philosophers have delighted to compare the
course of human life to that of a river; perhaps a still apter
simile might be found in the history of a glacier. Heaven-
descended in its origin, it yet takes its mould and conformation
from the hidden womb of the mountains which brought it forth.
At first soft and ductile, it acquires a character and firmness of
its own, as an inevitable destiny urges it on its onward career.
Jostled and constrained by the crosses and inequalities of its
prescribed path, hedged in by impassable barriers which fix
limits to its movements, it yields groaning to its fate, and still
travels forward seamed with the scars of many a conflict with
opposing obstacles. All this while, although wasting, it is
renewed by unseen power—it evaporates, but is not consumed.
On its surface it bears the spoils which during the progress of
existence it has made its own:—often weighty burdens devoid
of beauty or value—at times precious masses, sparkling with
gems or with ore. Having at length attained its greatest width
and extension, commanding admiration by its beauty and
power, waste predominates over supply, the vital springs begin
to fail; it stoops into an attitude of decrepitude; it drops the
burdens one by one, which it had borne so proudly aloft; its
dissolution is inevitable. But as it is resolved into its elements, it
takes all at once a new, and livelier, and disembarrassed form;
from the wreck of its members it arises, "another, yet the same,"
—a noble, full-bodied, arrowy stream, which leaps, rejoicing,
over the obstacles which before had stayed its progress, and
hastens through fertile valleys towards a freer existence, and a
final union in the ocean with the boundless and the infinite.

(The Tour of Mont Blanc and Monte Rosa, 1855.)

ALBERT SMITH
(1816-1860)
The Ascent of Mont Blanc

Albert Smith, a physician by profession, never lost one of his childhood's ambitions—to climb Mont Blanc. As a child, he had been given "The Peasants of Chamouni," which fired him to anticipate his subsequent success as a showman. "Finally I got up a small moving panorama of the horrors pertaining to Mont Blanc . . . and this I so painted up and exaggerated in my enthusiasm, that my little sister would become quite pale with fright." After gratifying his ambition he lectured for years on Mont Blanc at the Egyptian Hall, a popular entertainment which was attended, among others, by Queen Victoria. His book "Mont Blanc" is an engaging blend of genuine enthusiasm, bombast and melodramatic exaggerations. The "all but perpendicular iceberg" of the Mur de la Côte—"should the foot slip you would glide like lightning from one frozen crag to another"—is normally a steep snow slope down which a skier could descend in linked turns with nothing more alarming to fear than an innocuous slide to the bottom if he fell. Albert Smith was a great showman, but he did not climb Mont Blanc merely to exploit the adventure for commercial showmanship. He had a genuine love and reverence for the great mountain.

IT was now fearfully cold; and every now and then a sharp north-east wind nearly cut us into pieces, bringing with it a storm of spiculæ of ice, which were really very painful, as they blew against and past our faces and ears: so we took to our veils again, which all night long had been twisted round our hats. I felt very chilled and dispirited. I had now passed two nights without sleep; and I had really eaten nothing since the yesterday's morning but part of an egg, a piece of fowl, and a little bit of bread—for my illness had taken away all my appetite; and on this small diet I had been undergoing the greatest work. But none of us were complaining of nausea, or difficulty of breathing, or blood to the head, or any of the other symptoms which appear to have attacked most persons even on the Grand Plateau; so I plucked up fresh courage, and prepared for our next achievement.

This was no light affair. From the foot of the Rochers Rouges there runs a huge and slanting buttresss of ice, round which we had to climb from the north-east to the east. Its surface was at an angle of about sixty degrees. Above us, it terminated in a mighty cliff, entirely covered with icicles of marvellous length and beauty; below, it was impossible to see where it went, for it finished suddenly in an edge, which was believed to be the border of a great crevice. Along this we now had to go; and the journey was as hazardous a one as man might make along a barn-top with frozen snow on it. Jean Carrier went first, with his axe, and very cautiously cut every step in which we were to place our feet in the ice. It is difficult at times to walk along ice on a level; but when that ice is tilted up more than halfway towards the perpendicular, with a fathomless termination below, and no more foot and hand hold afforded than can be chipped out, it becomes a nervous affair enough. The cords came into requisition again; and we went along, leaning very much over to our right, and, I must say, paying little attention to our guides, who were continually pointing out spots for us to admire—the Jardin, Monte Rosa, and the Col du Géant—as they became visible. It took us nearly half an hour to creep round this hazardous slope, and then we came once more upon a vast undulating field of ice, looking straight down the Glacier du Tacul, towards the upper part of the Mer de Glace—the reverse of the view the visitor enjoys from the Jardin.

My eye-lids had felt very heavy for the last hour; and, but for the absolute mortal necessity of keeping them widely open, I believe would have closed before this; but now such a strange and irrepressible desire to go to sleep seized hold of me, that I almost fell fast off as I sat down for a few minutes on the snow to tie my shoes. But the foremost guides were on the march again, and I was compelled to go on with the caravan. From this point, on to the summit, for a space of two hours, I was in such a strange state of mingled unconsciousness and acute observation—of combined sleeping and waking—that the old-fashioned word "bewitched" is the only one that I can apply to the complete confusion and upsetting of sense in which I found myself plunged. With the perfect knowledge of where I was, and what I was about—even with such caution as was required to place my feet on particular places in the snow—I conjured up such a set of absurd and improbable phantoms about me, that the most spirit-ridden intruder upon a May-day festival on the Hartz mountains was never more beleaguered. I am not sufficiently versed in the finer theories of the psychology of sleep to know if such a state might be; but I believe for the greater part of this bewildering period I was fast asleep with my eyes open, and through them the wandering brain received external impressions; in the same manner as, upon awaking, the phantasms of our dreams are sometimes carried on, and connected with objects about the chamber. It is very difficult to explain the odd state in which I was, so to speak, entangled. A great many people I knew in London were accompanying me, and calling after me, as the stones did after Prince Pervis, in the *Arabian Nights*. Then there was some terribly elaborate affair that I could not settle, about two bedsteads, the whole blame of which transaction, whatever it was, lay on my shoulders; and then a literary friend came up, and told me he was sorry we could not pass over his ground on our way to the summit, but that the King of Prussia had forbidden it. Everything was as foolish and unconnected as this, but it worried me painfully; and my senses were under such little control; and I reeled and staggered about so, that when we had crossed the snow prairie, and arrived at the foot of an almost perpendicular wall of ice, four or five hundred feet high—the terrible Mur de la Côte—up which we had to climb, I sat down again on the snow, and told Tairraz that I would not go any further, but that they might leave me there if they pleased.

The Mont Blanc guides are used to these little varieties of temper, above the Grand Plateau. In spite of my mad determination to go to sleep, Balmat and another set me up on my legs again, and told me that if I did not exercise every caution, we should all be lost together, for the most really dangerous part of the whole ascent had arrived. I had the greatest difficulty in getting my wandering wits into order; but the risk called for the strongest mental effort; and, with just sense enough to see that our success in scaling this awful precipice was entirely dependent upon "pluck," I got ready for the climb. I have said the Mur de la Côte is some hundred feet high, and is an all but perpendicular iceberg. At one point you can reach it from the snow, but immediately after you begin to ascend it obliquely, there is nothing below but a chasm in the ice more frightful than anything yet passed. Should the foot slip, or the baton give way, there is no chance for life—you would glide like lightning from one frozen crag to another, and finally be dashed to pieces, hundreds and hundreds of feet below in the horrible depths of the glacier. Were it in the valley, simply rising up from a glacier *moraine*, its ascent would require great nerve and caution; but here, placed fourteen thousand feet above the level of the sea, terminating in an icy abyss so deep that the bottom is lost in obscurity; exposed, in a highly rarefied atmosphere, to a wind cold and violent beyond all conception; assailed, with muscular powers already taxed far beyond their strength, and nerves shaken by constantly increasing excitement and want of rest—with bloodshot eyes, and raging thirst, and a pulse leaping rather than beating—with all this, it may be imagined that the frightful Mur de la Côte calls for more than ordinary determination to mount it.

Of course every footstep had to be cut with the adzes; and my blood ran colder still as I saw the first guides creeping like flies upon its smooth glistening surface. The two Tairraz were in front of me, with the fore part of the rope, and François Favret, I think, behind. I scarcely knew what our relative positions were, for we had not spoken much to one another for the last hour; every word was an exertion, and our attention was solely confined to our own progress. In spite of all my exertions, my confusion of ideas and extraordinary drowsiness increased to such a painful degree, that, clinging to the handholes made in the ice, and surrounded by all this horror, I do believe, if we had halted on our climb for half a minute, I should have gone off asleep. But there was no pause. We kept progressing, very slowly indeed, but still going on—and up so steep a path, that I had to wait until the guide before me removed his foot before I could put my hand into the notch. I looked down below two or three times, but was not at all giddy, although the depth lost itself in the blue haze.

For upwards of half an hour we kept on slowly mounting this iceberg, until we reached the foot of the last ascent—the *calotte*, as it is called—the "cap" of Mont Blanc. The danger was now over, but not the labour, for this dome of ice was difficult to mount. The axe was again in requisition; and everybody was so "blown," in common parlance, that we had to stop every three or four minutes. My young companions kept bravely on, like fine fellows as they were, getting ahead even of some of the guides; but I was perfectly done up. Honest Tairraz had no sinecure to pull me after him, for I was stumbling about, as though completely intoxicated. I could not keep my eyes open,

and planted my feet anywhere but in the right place. I know I
was exceedingly cross. I have even a recollection of having
scolded my "team," because they did not go quicker; and I was
excessively indignant when one of them dared to call my
attention to Monte Rosa. At last, one or two went in front, and
thus somewhat quickened our progress. Gradually our speed
increased, until I was scrambling almost on my hands and
knees; and then, as I found myself on a level, it suddenly
stopped. I looked round, and saw there was nothing higher.
The batons were stuck in the snow, and the guides were grouped
about, some lying down, and others standing in little parties.
I was on the top of Mont Blanc!   (*Mont Blanc.*)

ALFRED WILLS
(1828-1912)

*Alfred Wills, later Mr. Justice Wills, made many recruits to mountaineering
by his book "Wanderings Among the High Alps" from which the following
passage is taken.*

*His ascent of the Wetterhorn was an important landmark in the history of
the Alpine Club. Indeed it was for long an accepted convention in the Alpine
Club to consider his ascent of the Wetterhorn as the first purely sporting climb,
with no ulterior motive such as scientific research. I exposed this fantastic
myth in my book "The Alps," published in 1912, but no less an authority than
Sir Martin Conway gave renewed currency to this myth as late as 1922. The
facts are as follows.*

*The Wetterhörner consists of three peaks of which the Rosenhorn
(12,111 ft.) was the first to be climbed. The Mittelhorn (12,165 ft.) is the
highest. The Hasle Jungfrau (12,150 ft.), which is the peak conspicuous
from Grindelwald, is popularly known as the Wetterhorn.*

*The exploration of the Wetterhörner was initiated by the companions of
Aggasiz, a distinguished Swiss scientist, who spent many weeks investigating
glacier motion on the Unteraar glacier, where he bivouacked under an overhanging rock, his shelter being humorously described as the Hotel des
Neuchâtelois. On August 27th, 1844, his colleagues Desor, Dollfus,
Dupasquier, and the engineer Stengel, with six guides headed by Währen, left
the "hotel" on the Unteraar, crossed to the Urbachtal, and on the following
day made the first ascent of the Rosenhorn, the first of the Wetterhörner to be
climbed.*

*A few days later Desor instructed the guides Jaun and Bannholzer of
Meiringen to attempt the Wetterhorn, and on August 31st, 1844, they made*

the first ascent of the Hasle Jungfrau, which as I have said is popularly known as the Wetterhorn. On July 7th, 1845, two Swiss amateurs, Dr. Roth and Förster Fankhauser, with Grindelwald guides made the first ascent of the Wetterhorn from Grindelwald, the previous ascent having been made from Rosenlaui. Nearly a hundred years later a contemporary newspaper account of this expedition was unearthed, and a climb which had till then been ignored by all Alpine historians found due recognition among mountaineers. On the following day (July 8th, 1845) the highest peak of the Wetterhörner, the Mittelhorn, was climbed from Rosenlaui by an Englishman, Speer, with the Meiringen guides, Jaun and Kaspar Ablanalp. On July 31st, 1845, Agassiz, Vogt and Bovet, with the guides Währen, Jaun and Bannholzer, made the third ascent of the Wetterhorn (Hasle Jungfrau) from the Dollfus via the Lauteraarjoch.

Nine years later the Wetterhorn (Hasle Jungfrau) was climbed from Rosenlaui at the beginning of June, 1854, by a young Englishman named Blackwell. On June 13th he climbed the Wetterhorn from Grindelwald, and planted a flag just below the summit. It has been argued that he did not reach the top and that his flag marked the highest point reached. This is absurd. Nobody doubts that he climbed the peak from Rosenlaui a few days before. Had there been a cornice—a bad cornice is rare in June—he must have forced a breach through it on the first ascent, and there is therefore not the slightest reason to suppose that he could have been checked by the cornice a few days later.

A few weeks later, on September 17th, 1845, Wills made what he believed to be the first ascent of the Wetterhorn (Hasle Jungfrau). Actually it was the sixth in all, and the third from Grindelwald. One of his guides, Peter Bohren, as Herr Carl Egger points out in his book "Pioniere der Alpen," had climbed the mountain from Grindelwald with the Swiss amateurs and again with Blackwell. Herr Egger expresses surprise that he should have concealed from Wills the fact of these previous ascents, but surely Bohren was alive to the economic value of gratified ambition, and was not so foolish as to rob his patron of the innocent illusion that he was "the first to scale that awful peak." The good villagers of Grindelwald seem to have done their best to aid and abet this innocent deception.

Many years later Mr. Justice Wills presided over a notorious trial, the trial of Oscar Wilde.

The Ascent of the Wetterhorn

WHILE we had been making our short halt at the edge of the plateau, we had been surprised to behold two other figures, creeping along the dangerous ridge of rocks we had just passed. They were at some little distance from us, but we saw that they were dressed in the guise of peasants, and when we first perceived them, Lauener (who was a great hunter himself) shouted excitedly, "Gemsjäger!" but a moment's reflection convinced us that no chamois-hunter would seek his game in this direction; and immediately afterwards we observed that one carried on his back a young fir tree, branches, leaves and all. We had turned aside a little to take our refreshment, and while we were so occupied, they passed us, and on our setting forth again, we saw them on the snow slopes, a good way ahead, making all the haste they could, and evidently determined to be the first at the summit. After all our trouble, expense and preparations, this excited the vehement indignation of my Chamouni guides—they declared that, at Chamouni, anyone who should thus dog the heels of explorers and attempt to rob them of their well-earned honours would be scouted; nor were they at all satisfied with the much milder view the Oberlanders took of the affair. The pacific Balmat was exceedingly wroth, and muttered something about "coups de poing," and they at length roused our Swiss companions to an energetic expostulation. A great shouting now took place between the two parties, the result of which was, that the piratical adventurers promised to wait for us on the rocks above, whither we arrived very soon after them. They turned out to be two chamois-hunters, who had heard of our intended ascent, and resolved to be even with us, and plant their tree side by side with our "Flagge." They had started very early in the morning, had crept up the precipices above the upper glacier of Grindelwald, before it was light, had seen us soon after daybreak, followed on our trail, and hunted us down. Balmat's anger was soon appeased, when he found they owned the reasonableness of his desire that they should not steal from us the distinction of being the *first* to scale that awful peak, and instead of administering the fisticuffs he had talked about, he declared they were "bons enfants" after all, and presented them with a cake of chocolate; thus the pipe of peace was smoked, and tranquillity reigned between the rival forces.

Once established on the rocks, and released from the ropes, we began to consider our next operations. A glance upwards showed that no easy task awaited us. In front rose a steep curtain of glacier, surmounted, about five or six hundred feet above us, by an overhanging cornice of ice and frozen snow, edged with a fantastic fringe of pendants and enormous icicles. This formidable obstacle bounded our view, and stretched from end to end of the ridge. What lay beyond it, we could only conjecture; but we all thought that it must be crowned by a swelling dome, which would constitute the actual summit. We foresaw great difficulty in forcing this imposing barrier; but after a short consultation, the plan of attack was agreed upon, and immediately carried into execution. Lauener and Sampson were sent forward to conduct our approaches which consisted of a series of short zigzags, ascending directly from where we were resting to the foot of the cornice. The steep surface of the glacier was covered with snow; but it soon became evident that it was not deep enough to afford any material assistance. It was loose and uncompacted, and lay to the thickness of two or three inches only; so that every step had to be hewn out of the solid ice. Lauener went first, and cut a hole just sufficient to afford him a foot-hold while he cut another. Sampson followed, and doubled the size of the step, so as to make a safe and firm resting-place. The line they took ascended, as I have said, directly above the rocks on which we were reclining, to the base of the overhanging fringe. Hence, the blocks of ice, as they were hewn out, rolled down upon us, and shooting past, fell over the brink of the arête by which we had been ascending, and were precipitated into a fathomless abyss beneath. We had to be on the *qui vive* to avoid these rapid missiles, which came accompanied by a very avalanche of dry and powdery snow. One, which I did not see in time, struck me a violent blow on the back of the head, which made me keep a better look out for its successors. I suggested that they should mount by longer zigzags, which would have the double advantage of sending the debris on one side, and of not filling up the footsteps already cut with the drifts of snow. Balmat's answer, delivered in a low, quiet tone, was conclusive: "Mais où tomberaient-ils, monsieur, si, par un malheur, ils glissaient? A présent, il y aurait la chance que nous pourrions les aider; mais si on glissait à côté—voilá, monsieur!" pointing to a block of ice which passed, a little on one side, and bounded into the frightful gulf.

For nearly an hour, the men laboured intently at their difficult task, in which it was impossible to give them help; but, at length, they neared the cornice, and it was thought advisable that we should begin to follow them. Balmat went first, then I, then Bohren, and the two chamois hunters, who now made common cause with us, brought up the rear. We were all tied together. We had to clear out all the foot-holes afresh, as they were filled with snow. A few paces after starting, when we were clear of the rocks, I ascertained the angle of the slope, by planting my alpenstock upright, and measuring the distance from a given point in it to the slope, in two directions, vertically and horizontally. I found the two measurements exactly equal; so that the inclination of the glacier was 45°; but at every step it became steeper; and when, at length, we reached the others, and stood, one below another, close to the base of the cornice, the angle of inclination was between 60° and 70°! I could not help being struck with the marvellous beauty of the barrier which lay, still to be overcome, between us and the attainment of our hopes. The cornice curled over towards us, like the crest of a wave, breaking at irregular intervals along the line into pendants and inverted pinnacles of ice, many of which hung down to the full length of a tall man's height. They cast a ragged shadow on the wall of ice behind, which was hard and glassy, not flecked with a spot of snow, and blue as the "brave o'erhanging" of the cloudless firmament. They seemed the battlements of an enchanted fortress, framed to defy the curiosity of man, and to laugh to scorn his audacious efforts.

A brief parley ensued. Lauener had chosen his course well, and had worked up to the most accessible point along the whole line, where a break in the series of icicles allowed him to approach close to the ice parapet, and where the projecting crest was narrowest and weakest. It was resolved to cut boldly into the ice, and endeavour to hew deep enough to get a sloping passage on to the dome beyond. He stood close, not facing the parapet, but turned half round, and struck out as far away from himself as he could. A few strokes of his powerful arm brought down the projecting crest, which, after rolling a few feet, fell headlong over the brink of the arête, and was out of sight in an instant. We all looked on in breathless anxiety; for it depended upon the success of this assault, whether that impregnable fortress was to be ours, or whether we were to return, slowly and sadly, foiled by its calm and massive strength.

Suddenly, a startling cry of surprise and triumph rang through the air. A great block of ice bounded from the top of the parapet, and before it had well lighted on the glacier, Lauener exclaimed, "Ich schaue den blauen Himmel!" (I see blue sky!). A thrill of astonishment and delight ran through our frames. Our enterprise had succeeded! We were almost upon the actual summit. That wave above us, frozen, as it seemed, in the act of falling over, into a strange and motionless magnificence, was the very peak itself! Lauener's blows flew with redoubled energy. In a few minutes, a practicable breach was made, through which he disappeared; and in a moment more, the sound of his axe was heard behind the battlement under whose cover we stood. In his excitement, he had forgotten us, and very soon the whole mass would have come crashing down upon our heads. A loud shout of warning from Sampson, who now occupied the gap, was echoed by five other eager voices, and he turned his energies in a safer direction. It was not long before Lauener and Sampson together had widened the opening; and then, at length, we crept slowly on. As I took the last step, Balmat disappeared from my sight; my left shoulder grazed against the angle of the icy embrasure, while, on the right, the glacier fell abruptly away beneath me, towards an unknown and awful abyss; a hand from an invisible person grasped mine; I stepped across, and had passed the ridge of the Wetterhorn!

The instant before, I had been face to face with a blank wall of ice. One step, and the eye took in a boundless expanse of crag and glacier, peak and precipice, mountain and valley, lake and plain. The whole world seemed to lie at my feet. The next moment, I was almost appalled by the awfulness of our position. The side we had come up was steep; but it was a gentle slope, compared with that which now fell away from where I stood. A few yards of glittering ice at our feet, and then, nothing beneath us and the green slopes of Grindelwald, nine thousand feet beneath. I am not ashamed to own that I experienced, as this sublime and wonderful prospect burst upon my view, a profound and almost irrepressible emotion—an emotion which, if I may judge by the low ejaculations of surprise, followed by a long pause of breathless silence, as each in turn stepped into the opening, was felt by others as well as myself. Balmat told me repeatedly, afterwards, that it was the most awful and startling moment he had known in the course of his long mountain experience. We felt as in the more immediate presence of Him who had reared this tremendous pinnacle, and beneath the "majestical roof" of whose deep blue Heaven we stood, poised, as it seemed, half way between the earth and sky.

THE REV. JOHN FREDERICK HARDY
(1826-1888)

The first volume of "Peaks, Passes and Glaciers ' was published in 1859, and was edited by John Ball, the first President of the Alpine Club. The following account of the first ascent of the Lyskamm, one of the principal peaks in the Monte Rosa chain, appeared in the second volume.

Hardy was a Fellow of Sidney Sussex College, Cambridge. He was a member of the first party to cross the Jungfraujoch and Fiescherjoch, and was the first Englishman to climb the Finsteraarhorn and Bernina.

Hardy's narrative is a perfect mid-Victorian period piece. The heartiness and the unsophisticated patriotism—what modern climber would sing the national anthem on reaching the summit of a virgin peak?—the facetiousness and the indulgent attitude to the ladies—"who, God bless them for the dear, inconsistent creatures they are!"—have the nostalgic charm of a vanished age.

The First Ascent of the Lyskamm (14,888)

"I SAY, old fellow, we're all going up Monte Rosa tomorrow; won't you join us? We shall have capital fun."

"What! Is that Hardy? Oh, yes, do come, there's a good fellow."

With these and similar kind invitations was I greeted as I emreged from Seiler's hotel at Zermatt on a pleasant morning in August, 1861, to join the crowd of loungers who were enjoying the warm sun, and snuffing up the pure mountain air that, defiant of dirty chalets and still dirtier inhabitants, rolled down into the little village. Before I had time to answer, a voice, afterwards discovered to be J. A. Hudson's, was heard to mention the Lyskamm, upon which hint I spake.

"Ah, the Lyskamm! that's the thing: leave Monte Rosa, and go in for the Lyskamm; anybody can do Monte Rosa, now the route's so well known; but the Lyskamm's quite another affair."

"Yes, indeed, I expect it is. Why, Stephen couldn't do it."

"He was only stopped by the bad state of the snow."

"Well, Tuckett failed too."

"He was turned back by a fog."

"So may we be."

"Certainly we may, also we mayn't; and in the present state of the weather the latter's the more likely of the two."

The end of the discussion was that Professor Ramsay, Dr.

Sibson, T. Rennison, J. A. Hudson, and W. E. Hall, agreed to join with me in seeking a highway up the Lyskamm, while Galton and Gray remained faithful to their original intention of climbing the Rosy mountain. My five friends pressed upon me the leadership and management of the expedition; and my first act of sovereignty was the very agreeable one of receiving the homage of two new subjects. C. H. Pilkington and R. Stephenson, with whom I had crossed the Alphubel, and spent several pleasant days in the neighbourhood of Zermatt, but who had threatened to leave for England that very afternoon, came to ask me if I would take two more. "Yes, to be sure," I replied, "if you're the two." And having thus raised the party to eight, I set to work at once to seek the best guides.

Jean Pierre Cachat, of Chamounix, and Franz Lochmatter, of Macugnaga, were soon engaged. The latter introduced a companion, Karl Herr, of whom he gave so good an account that I gladly put him on my list; still I was without any local guide save Stephen Taugwald, who was engaged to Dr. Sibson; and though Stephen is a very decent fellow, he's not made of the sort of stuff for a leader.

"But why has not Monsieur engaged Pierre Perren?" inquired Cachat.

"Il n'est pas ici."

"Mais, oui, Monsieur, il est ici," replied a voice which there was no contradicting, for it was Perren's own; and amid a shout of laughter he pushed his way through the little crowd, and brought his jolly, ugly, honest, intelligent face in front of mine. He had returned unexpectedly to Zermatt in consequence of the illness of the gentleman with whom he had been travelling, and was thus enabled to place his services at our disposal.

We had now, in my opinion, force enough; and as the guides insisted on my naming the terms of our engagement, I offered to give them forty francs apiece in any case, but fifty if we reached the summit, which arrangement, perhaps somewhat too liberal for any but first-class men, they gladly accepted. Joseph Marie Perren, a brother of my friend, was then engaged to act as porter for twenty francs; forty eggs were ordered to be boiled hard, and a few loaves to be set aside; for meat, cheese, and wine, we knew we could depend on the inn at the Riffelberg.

In the cool of the evening we strolled slowly up the slopes on which this tiny auberge stands; and having ordered dinner and beds, of which latter article we actually obtained seven, while the eighth man had a mattress on the floor, we sent for the guides to discuss the hour of starting. We English were all for midnight; but the natives insisted that the moon would not give us sufficient light to traverse the glacier, and that there was no advantage in starting till two hours later. A lengthy debate ended in a compromise; 30 minutes a.m. was to be the time. A light repast, followed by a cigar and a petit verre, insured us three hours of sound sleep.

A few minutes after twelve I awoke, looked at my watch by the moonlight; and after that short struggle between inclination and duty, which the best regulated mind endures when its proprietor is snugly ensconced between the blankets, I jumped out of bed, and proceeded to rouse the rest. . . .

· What with one delay and another it was 1.40 a.m. before we actually started; so that, after all, the guides gained their point within twenty minutes. The moon was brilliant and all but full; but, being somewhat low in the sky, she invested us with tremendously long shadows; and as including our Monte Rosa friends, we were nineteen in all, and were for the most part walking in single file, the effect was decidedly spectral. . . .

At 5 a.m we divided ourselves into the two parties, which had been previously arranged by lots, as we were far too numerous for one rope.

And now the work began in real earnest. The snow was in delightful condition; but the glacier was cut up by innumerable crevasses into the most superb seracs, and we had to thread our way as through a labyrinth. Backwards and forwards, now right, now left, we doubled like a Cambridgeshire hare; or rather as we wriggled in and out, with the head of our long party going perhaps south, and the tail north or east or west, we must have looked at a distance like a gigantic snake winding along among the everlasting snows. In general No. 2 followed quietly in the footsteps of No. 1, but once they had the audacity to select their own route,—a breach of discipline which could not be overlooked, especially as they had obviously taken the best line of country, and were actually in advance of us. With a few severe words, received, I fear, with derisive cheers, we passed again to the front, and gave them no second opportunity of repassing us.

The inclination of the glacier varied through almost every

conceivable angle, from 1° to 360°; but the snow was so crisp and pleasant that we had scarcely a step to cut. We had originally intended to follow the usual route to the Lys Col, and then bear away to the right till we reached the lower end of the Lyskamm arete; but about 7.30 Perren pointed out to me a rather stiffish snow-slope, lying to our immediate right, by which we might possibly reach the desired point at once, and thus save, at the very least, an hour's fatigue. . . . Away we all floundered through the snow, which was not quite as hard as we could have wished; but by judicious zigzagging, and by adopting that "haustum longum, haustem fortem, et haustum omnes simul," which Lord Dufferin so forcibly recommends, we gained the top of our slope and the base of the arete in less than an hour.

We had taken a slight breakfast while among the seracs, but we now settled down to the substantial meal of the day. The knapsacks were unpacked, eggs, meat, bread, and cheese devoured with avidity, and washed down by a delicious beverage invented by one of our party, and henceforth to be known as the Sibson mixture,—red country wine and Swiss champagne combined in equal proportions.

Breakfast finished, I addressed my followers, and very nearly excited a mutiny by suggesting that, if anyone doubted his power to last, he had better remain on this plateau, as there could be no turning back on the arete. I am proud to say that my suggestion was received with the contempt it deserved. In fact, such strong language was used with regard to all laggards, that I am inclined to think that even the supernumerary porter, had he understood English, would have felt it his duty to proceed further. As it was, we left him alone in his glory, smoking the pipe of idleness. Unless his meditations were of a more exciting character than I suppose, he must have been rather cold before we returned to him.

At nine o'clock, after a short reconnaissance, Perren started ahead and went up the arete in magnificent style, kicking and cutting steps with a skill and rapidity which I have seldom seen equalled, stopping only now and then to shout down to us a hoarse query as to the state of the snow above him, lest he should unwarily tread upon an overhanging cornice; and on receiving a satisfactory answer, turning to his work again with a wild halloo. . . .

After about an hour and a half's hard climbing we reached a small plateau, from which the summit itself was visible; and though we saw that there was still serious work before us, we felt certain of victory, and indulged in a preliminary dance of triumph.

And now onward for the final assault. The slope becomes steeper and narrower; happily there is little wind, but the air is perceptibly keener; the snow is harder and harder; kicking will do but little now; the axe is in constant requisition. Hark! what is that Perren says about the Gipfel?

"Herr Hardy, wollen Sie der Erste sein, der seinen Fuss auf den Gipfel setzt?"—"He wants to know if you'd like to be the first to set foot on the top."

"Oh, by all means,—Ja gewiss, Peter."

And so in another minute (at 11.40 a.m.) Peter stands aside, and I find myself at the top of all, 14,889 feet above the level of the sea. On come the rest of the conspirators, crowding eagerly to the tiny plateau, which will barely hold us all at the same time. There is universal shaking of hands, and patting of backs, and noisy congratulation. As for Perren he is wild with joy, and shrieks and chuckles, and seizing both my hands dances round me; when he puts his arm round my shoulder, and pats and fondles me, as though he were caressing a young horse, that he had tried and not found wanting.

At last something like order is restored, and Herr strikes up a German hymn, which rings out clear and pleasantly in the calm air, till, at a hint from Perren, he changes into "God save the Queen," and out burst fourteen voices, if not in perfect harmony, at least in perfect goodwill; and as we sing with uncovered heads, the noble old anthem fills our English hearts with happy thoughts of home and fatherland, and of the bright eyes that will sparkle, and the warm hearts that will rejoice, at our success. . . .

For somewhat more than half an hour we feasted our eyes with this magnificent panorama, till some one complaining that he felt cold, there was a general cry for more of the Sibson mixture. Perren, who knew the difficulties that were yet to come, was for drinking no more till we were fairly off the arete; but his prudent counsels were laughed to scorn by the others, who declared it would be a sottise to bring wine to the top of a mountain, and then carry it down untasted. After all two bottles among fourteen was not likely to affect our steadiness very materially; and the slight stimulant would probably do more good than harm. At all events the mixture was taken as before; and then at half an hour after noon commenced the really anxious part of the expedition,—the descent of the arete. . . .

Slowly and steadily, carefully trying each step before trusting to it,—sometimes, when the slope allowed, walking boldly forwards with alpenstocks thrown well back,—at others, turning face to snow, and letting ourselves down, hand under hand, while we looked through our legs for the foot-holes,— now and again one or another of us slipping away, but held safely up by the rope and the steady anchorage of his comrades' alpenstocks—here and there the steps of our ascent, all melted and useless, and our progress broken into a series of short halts, while the axe was doing its work,—with all our faculties, mental as well as bodily, in full tension,—with no words uttered but the occasional "arrêtez" or "en avant,"—still downwards, downwards for nearly two hours.

Now, however, we see a black spot in the plateau we have been slowly approaching; the black spot moves,—it shouts,—it is the supernumerary porter; a few minutes more of caution, and we are receiving his congratulations, and, what is more interesting to us, making another dive into the contents of the knapsacks.

It is all plain sailing now; we may laugh, and talk, and sing as we please; the business is over, the Lyskamm is conquered, without an accident, and without a breakdown, by a larger party than ever before attempted a new ascent. We found the snow soft and yielding on the slope leading down to the Monte Rosa glacier; and as we zigzagged downwards in our old steps, the foremost men got pretty heavily besprinkled by the masses which were dislodged by their followers. This, however, only gave rise to a little vigorous chaff, and we were soon doubling again amongst the seracs, and fighting our way in the half-melted snow to the Auf der Platte, which we gained at 4.35 p.m.

And now we are once more among vestiges of civilisation. Fragments of egg-shells, chicken bones, and broken bottles, tell of the numerous picnics that have been celebrated here.

"By the bye, Perren, we have a cache here ourselves."

"Ja, Herr, we have four bottles of wine here."

"Out with it then, by all means; here's the corkscrew."

What is this sudden horror that comes over his face? Has he fallen unexpectedly upon the traces of some terrible or inhuman crime? It is but too true,—robbery of the most aggravated character,—our cache has been discovered, and one of our cherished bottles has been feloniously emptied! . . .

We finished the three bottles that had been left to us; and crossing the Gorner glacier, with no worse misfortune than an occasional shoeful of water, we reached the Riffel Inn at seven. Here we paid our guides the fifty francs apiece which we had promised, giving Perren an extra douceur of ten francs, which he had well earned by his careful leadership throughout.

We decided on pushing on to Zermatt at once; and although one or two of the party lost their way in the woods, we were all comfortably reunited at dinner soon after nine o'clock. The news of our success had preceded us, for we had been seen, when on the summit, by some Englishmen who were on the opposite ridges of Monte Rosa. The hearty welcome of Seiler, who, according to his wont, insisted upon treating us to his best wine, and the warm congratulations of our English friends, especially of the ladies (who, God bless them for the dear inconsistent creatures they are! always entreat you not to run into danger, and always are intensely delighted when they think you have disobeyed them), brought a most agreeable day to a most agreeable conclusion.   (*Peaks, Passes and Glaciers.*)

JOHN RICHARD GREEN
(1837-1883)

As a debunker of mountaineering the eminent historian J. R. Green is far more effective than Ruskin. The following essay, which will be found in "Stray Studies," was written about 1870.

"Solid, Practical, Slightly Stupid"

THE hero of the Bell Alp or the Oeggischorn is naturally enough the Alpine Clubist. He has hurried silent and solitary through the lower country, he only blooms into real life at the sight of "high work." It is wonderful how lively the little

place becomes as he enters it, what a run there is on the landlord for information as to his projects, what endless consulta-
tions of the barometer, what pottering over the pages of *Peaks,
Passes and Glaciers*. How many guides will he take, has he a dog,
will he use the rope, what places has he done before?—a
thousand questions of this sort are buzzing about the room as
the hero sits quietly down to his dinner. The elderly spinster
remembers the fatal accident of last season, and ventures to ask
him what preparations he has made for the ascent. The hero
stops his dinner politely, and shows her the new little box of
lipsalve with which he intends to defy the terrors of the Alps.
To say the truth, the Alpine climber is not an imaginative man.
With him the climb which fills every bystander with awe is "a
good bit of work, but nothing out of the way you know." He
has never done this particular peak, and so he has to do it; but
it has been too often done before to fill him with any particular
interest in the matter. As for the ascent itself, he sets about
planning it as practically as if he were planning a run from
London to Lucerne. We see him sitting with his guides,
marking down the time-table of his route, ascertaining the
amount of meat and wine which will be required, distributing
among his followers their fair weights of blankets and ropes.
Then he tells us the hour at which he shall be back to-morrow,
and the file of porters set off with him quietly and steadily up
the hillside. We turn out and give him a cheer as he follows,
but the thought of the provisions takes a little of the edge off our
romance. Still, there is a great run that evening on *Peaks,
Passes and Glaciers*, and a constant little buzz round the fortunate
person who has found the one record of an ascent of this
particular peak.

What is it which makes men in Alpine travel-books write as
men never write elsewhere? What is the origin of a style unique
in literature, which misses both the sublime and the ridiculous,
and constantly hops from tall-talk to a mirth feeble and inane?
Why is it that the senior tutor, who is so hard on a bit of bad
Latin, plunges at the sight of an Alp into English inconceivable,
hideous? Why does page after page look as if it had been
dredged with French words through a pepper-castor? Why is
the sunrise or the scenery always "indescribable," while the
appetite of the guides lends itself to such reiterated description?
These are questions which suggest themselves to quiet critics,

but hardly to the group in the hotel. They have found the hole where the hero is to snatch a few hours of sleep before commencing the ascent. They have followed him in imagination round the edge of the crevasses. All the old awe and terror that disappeared in his presence revive at the eloquent description of the arête. There is a gloom over us as we retire to bed and think of the little company huddled in their blankets, waiting for the dawn. There is a gloom over us at breakfast as the spinster recalls one "dreadful place where you look down five thousand feet clear." The whole party breaks up into little groups, who set out for high points from which the first view of the returning hero will be caught. Everybody comes back certain they have seen him, till the landlord pronounces that everybody has mistaken the direction in which he must come. At last there is a distant *jodel*, and in an hour or so the hero arrives. He is impassive and good-humoured as before. When we crowd around him for the tidings of peril and adventure, he tells us, as he told us before he started, that it is "a good bit of work, but nothing out of the way." Pressed by the spinster, he replies, in the very words of *Peaks and Passes*, that the sunrise was "indescribable," and then, like the same inspired volume, enlarges freely on the appetite of his guides. Then he dines, and then he tells us that what he has really gained from his climb is entire faith in the efficacy of his little box for preventing all injury from sun or from snow. He is a little proud, too, to have done the peak in twenty minutes less time than Jones, and at ten shillings less cost. Altogether, it must be confessed, the Alpine Clubist is not an imaginative man. His one grief in life seems to be the failure of his new portable cooking apparatus, and he pronounces "Liebig's Extract" to be the great discovery of the age. But such as he is, solid, practical, slightly stupid, he is the hero of the Alpine hotel.

SIR LESLIE STEPHEN
(1832-1904)

Leslie Stephen was the only Alpine pioneer who achieved great eminence both in mountaineering and in literature. He made the first crossing of the Eigerjoch in 1859 and in the early sixties conquered a succession of great virgin peaks, notably the Schreckhorn, Zinal Rothorn, Bietschhorn, Blümlisalp, and the first crossing of the Jungfraujoch, Col des Hirondelles, etc. He was, perhaps, the most distinguished literary critic of his day, and will always be remembered outside mountaineering circles as the Editor of "The Dictionary of National Biography." He took Orders while a Don at Cambridge, but subsequently repudiated his clerical status and wrote "An Agnostic's Apology."

The Rewards of a Mountaineer

NOW the first merit of mountaineering is that it enables one to have what theologians would call an experimental faith in the size of mountains—to substitute a real living belief for a dead intellectual assent. It enables one, first, to assign something like its true magnitude to a rock or a snow-slope; and, secondly, to measure that magnitude in terms of muscular exertion instead of bare mathematical units. Suppose that we are standing upon the Wengern Alp; between the Mönch and the Eiger there stretches a round white bank, with a curved outline, which we may roughly compare to the back of one of Sir E. Landseer's lions. The ordinary tourists—the old man, the woman, or the cripple, who are supposed to appreciate the real beauties of Alpine scenery—may look at it comfortably from their hotel. They may see its graceful curve, the long straight lines that are ruled in delicate shading down its sides, and the contrast of the blinding white snow with the dark blue sky above; but they will probably guess it to be a mere bank—a snowdrift, perhaps, which has been piled by the last storm. If you pointed out to them one of the great rocky teeth that projected from its summit, and said that it was a guide, they would probably remark that he looked very small, and would fancy that he could jump over the bank with an effort. Now a mountaineer knows, to begin with, that it is a massive rocky rib, covered with snow, lying at a sharp angle, and varying perhaps from 500 to 1,000 feet in height. So far he might be accompanied by men of less soaring ambition; by an engineer who had been mapping the country, or an artist who had been carefully observing the mountains from their bases. They might learn in time to interpret correctly the real meaning of shapes at which the uninitiated guess at random. But the mountaineer can go a step further, and it is the next step which gives the real significance to those delicate curves and lines. He can translate the 500 or 1,000 feet of snow-slope into a more tangible

unit of measurement. To him, perhaps they recall the memory
of a toilsome ascent, the sun beating on his head for five or six
hours, the snow returning the glare with still more parching
effect; a stalwart guide toiling all the weary time, cutting steps
in hard blue ice, the fragments hissing and spinning down the
long straight grooves in the frozen snow till they lost themselves
in the yawning chasm below; and step after step taken along the
slippery staircase, till at length he triumphantly sprang upon
the summit of the tremendous wall that no human foot had
scaled before. The little black knobs that rise above the edge
represent for him huge impassable rocks, sinking on one side
in scarped slippery surfaces towards the snowfield, and on the
other stooping in one tremendous cliff to a distorted glacier
thousands of feet below. The faint blue line across the upper
névé, scarcely distinguishable to the eye, represents to one
observer nothing but a trifling undulation; a second, perhaps,
knows that it means a crevasse; the mountaineer remembers
that it is the top of a huge chasm, thirty feet across, and perhaps
ten times as deep, with perpendicular sides of glimmering blue
ice, and fringed by thick rows of enormous pendent icicles.
The marks that are scored in delicate lines, such as might be
ruled by a diamond on glass, have been cut by innumerable
streams trickling in hot weather from the everlasting snow, or
ploughed by succeeding avalanches that have slipped from the
huge upper snowfields above. In short, there is no insignificant
line or mark that has not its memory or its indication of the
strange phenomena of the upper world. True, the same picture
is painted upon the retina of all classes of observers; and so
Porson and a schoolboy and a peasant might receive the same
physical impression from a set of black and white marks on the
page of a Greek play; but to one they would be an incoherent
conglomeration of unmeaning and capricious lines, to another
they would represent certain sounds more or less corresponding
to some English words; whilst to the scholar they would reveal
some of the noblest poetry in the world, and all the associations
of successful intellectual labour. I do not say that the difference
is quite so great in the case of the mountains; still I am certain
that no one can decipher the natural writing on the face of a
snow-slope or a precipice who has not wandered amongst their
recesses, and learnt by slow experience what is indicated by
marks which an ignorant observer would scarcely notice. True,

even one who sees a mountain for the first time may know that, as a matter of fact, a scar on the face of a cliff means, for example, a recent fall of a rock; but between the bare knowledge and the acquaintance with all which that knowledge implies—the thunder of the fall, the crash of the smaller fragments, the bounding energy of the descending mass—there is almost as much difference as between hearing that a battle has been fought and being present at it yourself. We have read all descriptions of Waterloo till we are sick of the subject; but I imagine that our emotions on seeing the shattered well of Hougomont are very inferior to those of one of the Guard who should revisit the place where he held out for a long day against the assaults of the French army.

Now to an old mountaineer the Oberland cliffs are full of memories; and, more than this, he has learnt the language spoken by every crag and every wave of glacier. It is strange if they do not affect him rather more powerfully than the casual visitor who has never been initiated by practical experience into their difficulties. To him, the huge buttress which runs down from the Mönch is something more than irregular pyramid, purple with white patches at the bottom and pure white at the top. He fills up the bare outline supplied by the senses with a thousand lively images. He sees tier above tier of rock, rising in a gradually ascending scale of difficulty, covered at first by long lines of the debris that have been splintered by frost from the higher wall, and afterwards rising bare and black and threatening. He knows instinctively which of the ledges has a dangerous look—where such a bold mountaineer as John Lauener might slip on the polished surface, or be in danger of an avalanche from above. He sees the little shell-like swelling at the foot of the glacier crawling down the steep slope above, and knows that it means an almost inaccessible wall of ice; and the steep snowfields that rise towards the summit are suggestive of something very different from the picture which might have existed in the mind of a German student, who once asked me whether it was possible to make the ascent on a mule.

Hence, if mountains owe their influence upon the imagination in a great degree to their size and steepness, and apparent inaccessibility—as no one can doubt that they do, whatever may be the explanation of the fact that people like to look at big, steep, inaccessible objects—the advantages of the mountaineer are obvious. He can measure those qualities on a very different scale from the ordinary traveller. He measures the size, not by the vague abstract term of so many thousand feet, but by the hours of labour, divided into minutes—each separately felt—of strenuous muscular exertion. The steepness is not expressed in degrees, but by the memory of the sensation produced when a snow-slope seems to be rising up and smiting you in the face; when, far away from all human help, you are clinging like a fly to the slippery side of a mighty pinnacle in mid air. And as for the inaccessibility, no one can measure the difficulty of climbing a hill who has not wearied his muscles and brain in struggling against the opposing obstacles. Alpine travellers, it is said, have removed the romance from the mountains by climbing them. What they have really done is to prove that there exists a narrow line by which a way may be found to the top of any given mountain; but the clue leads through innumerable inaccessibilities; true, you can follow one path, but to right and left are cliffs which no human foot will ever tread, and whose terrors can only be realised when you are in their immediate neighbourhood. The cliffs of the Matterhorn do not bar the way to the top effectually, but it is only by forcing a passage through them that you can really appreciate their terrible significance.

Hence I say that the qualities which strike every sensitive observer are impressed upon the mountaineer with tenfold force and intensity. If he is as accessible to poetical influences as his neighbours—and I don't know why he should be less so—he has opened new avenues of access between the scenery and his mind. He has learnt a language which is but partially revealed to ordinary men. An artist is superior to an unlearned picture-seer, not merely because he has greater natural sensibility, but because he has improved it by methodical experience; because his senses have been sharpened by constant practice, till he can catch finer shades of colouring, and more delicate inflexions of line; because, also, the lines and colours have acquired new significance, and been associated with a thousand thoughts with which the mass of mankind has never cared to connect them. The mountaineer is improved by a similar process. But I know some sceptical critics will ask, does not the way in which he is accustomed to regard mountains rather deaden their poetical influence? Doesn't he come to look at them as mere instruments of sport, and overlook their more spiritual teaching? Does not all the excitement of personal adventure and the noisy apparatus of guides, and ropes, and axes, and tobacco, and the fun of climbing, rather dull his perceptions and incapacitate him from perceiving

> The silence that is in the starry sky,
> The sleep that is among the lonely hills?

Well, I have known some stupid and unpoetical mountaineers; and, since I have been dismounted from my favourite hobby, I think I have met some similar specimens among the humbler class of tourists. There are persons, I fancy, who "do" the Alps; who look upon the Lake of Lucerne as one more task ticked off from their memorandum book, and count up the list of summits visible from the Gornergrat without being penetrated with any keen sense of sublimity. And there are mountaineers who are capable of making a pun on the top of Mont Blanc—and capable of nothing more. Still I venture to deny that even punning is incompatible with poetry, or that those who make the pun can have no deeper feeling in their bosoms which they are perhaps too shamefaced to utter.

The fact is that that which gives its inexpressible charm to mountaineering is the incessant series of exquisite natural scenes, which are for the most part enjoyed by the mountaineer alone. This is, I am aware, a round assertion; but I will try to support it by a few of the visions which are recalled to me by these Oberland cliffs, and which I have seen profoundly enjoyed by men who perhaps never mentioned them again, and probably in describing their adventures scrupulously avoided the danger of being sentimental.

Thus every traveller has occasionally done a sunrise, and a more lamentable proceeding than the ordinary view of a sunrise can hardly be imagined. You are cold, miserable, breakfastless; have risen shivering from a warm bed, and in your heart long only to creep into bed again. To the mountaineer all this is changed. He is beginning a day full of the anticipation of a pleasant excitement. He has, perhaps, been waiting anxiously for fine weather, to try conclusions with some huge giant not yet scaled. He moves out with something of the feeling with which a soldier goes to the assault of a fortress, but without the same probability of coming home in fragments; the danger is trifling enough to be merely exhilatory, and to give a pleasant tension to the nerves; his muscles feel firm and springy, and his stomach—no small advantage to the enjoyment of scenery—is in excellent order. He looks at the sparkling stars with keen satisfaction, prepared to enjoy a fine sunrise with all his faculties at their best, and with the added pleasure of a good omen for his day's work. Then a huge dark mass begins to mould itself slowly out of the darkness, the sky begins to form a background of deep purple, against which the outline becomes gradually more definite; one by one, the peaks catch the exquisite Alpine glow, lighting up in rapid succession, like a vast illumination; and when at last the steady sunlight settles upon them, and shows every rock and glacier, without even a film of mist to obscure them, he feels his heart bound, and steps out gaily to the assault—just as the people on the Rigi are giving thanks that the show is over and that they may go to bed. Still grander is the sight when the mountaineer has already reached some lofty ridge, and, as the sun rises, stands between the day and the night—the valley still in deep sleep, with the mists lying between the folds of the hills, and the snow-peaks standing out clear and pale white just before the sun reaches them, whilst a broad band of orange light runs all round the vast horizon. The glory of sunsets is equally increased in the thin upper air. The grandest of all such sights that live in my memory is that of a sunset from the Aiguille du Goûter. The snow at our feet was glowing with rich light, and the shadows in our footsteps a vivid green by the contrast. Beneath us was a vast horizontal floor of thin level mists suspended in mid air, spread like a canopy over the whole boundless landscape, and tinged with every hue of sunset. Through its rents and gaps we could see the lower mountains, the distant plains, and a fragment of the Lake of Geneva lying in a more sober purple. Above us rose the solemn mass of Mont Blanc in the richest glow of an Alpine sunset. The sense of lonely sublimity was almost oppressive, and although half our party was suffering from sickness, I believe even the guides were moved to a sense of solemn beauty.

These grand scenic effects are occasionally seen by ordinary travellers, though the ordinary traveller is for the most part out of temper at 3 a.m. The mountaineer can enjoy them, both because his frame of mind is properly trained to receive the natural beauty, and because he alone sees them with their best accessories, amidst the silence of the eternal snow, and the vast panoramas visible from the loftier summits. And he has a similar advantage in most of the great natural phenomena of the cloud and the sunshine. No sight in the Alps is more impressive than the huge rocks of a black precipice suddenly frowning out through the chasms of a storm-cloud. But grand as such a sight may be from the safe verandahs of the inn at Grindelwald, it is far grander in the silence of the Central Alps amongst the savage wilderness of rock and snow. Another characteristic effect of the High Alps often presents itself when one has been climbing for two or three hours, with nothing in sight but the varying wreaths of mist that chased each other monotonously along the rocky ribs up whose snow-covered backbone we were laboriously fighting our way. Suddenly there is a puff of wind, and looking round we find that we have in an instant pierced the clouds, and emerged, as it were, on the surface of the ocean of vapour. Beneath us stretches for hundreds of miles the level fleecy floor, and above us shines out clear in the eternal sunshine every mountain, from Mont Blanc to Monte Rosa and the Jungfrau. What, again, in the lower regions, can equal the mysterious charm of gazing from the edge of a torn rocky parapet into an apparently fathomless abyss where nothing but what an Alpine traveller calls a "strange formless wreathing of vapour" indicates the storm-wind that is raging below us? I might go on indefinitely re-calling the strangely impressive scenes that frequently startle the traveller in the waste upper world; but language is feeble indeed to convey even a glimmering of what is to be seen to those who have not seen it for themselves, whilst to them it can be little more than a peg upon which to hang their own recol-lections. These glories, in which the mountain Spirit reveals himself to his true worshippers, are only to be gained by the appropriate service of climbing—at some risk, though a very trifling risk if he is approached with due form and ceremony—into the furthest recesses of his shrines. And without seeing them, I maintain that no man has really seen the Alps.

(*The Playground of Europe.*)

The Alps in Winter

THE winter Alps provide some such curtain. The very daylight has an unreal glow. The noisy summer life is suspended. A scarce audible hush seems to be whispered throughout the region. The first glacier stream that you meet strikes the key-note of the prevailing melody. In summer the torrent comes down like a charge of cavalry—all rush and roar and foam and fury—turbid with the dust ground from the mountain's flanks by the ice-share, and spluttering and writhing in its bed like a creature in the agonies of strangulation. In winter it is transformed into the likeness of one of the gentle brooks that creeps round the roots of Scawfell, or even one of those sparkling trout-streams that slides through a water-meadow beneath Stonehenge. It is perfectly transparent. It babbles round rocks instead of clearing them at a bound. It can at most fret away the edges of the huge white pillows of snow that cap the boulders. High up it can only show itself at intervals between smothering snowbeds which form continuous bridges. Even the thundering fall of the Handeck becomes a gentle thread of pure water creeping behind a broad sheet of ice more delicately carved and moulded than a lady's veil, and so diminished in volume that one wonders how it has managed to festoon the broad rock-faces with so vast a mass of pendent icicles. The pulse of the mountains is beating low; the huge arteries through which the life-blood courses so furiously in summer have become a world too wide for this trickle of pellucid water. If one is still forced to attribute personality to the peaks, they are clearly in a state of suspended animation. They are spell-bound, dreaming of dim abysses of past time or of the summer that is to recall them to life. They are in a trance like that of the Ancient Mariner when he heard strange spirit-voices conversing overhead in mysterious whispers. . . .

But it is time to descend to detail. The Alps in winter belong, I have said, to dreamland. From the moment when the traveller catches sight, from the terraces of the Jura, of the long encampment of peaks, from Mont Blanc to the Wetterhorn, to the time when he has penetrated to the innermost recesses of the chain, he is passing through a series of dreams within dreams. Each vision is a portal to one beyond and within, still more unsubstantial and solemn. One passes, by slow gradations, to the more and more shadowy regions, where the stream of life runs lower and the enchantment binds the senses with a more powerful opiate. Starting, for example, from the loveliest of all conceivable lakes, where the Blümlisalp, the Jungfrau and Schreckhorn form a marvellous background to the old towers of Thun, one comes under the dominion of the charm. The lake-waters, no longer clouded by turbid torrents, are mere liquid turquoise. They are of the colour of which Shelley was thinking when he described the blue Mediterranean awakened from his summer dreams "beside a pumice-isle in Baiæ's Bay." Between the lake and the snow-clad hills lie the withered forests, the delicate reds and browns of the deciduous foliage giving just the touch of warmth required to contrast the coolness of the surrounding scenery. And higher up, the pine-forests still display their broad zones of purple, not quite in that uncompromising spirit which reduces them in the intensity of summer shadow to mere patches of pitchy blackness, but mellowed by the misty air, and with their foliage judiciously softened with snow-dust like the powdered hair of a last-century beauty. There is no longer the fierce glare which gives a look of parched monotony to the stretches of lofty pasture under an August sun. The perpetual greens, denounced by painters, have disappeared, and in their place are ranges of novel hue and texture which painters may possibly dislike—for I am not familiar with their secrets—but which they may certainly despair of adequately rendering. The ranges are apparently formed of a delicate material of creamy whiteness, unlike the dazzling splendours of the eternal snows, at once so pure and so mellow that it suggests rather frozen milk than ordinary snow. If not so ethereal, it is softer and more tender than its rival on the loftier peaks. It is moulded into the same magic combination of softness and delicacy by shadows so pure in colour that they seem to be woven out of the bluest sky itself. Lake and forest and mountain are lighted by the low sun, casting strange misty shadows to portentous heights, to fade in the vast depths of the sky, or to lose themselves imperceptibly on the mountain flanks. As the steamboat runs into the shadow of the hills, a group of pine-trees on the sky-line comes near the sun, and is suddenly transformed into molten silver; or some snow-ridge, pale as death on the nearest side, is lighted up along its summit with a series of points glowing with intense brilliancy, as though the peaks were being kindled by a stupendous burning-glass. The great snow-mountains behind stand glaring in spectral calm, the cliffs hoary with frost, but scarcely changed in outline or detail from their summer aspect. When the sun sinks, and the broad glow of gorgeous colouring fades into darkness, or is absorbed by a wide expanse of phosphoric moonlight, one feels fairly in the outer court of dreamland.

(*The Playground of Europe*.)

THOMAS HARDY
(1840-1928)

In a letter to Leslie Stephen's biographer, Thomas Hardy describes how in the course of a visit to the Bernese Oberland in 1897 "the opening scenery revealed the formidable peak of the Great Schreckhorn" which Stephen was the first to climb. "Then and there," writes Hardy, "I suddenly had a vivid sense of him, as if his personality informed the mountain—gaunt and difficult, like himself.... As I lay awake that night, the more I thought of the mountain, the more permeated with him it seemed: I could not help remarking to my wife that I felt as if the Schreckhorn were Stephen in person; and I was moved to begin a sonnet to express the fancy, which I resolved to post to him when I got home. However, thinking that he might not care for it, I did not do so."
The sonnet is printed in "The Life and Letters of Leslie Stephen."

The Schreckhorn

ALOOF, as if a thing of mood and whim,
Now that its spare and desolate figure gleams
Upon my nearing vision, less it seems
A looming Alp-height than a guise of him
Who scaled its horn with ventured life and limb,
Drawn on by vague imaginings, maybe,
Of semblance to his personality
In its quaint glooms, keen lights, and rugged trim.

At his last change, when Life's dull coils unwind,
Will he, in old love, hitherward escape,
And the eternal essence of his mind
Enter this silent adamantine shape,
And his low voicing haunt its slipping snows
When dawn that calls the climber dyes them rose?

(*Collected Poems of Thomas Hardy*.)

EDWARD WHYMPER
(1840-1911)

Edward Whymper was the son of a wood engraver. He was taken away from school at the age of fourteen and apprenticed to his father's business. His work attracted the attention of William Longman, the publisher, who was in need of illustrations for a book on the Alps and who commissioned Edward Whymper for this purpose.

Whymper was twenty years of age when he left England for the Alps. He crossed the Channel on July 23rd, 1860, visited Kandersteg, crossed the Gemmi to Leuk, explored the Saas valley and sketched the view from the Fee Alp, one of the few Alpine views which excited his enthusiastic appreciation. From Saas Fee he went to Zermatt.

Mr. Frank Smythe, who has written the life of Whymper, makes an excellent point when he contrasts Whymper's first impressions of the Matterhorn, as recorded in his diary, with the sentiments which he put on record for the public:

"Saw, of course, the Matterhorn repeatedly; what precious stuff Ruskin has written about this, as well as about many other things. When one has a fair view of the mountain as I had, it may be compared to a sugar loaf set up on a table; the sugar loaf should have its head knocked on one side. Grand it is, but beautiful I think it is not."

And this is what he wrote, when he was writing for the public. The quotation is from "Scrambles amongst the Alps":

"Ages hence generations unborn will gaze upon its awful precipices and wonder at its unique form. However exalted may be their ideas, and however exaggerated their expectations, none will come to return disappointed!"

Whymper was a superb salesman. He sold the Matterhorn to the British public, and—like other salesmen—his private opinion of the commodity which he marketed did not always coincide with his publicity pronouncements. Few mountaineers had less appreciation of mountain beauty or a greater appreciation of mountain adventure.

Whymper returned to the Alps in 1861, made the second ascent of the Pelvoux and, emboldened by this success, attempted the Matterhorn from Italy. His seven unsuccessful attempts on the Matterhorn (1861-1865) were all directed against the Italian side of the mountain. His persistent neglect of what is now the normal route from Zermatt is difficult to explain.

Many of Whymper's attempts on the Matterhorn were made with the great Italian guide, J. A. Carrel. Carrel, an ardent patriot who had fought in the Italian wars of liberation, was determined to make the first ascent from Italy by the Italian ridge, and—if possible—to lead an Italian party to the summit. Carrel, like Whymper, had something of the undisciplined nature of the mountain he loved. Like Whymper, he was a born leader, and, like Whymper, he did not readily consent to play second fiddle. It is not surprising that Whymper and Carrel did not form a successful partnership.

Early in July 1865, Whymper, who was twenty-five years of age, arrived at Breuil hoping to engage Carrel for yet another attempt on the Matterhorn, but Carrel had previously been engaged by two Italians (Giordano and Sella), who shared Carrel's desire that the conquest of the Matterhorn should be an Italian triumph. Carrel told Whymper that he had been "engaged by a party of distinction," and it was only after Carrel had left for the Matterhorn that Whymper realised that he had been "bamboozled and humbugged."

Whymper decided to cross the Théodule to Zermatt and engage the first competent guide he could find for an attack on the mountain from Switzerland. It was at this point that Lord Francis Douglas, brother of the Marquess of Queensberry, arrived from Zermatt. Douglas was fresh from his conquest of the Gabelhorn, the first ascent from Zinal. He confided to Whymper that old Peter Taugwalder had prospected the East face of the Matterhorn and was confident that the mountain could be climbed by that route. Douglas had decided to attempt the ascent and was readily persuaded to join forces with Whymper.

On the following day they crossed the Théodule to Zermatt, where they learned that the Rev. Charles Hudson had just arrived in company with Michel Croz, with whom he was proposing to attempt the Matterhorn.

Hudson, who according to Leslie Stephen was "as simple and noble a character as ever carried out the precepts of muscular Christianity without talking its cant," was the greatest amateur of the day, a pioneer of guideless climbing who had led a guideless party up Mont Blanc by a new route. He had not wasted years in exploring the more difficult routes to the summit. He went straight for the easiest route, and had no difficulty in persuading Michel Croz to accompany him. The late Captain Farrar, in a scholarly article, contrasts the ease with which Hudson imposed his views on Croz with Croz's reluctance to try this route when it was suggested by Whymper.

Whymper and Douglas persuaded Hudson that it would be undesirable for two parties to be on the mountain at the same time. They agreed to join forces, and to include in the party a young man of nineteen, Douglas Hadow, who "had done Mont Blanc in less time than most men." Hadow, though a strong walker, was an inexperienced climber, and was destined to prove the weak link in the chain.

They left Zermatt on July 13th, 1865, and reached the summit next day. The East face up to the "Shoulder," less than a thousand feet below the summit, was so easy that they did not even bother to rope. From the "Shoulder" they turned over on to the North face, and here the climbing was difficult, but far easier than the final section of the Italian route.

In the course of the descent, a little distance below the summit, Hadow fell. The rope broke between old Taugwalder and Francis Douglas. Hudson, Hadow, Douglas and Croz fell; Whymper and the two Taugwalders survived to tell the tale.

Old Taugwalder, according to Whymper, laboured for many years under the suspicion that he had cut the rope. He left his native valley for America, returning only to die. This suspicion, as Whymper points out, was absurd. It would have been impossible to cut the rope in the second that elapsed before it tightened, and pointless to cut it after it tightened, for if a slip on rocks can be checked, all danger is over.

It was ungenerous of Whymper to point out that "an old and weak rope" had been selected by Taugwalder as the link between him and Douglas, for I do not think that Whymper really believed this selection to have been deliberate.

C. Egger, a distinguished Swiss mountaineer, suggests "that Whymper, consciously or unconsciously, wished to deflect attention from himself to his guides, in order to diminish his own responsibility for the accident. For Whymper tied himself on to Taugwalder after the delay caused by depositing the names on the summit; he ought, therefore, to have perceived that it was the weakest rope which united Taugwalder to Douglas, all the more so as he had himself provided the ropes."

Whymper subsequently made some fine pioneer ascents in the Alps and the Rockies. There is little evidence in his writing of any love of mountain scenery or indeed of mountains, except as problems to be solved and as the arena for athletic feats. The true mountain lover is happy on a mountain even when he is repeating a familiar ascent. Whymper hardly ever climbed a mountain which he had climbed before, and indeed had little interest in peaks which other people had climbed. He only climbed five mountains of whose previous ascent he was certain at the time he climbed them.

A comparison between Whymper's account of the Matterhorn conquest in his letter to "The Times" (August 7th, 1865) and his "Scrambles amongst the Alps" is as interesting as a contrast between Whymper's impression of the Matterhorn in his journal and the finished rhetoric of "Scrambles amongst the Alps." Some of the differences between "The Times" letter and the book are mere stylistic improvements; thus "we were happy that night in camp and feared no evil" is an obvious improvement on "we were happy that night in camp and did not dream of calamity."

In the letter to "The Times" he quotes Croz as remarking: "I would rather go down with you and another guide alone than with those who are going." This sentence does not appear in his book, possibly because Croz's remark may have been resented by the relations of those who had died.

In an unpublished letter to Sir Edward Davidson, written in 1909, Whymper quotes again this remark of Croz and complacently takes great credit for never having given publicity to it for fear of distressing the relatives. Many picturesque details in the book are not in the original letters, such as Whymper's attempt to attract Carrel's attention by hurling stones down the cliff (not, of course, as a recent writer seems to have believed, on to the route which Carrel was climbing).

It is interesting to compare Whymper's account of what Carrel said on returning, "It is true. We saw them ourselves—they hurled stones at us!

The old traditions are *true—there are spirits on the top of the Matterhorn,"* with the sober version of what the Carrels actually said in the letter which Giordano wrote immediately after their return. Carrel, in point of fact, did not mistake Whymper for a demon, for he recognised him by his white trousers. The "sharp-eyed" lad who thought he saw an avalanche on the Matterhorn and the cross in the sky which Whymper imagined he saw after the accident both make their first appearance in the book.

Whymper was a dramatic writer and did not always confine himself to what Clough calls "the mere it was." Thus in his account of the descent of the Ecrins he describes a dramatic leap over a big gap in the ridge which no subsequent mountaineer has discovered.

As a man Whymper had more personality than charm. He made no lasting friendships either among the amateurs or guides with whom he climbed. He regarded his guides, as Mr. Smythe tells us, not as partners in a joint enterprise, but as employees, and he insisted on "unquestioning obedience to all orders," an attitude which led to serious trouble when the guides were men of forceful independence such as Klucker or the Carrels. "Whymper," writes Mr. Smythe, "was a hard taskmaster to himself and his guides, and the gulf between them was absolute."

His origins were humble and to the end he had some difficulty with his aspirates, but he never suffered from an inferiority complex. He neither rebelled against the social hierarchy nor attempted to conform to its demands. He was wholly uninfluenced by convention which he neither accepted nor repudiated. His nephew describes him lunching at Anderton's Hotel in Fleet Street "in a sweater that showed his bare, bull-like neck to perfection; he seldom wore anything under the sweater." He smoked the strongest possible shag, and the carpets, tablecloths, upholstered chairs, etc., in his vicinity were frequently burnt full of holes. He invariably smoked in bed, "and not only were his bedclothes soon riddled with holes but his own chest became scarred by hot ashes too."

Whymper's first contact with English mountaineers was at Zermatt. He was on his first visit to the Alps. He had no climbs to his credit, but this young man of twenty seems to have been serenely unconscious of the social gulf between him and the great men of the A.C.

Whymper had something of the indomitable granite quality of the mountain which he conquered, with the result that we tend, as Mr. Winthrop Young rightly says, to identify him in our memories with the greatness of the Matterhorn. "Through the attitudes of the protagonists (of mountaineering)," writes Mr. Young, "he crashed with a rude personal vehemence that remains hopelessly individual."

My interpretation of Whymper's character differs in many respects from Frank Smythe's and is perhaps more critical. Thus, for instance, whereas Smythe endorses Whymper's attack on the Taugwalders, my sympathies are with the guides.

Leslie Stephen's verdict is far less favourable than Frank Smythe's. In an *article which has never been republished (Macmillan's, August 1871) he writes):*

"*Mr. Whymper very properly denounces the absurd fable that the elder Taugwald cut the rope. It was a simple impossibility for him to do so; and if the rope had not instantaneously snapped, the whole party must have been killed. In fact, three survivors probably owe their lives to Taugwald's presence of mind, to which Mr. Whymper does justice. But I rather regret that he should not reject decidedly another grave, though less serious accusation, which comes in fact to this, that Taugwald intentionally used a weak rope in fastening himself to Lord F. Douglas in order to have a chance of being separated from him in case of accident. Knowing the carelessness too often displayed on such occasions, the confidence which guides will show in weak ropes, and the probable state of excitement of the whole party, which would easily account for such an oversight, I think that the hypothesis of deliberate intention on Taugwald's part is in the highest degree improbable; and there is not a particle of direct evidence in its favour. The presumption would be that Croz was almost equally responsible; and, at any rate, such accusations should have some more tangible ground than a vague possibility. A discussion of the point would be out of place here, and I venture upon this digression merely for the sake of an old guide, who has always had a high character, and, to the best of my knowledge, has well deserved it.*"

But in point of fact no native of Zermatt ever believed that Taugwalder cut the rope. So I have been assured by a Zermatter who has made a special study of the Matterhorn history. The fact that Whymper ostentatiously defended Taugwalder against a charge which was never made by any Zermatter or responsible mountaineer gave weight to equally absurd accusations which originated with Whymper. It is also, I am told, false to imply that Taugwalder emigrated for any other reason than that emigration to America was, at that time, very frequent among Zermatters.

Whymper alleges in his book that old Taugwalder suggested that he should write in his Führerbuch that he had not been paid, in order that the sympathy thus aroused might indirectly secure him new employers. The conversation is stated to have taken place in French. Taugwalder's French was as rudimentary as Whymper's. Probably he merely asked for some statement in his Führerbuch which would absolve him for responsibility for the accident.

The Matterhorn Legends

IT is unnecessary to enter into a minute description of the Matterhorn, after all that has been written about that famous mountain. Those by whom this book is likely to be read will know that the summit of the peak is nearly 15,000 feet above the level of the sea, and that it rises abruptly, by a

WEISSHORN

Photo: E. Gyger, Adelboden

THE MATTERHORN FROM THE RIFFELSEE

Photo: E. Gyger, Adelboden

series of cliffs which may properly be termed precipices, a clear 5,000 feet above the glaciers which surround its base. They will know too that it was the last great Alpine peak which remained unscaled,—less on account of the difficulty of doing so, than from the terror inspired by its invincible appearance. There seemed to be a *cordon* drawn around it, up to which one might go, but no farther. Within that invisible line gins and effreets were supposed to exist—the Wandering Jew and the spirits of the damned. The superstitious natives in the surrounding valleys (many of whom firmly believed it to be not only the highest mountain in the Alps, but in the world) spoke of a ruined city on its summit wherein the spirits dwelt; and if you laughed, they gravely shook their heads; told you to look yourself to see the castles and the walls, and warned one against a rash approach, lest the infuriate demons from their impregnable heights might hurl down vengeance for one's derision. Such were the traditions of the natives. Stronger minds felt the influence of the wonderful form, and men who ordinarily spoke or wrote like rational beings, when they came under its power seemed to quit their senses, and ranted, and rhapsodised, losing for a time all common forms of speech. Even the sober De Saussure was moved to enthusiasm when he saw the mountain, and—inspired by the spectacle—he anticipated the speculations of later geologists, in the striking sentences which are placed at the head of this chapter. *(Scrambles amongst the Alps.)*

The Conquest of the Matterhorn

YOU must now carry your thoughts back to the seven Italians who started from Breuil on the 11th of July. Four days had passed since their departure, and we were tormented with anxiety lest they should arrive on the top before us. All the way up we had talked of them, and many false alarms of "men on the summit" had been raised. The higher we rose, the more intense became the excitement. What if we should be beaten at the last moment? The slope eased off, at length we could be detached, and Croz and I, dashing away, ran a neck-and-neck race, which ended in a dead heat. At 1.40 p.m. the world was at our feet, and the Matterhorn was conquered. Hurrah! Not a footstep could be seen.

It was not yet certain that we had not been beaten. The summit of the Matterhorn was formed of a rudely level ridge, about 350 feet long, and the Italians might have been at its farther extremity. I hastened to the southern end, scanning the snow right and left eagerly. Hurrah! again; it was untrodden. "Where were the men?" I peered over the cliff, half doubting, half expectant, and saw them immediately—mere dots on the ridge, at an immense distance below. Up went my arms and my hat. "Croz! Croz! come here!" "Where are they, Monsieur?" "There, don't you see them, down there?" "Ah! the *coquins*, they are low down." "Croz, we must make those fellows hear us." We yelled until we were hoarse. The Italians seemed to regard us—we could not be certain. "Croz, we *must* make them hear us; they *shall* hear us!" I seized a block of rock and hurled it down, and called upon my companion, in the name of friendship, to do the same. We drove our sticks in, and prised away the crags, and soon a torrent of stones poured down the cliffs. There was no mistake about it this time. The Italians turned and fled.

Still, I would that the leader of that party could have stood with us at that moment, for our victorious shouts conveyed to him the disappointment of the ambition of a lifetime. He was *the* man, of all those who attempted the ascent of the Matterhorn, who most deserved to be the first upon its summit. He was the first to doubt its inaccessibility, and he was the only man who persisted in believing that its ascent would be accomplished. It was the aim of his life to make the ascent from the side of Italy, for the honour of his native valley. For a time he had the game in his hands: he played it as he thought best; but he made a false move, and he lost it.

The others had arrived, so we went back to the northern end of the ridge. Croz now took the tent-pole, and planted it in the highest snow. "Yes," we said, "there is the flag-staff, but where is the flag?" "Here it is," he answered, pulling off his blouse and fixing it to the stick. It made a poor flag, and there was no wind to float it out, yet it was seen all around. They saw it at Zermatt—at the Riffel—in the Val Tournanche. At Breuil, the watchers cried, "Victory is ours!" They raised "bravos" for Carrel, and "vivas" for Italy and hastened to put themselves *en fête*. On the morrow they were undeceived. "All was changed; the explorers returned sad—cast down—dis-

heartened—confounded—gloomy. ' It is true,' said the men.
' We saw them ourselves—they hurled stones at us! The old
traditions *are* true,—there are spirits on the top of the Matterhorn! ' "   (*Scrambles amongst the Alps.*)

The Accident

A FEW minutes later, a sharp-eyed lad ran into the Monte
Rosa hotel, to Seiler, saying that he had seen an avalanche
fall from the summit of the Matterhorn on to the Matterhorngletscher. The boy was reproved for telling idle stories; he was
right, nevertheless, and this was what he saw.

Michel Croz had laid aside his axe, and in order to give Mr.
Hadow greater security, was absolutely taking hold of his legs,
and putting his feet, one by one, into their proper positions.
So far as I know, no one was actually descending. I cannot
speak with certainty, because the two leading men were partially
hidden from my sight by an intervening mass of rock, but it is
my belief, from the movements of their shoulders, that Croz,
having done as I have said, was in the act of turning round, to
go down a step or two himself; at this moment Mr. Hadow
slipped, fell against him, and knocked him over. I heard one
startled exclamation from Croz, then saw him and Mr. Hadow
flying downwards; in another moment Hudson was dragged
from his steps, and Lord F. Douglas immediately after him.
All this was the work of a moment. Immediately we heard
Croz's exclamation, old Peter and I planted ourselves as firmly
as the rocks would permit: the rope was taut between us, and
the jerk came on us both as on one man. We held: but the rope
broke midway between Taugwalder and Lord Francis Douglas.
For a few seconds we saw our unfortunate companions sliding
downwards on their backs, and spreading out their hands,
endeavouring to save themselves. They passed from our sight
uninjured, disappeared one by one, and fell from precipice to
precipice on to the Matterhorngletscher below, a distance of
nearly 4,000 feet in height. From the moment the rope broke
it was impossible to help them.

(*Scrambles amongst the Alps.*)

Afterthoughts

SO the traditional inaccessibility of the Matterhorn was vanquished, and was replaced by legends of a more real character. Others will essay to scale its proud cliffs, but to none will it be the mountain that it was to its early explorers. Others may tread its summit-snows, but none will ever know the feelings of those who first gazed upon its marvellous panorama; and none, I trust, will ever be compelled to tell of joy turned into grief, and of laughter into mourning. It proved to be a stubborn foe; it resisted long, and gave many a hard blow; it was defeated at last with an ease that none could have anticipated, but, like a relentless enemy—conquered but not crushed—it took terrible vengeance. The time may come when the Matterhorn shall have passed away, and nothing, save a heap of shapeless fragments, will mark the spot where the great mountain stood; for, atom by atom, inch by inch, and yard by yard, it yields to forces which nothing can withstand. That time is far distant; and, ages hence, generations unborn will gaze upon its awful precipices, and wonder at its unique form. However exalted may be their ideas, and however exaggerated their expectations, none will come to return disappointed!

(Scrambles amongst the Alps.)

ALFRED LORD TENNYSON
(1802-1892)

The Dawn from Milan

I CLIMB'D the roofs at break of day;
  Sun-smitten Alps before me lay.
    I stood among the silent statues,
And statued pinnacles, mute as they.

How faintly-flush'd, how phantom-fair,
  Was Monte Rosa, hanging there
    A thousand shadowy-pencill'd valleys
And snowy dells in a golden air.

(The Daisy.)

FREDERICK LOCKER-LAMPSON

Reminiscences of Tennyson in Switzerland (1869)

MÜRREN.—We were looking towards the higher Alps, and Tennyson said that perhaps this earth and all that is on it —storms, mountains, cataracts, the sun and the skies—are the Almighty; in fact, that such is our petty nature, we cannot see Him, but we see His shadow, as it were, a distorted shadow.

Schaffhausen.—It was exceedingly sultry at the falls of Schaffhausen. These were very impressive, but to escape the sun we were glad to take refuge in a shed pervaded by an atrocious odour of decayed cheeses, or some such horror. "This is my usual luck," says Tennyson. "I never go to see anything which is very impressive, without encountering something mean or repulsive. Now this sublime cataract, and this disgusting stench, will for ever dwell together in my memory."

Grindelwald.—Today we bought two large carved bears, for which, after breaking a good deal of French over the dealer, we agreed that Tennyson should pay one hundred francs. These bears are now in the entrance hall at Aldoworth, keeping watch and ward, quite ready to welcome the arriving guest with a friendly hug. . . . The Aigle (Adler) is a huge hungry-looking caravansary, with curiously uncomfortable beds. Tennyson's especially, had none of the caressing and consenting softness of that to which he had been accustomed; suggestive of anything but sleep, it was hard and lumpy, and of the pronounced German type. . . .

The glacier nearest the hotel is much discoloured by the debris from the mountain. Tennyson's farewell words were: "That glacier is a filthy thing; it looks as if a thousand London seasons had passed over it."

Wengern Alps.—We came across a man who blew a loud blast through a cow's horn, which produced a varied and prodigiously prolonged blast. Tennyson said: "You'll have to pay half a franc for that noise. The man subsists on the ghost of a sound."

Packing.—One afternoon I was packing Tennyson's portmanteau, packing for both of us, as he was suffering from gout. The weather was so hot that we had taken off our coats, he, the while, being seated on the edge of his bed, smoking his pipe . . . the dear fellow volunteered something very kind about the trouble I took for him. I assured him it was no trouble, quite the contrary. He was silent for a while and then he said: "Locker, I think you have a physical pleasure in packing."

ROBERT LOUIS STEVENSON
(1856-1894)

Davos in Winter

A LONG straight reach of valley, wall-like mountains upon either hand that rise higher and higher and shoot up new summits the higher you climb; a few noble peaks seen even from the valley; a village of hotels; a world of black and white—black pinewoods, clinging to the sides of the valley, and white snow flouring it, and papering it between the pinewoods, and covering all the mountains with a dazzling curd; add a few score invalids marching to and fro upon the snowy road, or skating on the ice-rinks, possibly to music, or sitting under sunshades by the door of the hotel—and you have the larger features of a mountain sanatorium. A certain furious river runs curving down the valley; its pace never varies, it has not a pool for as far as you can follow it; and its unchanging, senseless hurry is strangely tedious to witness. It is a river that a man could grow to hate. Day after day breaks with the rarest gold upon the mountain spires, and creeps, growing and glowing, down into the valley. From end to end the snow reverberates the sunshine; from end to end the air tingles with the light, clear and dry like crystal. Only along the course of the river, but high above it, there hangs far into the noon one waving scarf of vapour. It were hard to fancy a more engaging feature in a landscape; perhaps it is harder to believe that delicate, long-lasting phantom of the atmosphere, a creature of the incontinent stream whose course it follows. By noon the sky is arrayed in an unrivalled pomp of colour—mild and pale and melting in the north, but towards the zenith, dark with an intensity of purple blue. What with this darkness of heaven and the intolerable lustre of the snow, space is reduced again to chaos. An

English painter, coming to France late in life, declared with natural anger that "the values were all wrong." Had he got among the Alps on a bright day he might have lost his reason. And even to anyone who has looked at landscape with any care, and in any way through the spectacles of representative art, the scene has a character of insanity. The distant shining mountain peak is here beside your eye; the neighbouring dull-coloured house in comparison is miles away; the summit, which is all of splendid snow, is close at hand; the nigh slopes, which are black with pine-trees, bear it no relation, and might be in another sphere. Here there are none of those delicate grada-tions, those intimate, misty joinings-on and spreadings-out into the distance, nothing of that art of air and light by which the face of nature explains and veils itself in climes which we may be allowed to think more lovely. A glaring piece of crudity, where everything that is not white is a solecism and defies the judge-ment of the eyesight; a scene of blinding definition; a parade of daylight, almost scenically vulgar, more than scenically trying, and yet hearty and healthy, making the nerves to tighten and the mouth to smile: such is the winter daytime in the Alps. With the approach of evening all is changed. A mountain will suddenly intercept the sun; a shadow fall upon the valley; in ten minutes the thermometer will drop as many degrees; the peaks that are no longer shone upon dwindle into ghosts; and mean-while, overhead, if the weather be rightly characteristic of the place, the sky fades towards night through a surprising key of colours. The latest gold leaps from the last mountain. Soon, perhaps, the moon shall rise, and in her gentler light the valley shall be mellowed and misted, and here and there a wisp of silver cloud upon a hill-top, and here and there a warmly glowing window in a house, between fire and starlight, kind and homely in the fields of snow.

But the valley is not seated so high among the clouds as to be eternally exempt from changes. The clouds gather, black as ink; the wind bursts rudely in; day after day the mists drive overhead, the snowflakes flutter down in blinding disarray; daily the mail comes in later from the top of the pass; people peer through their windows and foresee no end but an entire seclusion from Europe, and death by gradual dry-rot, each in his indifferent inn; and when at last the storm goes, and the sun comes again, behold a world of unpolluted snow, glossy like fur, bright like daylight, a joy to wallowing dogs and cheerful to the souls of men. Or perhaps from across storied and malarious Italy, a wind cunningly winds about the mountains and breaks, warm and unclean, upon our mountain valley. Every nerve is set ajar; the conscience recognises, at a gust, a load of sins and negligences hitherto unknown; and the whole invalid world huddles into its private chambers, and silently recognises the empire of the Föhn. (*Essays of Travel.*)

GEORGE MEREDITH
(1828-1909)
The Mountain Fever

CARRY your fever to the Alps, you of minds diseased: not to sit down in sight of them ruminating, for bodily ease and comfort will trick the soul and set you measuring our lean humanity against yonder sublime and infinite; but mount, rack the limbs, wrestle it out among the peaks; taste danger, sweat, earn rest: learn to discover ungrudgingly that haggard fatigue is the fair vision you have run to earth, and that rest is your uttermost reward. Would you know what it is to hope again, and have all your hopes at hand?—hang upon the crags at a gradient that makes your next step a debate between the thing you are and the thing you may become. There the merry little hopes grow for the climber like flowers and food, immediate, prompt to prove their uses, sufficient if just within the grasp, as mortal hopes should be. How the old lax life closes in about you there! You are the man of your faculties, nothing more. Why should a man pretend to more? We ask it wonderingly when we are healthy. Poetic rhapsodists in the vales below may tell of the joy and grandeur of the upper regions, they cannot pluck you the medical herb. He gets that for himself who wanders the marshy ledge at nightfall to behold the distant Sennhüttchen twinkle, who leaps the green-eyed crevasses, and in the solitude of an emerald alp stretches a salt hand to the mountain kine.

(*The Adventures of Harry Richmond.*)

JOHN ADDINGTON SYMONDS
(1840-1893)
The Love of the Alps

OF all the joys in life, none is greater than the joy of arriving
on the outskirts of Switzerland at the end of a long dusty
day's journey from Paris. The true epicure in refined pleasures
will never travel to Basle by night. He courts the heat of the
sun and the uninteresting monotony of French plains,—their
sluggish streams and never-ending poplar trees,—for the sake
of the evening coolness and the gradual approach to the great
Alps which await him at the close of day. It is about Mul-
hausen that he begins to feel a change in the landscape. The
fields broaden into rolling downs, watered by clear and running
streams; the green Swiss thistle grows by river-side and cowshed;
pines begin to tuft the slopes of gently rising hills; and now the
sun has set, the stars come out, first Hesper, then the troop of
lesser lights; and he feels,—yes, indeed, there is now no mistake,
—the well-known, well-loved, magical fresh air that never fails
to blow from snowy mountains and meadows watered by
perennial streams. The last hour is one of exquisite enjoyment,
and when he reaches Basle, he scarcely sleeps all night for
hearing the swift Rhine beneath the balconies, and knowing
that the moon is shining on its waters, through the town,
beneath the bridges, between pasture lands and copses, up the
still mountain-girded valleys to the ice-caves where the water
springs. There is nothing in all experience of travelling like
this. We may greet the Mediterranean at Marseilles with
enthusiasm; on entering Rome by the Porta del Popolo, we may
reflect with pride that we have reached the goal of our pilgrimage, and are at last among world-shaking memories. But
neither Rome nor the Riviera wins our hearts like Switzerland.
We do not lie awake in London thinking of them; we do not
long so intensely, as the year comes round, to revisit them. Our
affection is less a passion than that which we cherish for
Switzerland. . . .

After passing many weeks among the high Alps it is a great
pleasure to descend into the plains. The sunset, and sunrise,
and the stars of Lombardy, its level horizons and vague misty

distances, are a source of absolute relief after the narrow skies and embarrassed prospects of a mountain valley. Nor are the Alps themselves ever more imposing than when seen from Milan or the terrace of Novara, with a foreground of Italian corn-fields and old city towers, and rice-grounds golden green beneath a Lombard sun. Half-veiled by clouds the mountains rise like visionary fortress walls of a celestial city—unapproach-able, beyond the range of mortal feet. But those who know by old experience what friendly chalets, and cool meadows, and clear streams are hidden in their folds and valleys, send forth fond thoughts and messages, like carrier-pigeons, from the marble parapets of Milan, crying, "Before another sun has set I too shall rest beneath the shadow of their pines!" It is in truth not more than a day's journey from Milan to the brink of snow at Macugnaga. But very sad it is to leave the Alps, to stand upon the terraces of Berne and waft our ineffectual farewells. The unsympathizing Aar rushes beneath; and the snow-peaks, whom we love like friends, abide untroubled by the coming and the going of the world. The clouds drift over them—the sunset warms them with a fiery kiss. Night comes, and we are hurried far away to wake upon the shores of unfamiliar Seine, remem-bering, with a pang of jealous passion, that the flowers on Alpine meadows are still blooming, and the rivulets still flowing with a ceaseless song, while Paris shops are all we see, and all we hear is the dull clatter of a Paris crowd.

(*The Love of the Alps.*)

ALFRED FREDERICK MUMMERY
(1855-1895)

During the Golden age of mountaineering which closed with the conquest of the Matterhorn in 1865 the pioneers were mainly interested in the conquest of the virgin peaks. In the Silver age the pioneering instinct found expression in the conquest of virgin ridges and virgin faces of peaks already climbed, and also in the attack on difficult rock pinnacles, such as the Chamonix aiguilles. Just as Whymper and Leslie Stephen dominated the Golden age, so Mummery dominated the Silver age of Alpine exploration. Mummery's most famous climb was the conquest of the Grépon in 1881. In 1892 he led a guideless party (Collie, Pasteur and G. Hastings) up the Grépon, and the account of that expedition, quoted from "My Climbs in the Alps and Caucasus," begins with

Mummery's description of his lead up the Mummery crack. Mummery disappeared on an exploration of Nanga Parbat, and his body has never been found.

The Mummery Crack

POSSIBLY the knowledge that I was going to try to lead up to it made it look worse than it really was, but for the moment I was startled at its steepness. With the exception of two steps where the rock sets back slightly (to the extent, perhaps, of two feet in all), the whole is absolutely perpendicular. In this estimate I exclude a preliminary section of seven or eight feet, which bulges out and overhangs in a most painful manner. On the other hand, it was distinctly more broken than I had expected, and the longer we looked the better we liked it, till with fair hopes of success I climbed down to the foot of the crack, scrambled on to Hastings' shoulders, and tackled the toughest bit of rock-climbing I have ever attempted. For the first twenty feet or so the climber is to some extent protected by the rope, which can be hitched round a great splinter close to the col; beyond that point the rope is simply worn as an ornament, though doubtless it supplies one's companions with pleasing sensations whenever a slip seems imminent. About half-way up is an excellent step on which one can take breath. When I say excellent, I only mean relatively to the rest of the crack, not that it is suitable for lunch, or even that one can balance on it without holding on; indeed, on the first occasion that I ascended, my meditations at this point were rudely interrupted by my foot slipping on the shelving rock, and I was launched into thin air. Wiser by this memory, I hung on with my fingers as well as the absence of anything to hang on to would permit, and then, having somewhat regained my wind, began the second half of the ascent. This section was, by the general consent of the party, voted the hardest. There is really very little hold for the hands, and nothing at all for the feet, the climber proceeding chiefly by a pious reliance on Providence, eked out at intervals by loose stones wedged into a doubtful, wobbling sort of semi-security into the crack. Above, the need for piety is replaced by excellent hand-hold on the right, though the gasping and exhausted climber still finds it difficult to propel his weight upwards. Ledges then become more numerous, and at length one's arms and head hang down the Grépon side of the slab, whilst one's legs are still struggling with the concluding difficulties of the other side. At this juncture wild cheers broke from the party below, and awoke in me the dread that the porters would regard them as the wished-for signal and fly incontinently to Chamonix. In the intervals of gasping for breath, I suggested these fears to my companions, and a silence, as of death, instantly showed their appreciation of the danger.

In order to prevent the remainder of the party scrambling up with undue facility and thus exposing the Grépon to scorn, I judiciously urged them not to waste time by sending up the axes and luggage on the rope, but to sling the axes on their arms and distribute the luggage amongst the rest of the party. I found this eminently successful, and a most material aid in impressing my companions with a due respect for the crag.

We then scrambled up the gully and through the "Kanones Loch," and with our hopes rising at every advance, we followed my old route to the top of the great gap. Here we fixed a hundred feet of rope, and the party went down one by one. As I was descending last, having just passed a perfectly smooth and precipitous section of the cliff relying exclusively on the rope, I rested a moment on a trifling irregularity in the rock. When I essayed to continue the descent, the rope came to me as I pulled. With a great effort I succeeded in keeping my balance on the insecure footing where I had been resting, but for a moment I felt supremely uncomfortable. The rope was apparently quite loose above, and there appeared to be no means of climbing down the rock to the gap without its aid. However, after about ten feet of it had been hauled in, no more would come, and it resisted the united efforts of my companions in the gap. Collie also managed to see an apparently possible line of descent, and skilfully coached by him, keeping the rope in my hand merely as a *dernier ressort*, I succeeded in reaching the welcome security of Hastings' grip and was landed in the gap.

So far as we could see, the rope had slipped off the top of the tower on to the Nantillon face, and caught in a hitch some ten feet down. We could not see whether this hitch was reliable or not, but we all agreed that the first man to go up from our present position would have an unpleasant task. As it was still doutbful whether we could scale the final peak, and thus get on to the C.P. route, this was not an impossible contingency, and we hastened forward to set the question at rest.

This final peak had nearly baffled Burgener and Venetz, and we scarcely hoped to be able to climb it by fair means. We had determined, in consequence, to try and win the summit by throwing a rope over the top. It is true Burgener and I had failed signally in so doing, but on this occasion we had a light rope with us, far better adapted for that purpose than the ordinary Alpine Club rope we had used in 1881. Collie, on the way along the ridge, selected two excellent stones wherewith to weight the rope and give it some chance of facing the furious gale. With much discomfort to himself and grave damage to the pockets of his coat, he conveyed these murderous weapons through various difficulties to the very foot of the final climb.

The preparations for a preliminary assault by fair and legitimate methods were in progress, when Pasteur joyfully shouted that we had already joined the C.P. route, and could ascend by a perfectly simple and fairly easy line. . . . Pasteur gave me a shoulder, and in a few minutes we all crowded round the ice-axe and its fluttering flag.

The wind was howling across the ridge with such fury that we could only crouch under one of the stones, and we soon determined to go down to warmer quarters. We scrambled off the summit, and, sheltering under its lee, rejoiced in victory and lunch. Pasteur, who had been previously on this side of the mountain, now took the lead. He slipped a spare rope through a "piton" left by M. Dunod, and we all quickly slid down to a broad shelf. When I say all, however, I must except Hastings, who unluckily inserted his foot into a tempting crack, and found that no effort could subsequently release it. All hands heaved on the rope, but it was of no avail, and he bid fair—save for the dearth of eagles—to rival Prometheus. Someone at last suggested that he should take off his boot. The idea was hailed with approval, and we all shouted and yelled the advice. When, however, one is supported on a steep, not to say perpendicular, slab by one foot jammed in a crack some twelve inches from the surface, it is a problem of no slight complexity to unlace and remove an offending boot. The task was, however, accomplished; but then a second difficulty arose, what was to be done with it? Happily a pocket was discovered large enough to contain the property, and the ledge was soon reached in safety.

A short ascent by an easy gully led us to the gap between the Pic Balfour and the summit. From thence easy ledges brought us down to the C.P. cleft. Our porters greeted us with shouts, and let down a rope for our help. It was obvious, however, that a rock bridge, not, perhaps, wholly easy of access, would have enabled us to turn the obstruction without extraneous aid. Since, however, the porters were at hand, we thought they might as well have the privilege of pulling us up. Safely arrived in the neighbourhood of the knapsack, we "lay beside our nectar" till such time as the nectar was consumed. We subsequently raced down to the breakfasting rocks, descended to the lower glacier, and finally got back to the Montenvers about 5 p.m. Kind friends, who saw our approach, welcomed us with a vast pot— the pride and joy of the Montenvers Hotel—full of tea, and under its stimulating influence the crags became steeper and more terrible, until it seemed incredible that mere mortals could have faced such awful difficulties and perils. . . .

The True Mountaineer

BEFORE, however, quitting the summit of one of the steepest rocks in the Alps, I may perhaps be permitted to ask certain critics whether the love of rock-climbing is so heinous and debasing a sin that its votaries are no longer worthy to be ranked as mountaineers, but are to be relegated to a despised and special class of "mere gymnasts."

It would appear at the outset wholly illogical to deny the term "mountaineer" to any man who is skilled in the art of making his way with facility in mountain countries. To say that a man who climbs because he is fond of mountaineering work is not a mountaineer, whilst a man who climbs because it is essential to some scientific pursuit in which he is interested is a mountaineer, is contrary to the first principles of a logical definition, and I trust will never become general. It may be freely admitted that science has a higher social value than sport, but that does not alter the fact that mountaineering is a sport, and by no possible method can be converted into geology, or botany, or topography. That the technique of our sport has made rapid progress is alleged against us as a sort of crime, but I venture to say, in reality, it is a matter, not for regret, but for congratulation. To emulate the skill of their guides was the ideal of the early climbers, and I trust it will still be the ideal that we set before ourselves. A terminology which suggests that as a man approaches this goal, as he increases in mountaineering skill he ceases to be a mountaineer, stands self-condemned and must be remorselessly eliminated from the literature of our sport.

Probably most mountaineers would agree that the charm of mountain scenery is to be found in every step taken in the upper world. The strange interfolding of the snows, the gaunt, weird crags of the ridges, the vast, blue, icicle-fringed crevasse, or the great smooth slabs sloping downwards through apparently bottomless space, are each and all no less lovely than the boundless horizon of the summit view. The self-dubbed mountaineers, however, fail to grasp this essential fact. To them the right way up a peak is the easiest way, and all the other ways are wrong ways. Thus would they say, to take an instance from a well-known peak, if a man goes up the Matterhorn to enjoy the scenery, he will go by the Hörnli route; if he goes by the Zmutt ridge, it is, they allege, merely the difficulties of the climb that attract him. Now, this reasoning would appear to be wholly fallacious. Among the visions of mountain loveliness that rise before my mind none are fairer than the stupendous cliffs and fantastic crags of the Zmutt ridge. To say that this route with its continuously glorious scenery is, from an æsthetic point of view, the wrong way, while the Hörnli route which, despite the noble distant prospect, is marred by the meanness of its screes and its paper-besprinkled slopes, is the right, involves a total insensibility to the true mountain feeling.

The suspicion, indeed, sometimes crosses my mind that the so-called mountaineer confounds the pleasure he derives from photography or from geological or other research with the purely æsthetic enjoyment of noble scenery. Doubtless, the summit of a peak is peculiarly well adapted to these semi-scientific pursuits, and if the summit is the only thing desired, the easiest way up is obviously the right way; but from a purely æsthetic standpoint, the Col du Lion, the teeth of the Zmutt ridge, or Carrel's Corridor, whilst affording as exquisite a distant prospect, combine with it the dramatic force of a splendid foreground of jagged ridge, appalling precipice, and towering mist-veiled height.

The importance of foreground cannot, I think, be overrated, and it is obvious that the more difficult an ascent the bolder and more significant will usually be the immediate surroundings of the traveller. In other words, the æsthetic value of an ascent generally varies with its difficulty. This, necessarily, leads us to the conclusion that the most difficult way up the most difficult peaks is always the right thing to attempt, whilst the easy slopes of ugly screes may with propriety be left to the scientists, with M. Janssen at their head. To those who, like myself, take a non-utilitarian view of the mountains, the great ridge of the Grépon may be safely recommended, for nowhere can the climber find bolder towers, wilder clefts, or more terrific precipices; nowhere a fairer vision of lake and mountain, mist-filled valleys, and riven ice.

LORD CONWAY OF ALLINGTON
(1856-1937)

Martin Conway was one of the most versatile of the pioneers. He was an explorer, mountaineer, art critic and politician. In the Himalaya he made the first recorded crossing of the longest snow pass, the Hispar, outside the Arctic regions. He made the first crossing of Spitzbergen, and the first ascent in the Andes of Illimani. He crossed the Alps from end to end, and produced the first of a long series of climbers' guides. He was Slade Professor of Fine Arts at Cambridge University. His book "Early Flemish Artists" is not only erudite and scholarly but also readable. He was for many years M.P. for the combined English Universities.

This great art critic looked at mountains with an eye trained to perceive the subtlest effects. "Any goose sees glory" in the Matterhorn, but only a connoisseur of mountain form could have appreciated the delicate loveliness of the Plaine Morte.

Piz Palü and Piz Bernina

THAT same evening I slept out for Piz Palü, and traversed its long crest next day, reaching Pontresina just in time to hurry off to yet another gîte and sleep out for the third night in succession in order to capture the Piz Roseg while the fine weather held. How could one feel fatigue amid such experiences? The third climb was the longest and most sensational.

THE PLAINE MORTE
(Mischabel, Weisshorn, and Zinal Rothorn)

Photo: E. Gyger, Adelboden

PIZ BERNINA AND PIZ ROSEG

Photo: A. Pedrett, St. Moritz

Palü's snowcrest, festooned from peak to peak, is in places narrow, but is far surpassed in dramatic quality by the arête of Piz Roseg. Like a giant spear held aloft the summit burst with startling defiance upon our vision at the moment of arrival upon the lower peak, after seven hours' ascent from the hut. We were forewarned and expectant, but the thing beheld surpassed expectation. We had climbed in a gale of wind and with little hope of final success. The gale added to the effect. Slenderer and longer arêtes than that which connects the two summits exist, but this is slender and long enough. The slopes on either hand plunge to abysses that seem immeasurable. That on the right is a cliff of rock; the other is a sheer curtain of ice, smooth and relentless. It leads down to the crest of the saddle, known as Güssfeldt's, from which a famous ice-wall falls to the glacier-floor. The precipices of Bernina impend beyond a narrow glacier-arm. In the midst of these majestic surroundings the knife-edged arête rises like the flight of an arrow to the highest peak. Adding to its beauty at that moment, a delicately transparent veil of countless tiny ice-particles carried by the wind waved upon the crest. They swept hissing up the slope on one side, curled gracefully over the top, and fell on the other. Ice crystals glittered everywhere in the bright sunshine. The cold was bitter. It seemed as though any creature that stood upon that narrow ridge must be blown away. Nevertheless we advanced toward it. As we approached the gale dropped; the sun warmed us, and we could accomplish the tight-rope performance quickly. In thirty-five minutes we had chopped off the sharp snow summit and stood one by one in its place. Just down on the west side the rocks formed natural arm-chairs, with nothing between them and remote Mont Blanc; we rested there for two glorious hours before turning to descend.

A spell of enforced idleness followed these three exciting days. When the weather settled I was able to climb Piz Bernina. The route followed led me for the first time through really superb ice-scenery. We had to turn the great ice-fall of the Morteratsch glacier by a traverse across a slope of ice under overhanging seracs and above a vertical cliff. The piled debris of fallen seracs at the foot of the cliff showed the dangers of the way; not that such evidence was necessary, for the huge ice-towers in many places overhung, and it was evident that some of them were doomed to fall. So early in the morning, frost doubtless held them fast, but it would be otherwise in the after-noon, when we must return by the same route.

On the main body of the mountain we wrought a way among the yawning crevasses of a much-tortured névé. The magic bergschrund I had looked into on the way up our pass was tri-fling in comparison with these immense caverns. The surface through which they opened shone blindingly white under the high sun. Their depths were indigo-blue. The walls shimmered with every intervening tint. They were not mere slab-sided ditches, but variegated with every conceivable intricacy of form: here opening into grottoes, there piled with fallen masses of banded ice; here bulging, there overhanging, and everywhere draped with fringes of icicles slender as a twig or massive as the trunks of ancient trees. Fancy cannot picture a more romantic scene than these névé crevasses displayed. Moreover they were not parallel gashes in an even slope, but steps in a giant stair-case, ruinous as vast. High walls of ice stood up, and longi-tudinal sections cut the great steps into cubes which sloped this way and that. Towers and spires had cracked off from the larger masses, and leaned to one side or the other. We had to cut steps and swarm up such a pinnacle as the only way to attain an upper level against which it rested. Usually we found bridges of ice, massive or frail, but always of unexpected form and entrancing architecture. Some two hours may have been spent in this exotic fairyland before the main arête was reached. It is of rock, with one short wall of snow, excessively narrow—so narrow, in fact, that you cannot traverse on either side, but must walk balanced on its very crest in steps carefully fashioned, a rare experience.

If we lingered long on the cloudless summit and were slow in the descent, it was because that return traverse under the impending seracs threatened in the background of our minds. Assuredly it dyed all the emotions of the day for me, not always unpleasantly, not to the exclusion but rather to the heightening of merriment, yet infusing into each vision of wonder or beauty a certain solemnity, as of a sight beheld not for the first time only, but it might be for the last. It created a mood which was projected on to the scenery. When Matthew Arnold wrote:

> The solemn peaks but to the stars are known,
>   But to the stars and the pale moonlight's beams;
> Alone the sun uprises and alone
>   Spring the great streams,

he was expressing a subjective mood by a series of statements, each separately untrue. The solemn peaks are known to the sun and the clouds and so forth as much as to stars and moonlight; but the mood of a man embraces and refashions all he beholds, and thus comes back to him from Nature. He sees his own heart in the landscape and, truthfully expressing his emotion, describes it in terms of the external world. Not only will the eye be blind to such visions as it has not previously acquired power to see, but the heart will not throb save to emotions already potential within itself. Even the sight of danger will not appal one who has not the knowledge to recognise it, while a safe situation will affright when it is believed to be perilous. Thus also the eye will only weep in the presence of a glory which the imagination has flung over the bare prose of Nature. To the believer alone will God be manifest in the material world. *(Mountain Memories.)*

The Antiquity of Alpine Life

I HAD been a climber through many seasons before coming to realize this antiquity of Alpine life. Inquiry brought to light much published record of the history of the peasant communities into whose midst we came for a few weeks in summer to live our own lives of sport which barely touched theirs, only affecting them as bringing to their villages a market for their milk and a new occupation for their adventurous young men. I believe it was during the days of storm this September that I happened upon a little printed pedigree-book of the Zermatt families, and discovered that the Taugwalders, the Bieners, and all the rest of them (our porters, muleteers and guides) belonged to families which had been settled about Zermatt as far back as the thirteenth century. It also appeared that the constitution of the Commune still preserved features then impressed upon it, and that the names of fields and alps were of like antiquity. Ancient treaties between village and village, regulating the supply of water by mountain-canals and its distribution hour by hour to every man's property, were found to be still in accepted and successful operation. The whole landscape of the grazed alps took on a new significance. Small torrents of water captured from a glacier stream, led by skilful engineering across hillsides, and finally discharged by countless little rivulets upon every yard of the grass-land, were found to be of hoary antiquity, and the ridged surface of the ground to be due to centuries of deposition of fine glacier-mud in the beds of the little channels or at the points of their final discharge. As understanding of these matters increased, the visible landscape of the region immediately below the snow-line and down to the valley-floors took on a new significance. Its picturesqueness became involved in a tangle of human memories, accumulated activities, monu-mental accomplishments of successive bygone generations. But by however much this region was thus humanised, by just so much was the aloofness of the abode of snow increased. The Cervin attained a new dignity from its age-long association with the dwellers at its foot, who had one and all regarded it and the heights, its neighbours, as part of that other world which was the home of ghosts and mysterious powers. Folk-lore and local history thus added themselves as desirable subjects of study to the plain topographical, geographical, glaciological, botanical and other scientific inquiries which had been the occupation of my previous seasons in the Alps.

The First "Climbers' Guide"

THE experiences of the season of 1878 had two effects. They confirmed and enlarged my interest in mountain topography and history, and they emphasised the attraction of "New Expeditions." Thenceforward I cared only for such climbs as were in the nature of exploration, either as travers-ing ground for the first time, or as revealing the structure of mountain districts which could not be comprehended without personal investigation on the spot. The following year was mainly spent upon researches in Continental libraries in respect of subjects with which this book is not concerned. It is only germane to notice that the same process which was applied to the collection and co-ordination of facts connected with a certain category of works of art and their historical development could be applied with little change to the col-lection and ordering of facts connected with the structure of mountains and the history of mountaineering. The two re-searches, apparently so different in aim, could be and were carried on simultaneously; they acted and reacted on one another. . . .

No sooner was the Pocket-book in the hands of climbers and in actual use than its deficiencies became apparent. I heard little from those who found themselves correctly guided, but was deluged with complaints from less fortunate individuals who had been insufficiently or wrongly directed. A list of obscurities requiring elucidation thus rapidly formed and grew. Scarcely was the ink dry on the first edition than materials were collecting for another.

(Mountain Memories.)

The Plaine Morte

IT was a spot worth halting at. Behind were Mont Blanc and the Grand Combin "smoking their pipes," as Aymonod put it, but we did not look much at them. Ahead was the sight worth coming thus far to see. Twenty-two years before, on the occasion of my first visit to the Alps, I purchased certain sheets of the Dufour map, cut out so much of them as liberally included the Bernese Oberland and pasted the pieces together. In the corner of that map (it lay before me as I sat on the rock mound) is a considerable white patch, almost featureless, marked *Glacier de la Plaine Morte.* Well do I remember the curiosity that patch raised in me. What could the great cup-shaped snow-field, that had no exit, be like? And the same question often recurred, when, from the summits of Pennine peaks, I beheld, along the northern boundary of the view, the mass of the Wildstrubel and perhaps a suggestion of the great cup's edge along the crest of the Autannaz ridge, which forms its southern lip. Now the whole white area was before us, doubtless one of the most remarkable sights in the Alps. It is so large, so simple, so secluded. It seems like a portion of some strange world. Its effect of size is increased by the insignificance of the wall that surrounds it—enough to shut out all distant views and no more. The sense of novelty, of strangeness came upon me, such as I felt when all the Hispar glacier under its dark roof of cloud first opened on my view. Beautiful too it was, with the beauty of all great snow-fields; its large undulations, its rippled surface, glinting under the touch of the low risen sun. To add to its mystery, there came over the sky a veil of mist, which presently reduced the brilliancy of the day, increasing the apparent size of everything and lengthening all distances. Two birds, like swallows, twittered around, and seemed out of place. . . . We advanced at an easy pace, treading on the crests of the ripples, and passing over slight undulations. The further we went the more profound was the solitude. Here a man might come and, setting up his tent for a week, learn what it is to be alone. He might wander safely in any direction and, climbing the wall at any point, look out upon the world of hotels and tourists; then returning to his lone abode, he might kindle his solitary lamp and cook for himself the cup of contemplation.   (*The Alps from End to End.*)

HILAIRE BELLOC

A Revelation of the Alps

I SAW between the branches of the trees in front of me a sight in the sky that made me stop breathing, just as great danger at sea, or great surprise in love, or a great deliverance will make a man stop breathing. I saw something I had known in the West as a boy, something I had never seen so grandly discovered as was this. In between the branches of the trees was a great promise of unexpected lights beyond.

I pushed left and right along that edge of the forest and along the fence that bound it, until I found a place where the pine-trees stopped, leaving a gap, and where on the right, beyond the gap, was a tree whose leaves had failed; there the ground broke away steeply below me, and the beeches fell, one below the other, like a vast cascade, towards the limestone cliffs that dipped down still further beyond my sight. I looked through this framing hollow and praised God. For there below me, thousands of feet below me, was what seemed an illimitable plain; at the end of that world was an horizon, and the dim bluish sky that overhangs an horizon.

There was brume in it and thickness. One saw the sky beyond the edge of the world getting purer as the vault rose. But right up—a belt in that empyrean—ran peak and field and needle of intense ice, remote, remote from the world. Sky beneath them and sky above them, a steadfast legion, they glittered as though with the armour of the immovable armies of heaven. Two days' march, three days' march away, they stood up like the walls of Eden. I say it again, they stopped my breath. I had seen them.

So little are we, we men; so much are we immersed in our muddy and immediate interests that we think, by numbers and recitals, to comprehend distance or time, or any of our limiting infinities. Here were these magnificent creatures of God, I mean the Alps, which now for the first time I saw from the height of the Jura; and because they were fifty or sixty miles away, and because they were a mile or two high, they were become something different from us others, and could strike one motionless with the awe of supernatural things. Up there in the sky, to which only clouds belong and birds and the last trembling colours of pure light, they stood fast and hard; not moving as do the things of the sky. They were as distant as the little upper clouds of summer, as fine and tenuous; but in their reflection and in their quality as it were of weapons (like spears and shields of an unknown array) they occupied the sky with a sublime invasion: and the things proper to the sky were forgotten by me in their presence as I gazed.

To what emotion shall I compare this astonishment? So, in first love one finds that *this* can belong to *me*.

Their sharp steadfastness and their clean uplifted lines compelled my adoration. Up there, the sky above and below them, part of the sky, but part of us, the great peaks made communion between that homing creeping part of me which loves vineyards and dances and a slow movement among pastures, and that other part which is only properly at home in Heaven. I say that this kind of description is useless, and that it is better to address prayers to such things than to attempt to interpret them for others.

These, the great Alps, seen thus, link one in some way to one's immortality. Nor is it possible to convey, or even to suggest, those few fifty miles, and those few thousand feet; there is something more. Let me put it thus: that from the height of Weissenstein I saw, as it were, my religion. I mean, humility, the fear of death, the terror of height and of distance, the glory of God, the infinite potentiality of reception whence springs that divine thirst of the soul; my aspiration also towards completion, and my confidence in the dual destiny. For I know that we laughers have a gross cousinship with the most high, and it is this contrast and perpetual quarrel which feeds a spring of merriment in the soul of a sane man.

Since I could now see such a wonder and it could work such things in my mind, therefore, some day I should be part of it. That is what I felt.

That it is also which leads some men to climb mountain-tops, but not me, for I am afraid of slipping down.

(*The Path to Rome.*)

Tourists

IT was the first part of the afternoon when I got to a place called Meiringen, and I thought that there I would eat and drink a little more. So I steered into the main street, but there I found such a yelling and roaring as I had never heard before, and very damnable it was; as though men were determined to do common evil wherever God has given them a chance of living in awe and worship.

For they were all bawling and howling, with great placards and tickets, and saying, "This way to the Extraordinary Water-fall; that way to the Strange Cave. Come with me and you shall see the never-to-be-forgotten Falls of the Aar," and so forth. So that my illusion of being alone in the roots of the world dropped off me very quickly, and I wondered how people could be so helpless and foolish as to travel about in Switzerland as tourists and meet with all this vulgarity and beastliness.

If a man goes to drink good wine he does not say, "So that the wine be good I do not mind eating strong pepper and smelling hartshorn as I drink it," and if a man goes to read good verse, for instance Jean Richepin, he does not say, "Go on playing the trombone, go on banging the cymbals; so long as I am reading good verse I am content." Yet men now go into the vast hills and sleep and live in their recesses, and pretend to be indifferent to all the touts and shouters and hurry and hotels and high prices and abominations. Thank God, it goes in grooves! I say it again, thank God, the railways are trenches that drain our modern marsh, for you have but to avoid railways, even by five miles, and you can get more peace than would fill a nosebag. All the world is my garden since they built railways, and gave me leave to keep off them.

Also I vowed a franc to the Black Virgin of La Délivrance (next time I should be passing there) because I was delivered from being a tourist, and because all this horrible noise was not being dinned at me (who was a poor and dirty pilgrim, and no kind of prey for these cabmen, and busmen, and guides and couriers), but at a crowd of drawn, sad, jaded tourists that had come in by a train.   (*The Path to Rome.*)

The Italian Lakes

THE Italian lakes have that in them and their air which removes them from common living. Their beauty is not tae beauty which each of us sees for himself in the world; it is rather the beauty of a special creation; the expression of some mind. To eyes innocent, and first freshly noting our great temporal inheritance—I mean to the eyes of a boy and girl just entered upon the estate of this glorious earth, and thinking themselves immortal, this shrine of Europe might remain for ever in the memory; an enchanted experience, in which the single sense of sight had almost touched the boundary of music. They would remember these lakes as the central emotion of their youth. To mean men also who, in spite of years and of a full foreknowledge of death, yet attempt nothing but the satisfaction of sense, and pride themselves upon the taste and fineness with which they achieve this satisfaction, the Italian lakes would seem a place for habitation, and there such a man might build his house contentedly. But to ordinary Christians I am sure there is something unnatural in this beauty of theirs, and they find in it either a paradise only to be won by a much longer road or a bait and veil of sorcery, behind which lies great peril. Now, for all we know, beauty beyond the world may not really bear this double aspect; but to us on earth—if we are ordinary men—beauty of this kind has something evil. Have you not read in books how men when they see even divine visions are terrified? So as I looked at Lake Major in its halo I also was afraid, and I was glad to cross the ridge and crest of the hill and to shut out that picture framed all round with glory.   (*The Path to Rome.*)

COLONEL EDWARD LISLE STRUTT,
C.B.E., D.S.O.

Colonel Strutt is a pioneer of winter mountaineering, and a great authority on the Engadine and Bregaglia. He was second-in-command of the Everest 1922 expedition. He is an ex-President of the Alpine Club, and an ex-Editor of the "Alpine Journal."

A Great Guide: Christian Klucker

ON December 21st, 1928, Christian Klucker, following his invariable custom, summer or winter, of wearing no over-coat, but per contra carrying a walking-stick, left his home at Fex and walked down to Sils Maria. He called on his friend, Herr Kienberger, at the Hotel Waldhaus en route and com-plained of feeling slight heart trouble. He stated that he would see the doctor. On arrival in the village, he asked for a cup of tea in a restaurant, but before consuming it, quietly and painlessly expired. He was buried in the little churchyard of Fex on December 24th. The whole Upper Engadine was represented at the funeral, the coffin disappeared beneath a mountain of wreaths, while deputations from Basle, Zürich, Coire, and other towns attended. Snow finches, the rare winter visitors he loved so well, circled over Klucker's grave.

A very wise and learned friend, the late Sir Edward Davidson, once warned the writer against the use of superlatives. Yet I cannot help thinking that in speaking or writing of Christian Klucker, even a Davidson might acquiesce.

Klucker was far more than a doyen of first-class guides. This "grand old gentleman," to quote the last of many com-ments made on him in the *Alpine Journal*, could have filled with distinction almost any rôle in life. He was the Sils schoolmaster, latterly an inspector of schools; "Papa Klucker" was a constant and affectionate cry raised by children.

A first-class public speaker, an expert in map-reading and the use of the compass in days when guides and some amateurs were wont to treat such articles with contempt. An ardent lover and collector of books, with an extraordinary knowledge of topography and Alpine History ancient and modern. I feel that the *Journal* has lost in him one of its most distinguished assistants—"the *fine fleur* of professional culture," abstemious to a fault, in general knowledge and education surpassing all guides and most others. An excellent geologist, botanist and biologist, there was hardly a limit to his versatile accomplishments.

His name was omitted from a somewhat ambitious and unequal work for the obscure reason that he belonged to Eastern Switzerland. Not many of the Pioneers of the Alps could show a record like his! In a career commencing in 1874 no less than 44 first ascents and 88 new routes—in all parts of the Alps, Dauphiné to Dolomites, but of course largely in the Pennine, Bernina and Rhætian Alps—stand to his credit. He accompanied Whymper to the Canadian Rockies in 1901.

Without a superior as guide or mountaineer, a born leader with humorous and epigrammatic insight into his companions' psychology and powers, his equals might be counted on less, perhaps, than the fingers of one hand. Many of us are content to hear of our best expeditions, first repeated again and again in half the time, finally spoken of with contempt. Not so Christian Klucker. He vied with the younger men in modern desperate climbs; at the age of 74 he was accomplishing new routes; two months before his death he led—was there ever an expedition in which Klucker did *not* lead?—in the climb of Punta Rasica (without any rope-throwing), Cima del Largo traverse, Ago di Sciora, all first ascents of his thirty to forty years ago.

He towered, as Piz Badile over Bondo, above all Engadine guides past and present, with Martin Schocher an honourable second. Severe judges such as Edward Davidson, with his un-rivalled experience of the best professionals of two generations, have bracketed Klucker with Josef Pollinger and Franz Loch-matter as the best step-cutters ever known. The precipitous slabs and ridges of the Mont Blanc Aiguilles and the Bregaglia; the crumbling walls, the decaying chimneys of Rhætikon or Dolomites will acknowledge no superior cragsman. Small and thick-set, short in the reach but gifted with enormous strength, his grace on rocks was extraordinary, while on ice, like Alexander Burgener, he seemed to dilate into a very giant of power. . . .

Yet with all his dash, with all his almost matchless skill, there was no more careful climber. He was master of the mountain as he was of his party. The great peaks' hidden dangers were as an open book, easily read, to him. No risk, humanly to be avoided, was run by him. He led his party to victory, never towards defeat, far less disaster.

"Since 1874 I have had the luck to climb every summer and winter in my beloved mountains, and never once in all these fifty years has a serious mishap occurred. No search parties have had to be called upon, and, although I have traversed many difficult glaciers, I have never had both feet in a crevasse! Now I am seventy-two years old and perhaps twilight is approaching."

So wrote Christian Klucker to me more than four years ago. That "twilight" never approached: alone, as he had lived, save for countless friends and admirers, his unconquerable spirit met the end he would have desired. For the rest—let it stand as the epitaph of a great, of a deathless, Mountaineer.

(*The Alpine Journal*, xli.)

GEOFFREY WINTHROP YOUNG

Geoffrey Winthrop Young stood in much the same relation to the Indian summer of Alpine exploration as Whymper to the Golden Age and Mummery to the Silver Age. No climber of the period has a longer list of classic first ascents to his credit. His story of the first ascent of the south face of the Täschhorn, perhaps the greatest adventure story in Alpine literature, and of the first ascent of the Mer de Glace face of the Grépon have been published in other anthologies. His pioneer ascents on the Jorasses and Weisshorn are quoted in "The Englishman in the Alps." I have therefore selected, from his memorable book "On High Hills," a passage from his description of the first ascent of the south-east ridge of the Nesthorn, one of the very few first-class pioneer ascents which was carried through by an all-British guide-less party.

Though the love of mountains has inspired many poets, Geoffrey Young was the first poet to interpret for mountaineers the romance of mountaineering. All his earlier mountain poems are reproduced in "The Englishman in the Alps," but "I Hold the Heights" was not written when "The Englishman in the Alps" was published. During the First World War Geoffrey Young lost a leg while in command of an Ambulance on the Italian front. It was after his leg had been amputated (above the knee) that he wrote these moving and beautiful lines which are quoted below. In spite of his shattering handicap he returned to the mountains and climbed the Matterhorn and the Grépon.

A New Route up the Nesthorn

MEANWHILE, George had been making his own exami-
nation of the flutings on the south face, and on my return
to the mantelpiece he remarked confidently that he thought it
would go. The effortless ease with which he wound up rocks
which reduced me to convulsive struggling gave me reason to
hope that he might be right. It was for emergencies such as this
that the younger and more brilliant cragsmen of the party had
been so far, somewhat selfishly, kept in reserve upon the rope.
And selfishness had still another share in the decision; because
a change of leader at this point would mean some useful rest
before we began the race with darkness down the crevassed
glaciers of the north face: a last lap, for which every hoarded
faculty and every pound of energy and experience might be
needed.

We changed places on the rope. At about my shoulder level,
as I leaned against it, there was a nick on the extreme south
corner of the slab. Across this I could pass George's rope, and
as my footing was good and my two hands could hold and spring
the rope conveniently on either side of the nick, I felt certain of
keeping the belay sufficiently "indirect" to be sound. George
traversed out from our shelf, moving subtly across the red rib
and hollow of the vertical face; then he disappeared behind a
farther volute. I could hear him; but the rope ceased to run
out. The minutes passed. He was trying for some possible line
up the smooth flutings, clinging to the wall, and with the overhang above checking each attempt. The long-continued effort
must have been exhausting, for the holds over all this wall were
few and inadequate, up to the level at which they ceased
altogether. It was a relief to see him returning into sight,
swinging agilely across the cliff on a broken line of finger-holds.

But, unexpectedly, when he reached the scoop between the
two nearest upright slats, about ten feet away from me, I saw
him glance upward, pause, and then begin to wrestle up it.
The sight of my shelf, recalling our dangerous alternative route
up the north face, may have suggested to him a last attempt on
the south wall as a preferable course. So far as I could see, he
had no real holds at all; but he fought his way up magnificently,
until all that remained below the rock cornice, which cut off
everything else above from my sight, was his two boots. They

were clinging, cat-like, and continued to cling for long seconds, to almost imperceptible irregularities on the walls of the rift. The mere sight of them made me breathless; and I tightened every muscle, ready to spring the rope on its nick. For, on such foot-hold no climber would choose to wait long, were his hand-holds adequate for a lift; and if George's hand-holds were *not* adequate——!

Anyway, they did not serve for the gymnastic backward swing, outward and upward, which he was forced to risk. I saw the boots flash from the wall without even a scrape; and, equally soundlessly, a grey streak flickered downward, and past me, and out of sight. So much did the wall, to which he had clung so long, overhang that from the instant he lost hold he touched nothing until the rope stopped him in mid-air over the glacier. I had had time to think, as I flung my body forward on to the belayed rope, grinding it and my hands against the slab, that no rope could stand such a jerk; and even to think out what our next action must be—so instantaneous is thought. The boots had been standing some fifteen to twenty feet above me, so that the clear fall could not have been much less than forty feet. But the rope held, springing like an elastic band, and cracking under my chest and hands on the rock. We were using that year a then rather popular Austrian woven rope, since entirely condemned. Whenever, in later years, I have looked back at the tabulated rope-tests, which show that this rope is warranted to snap like straw under the jerk of a man's weight falling from, I think, five feet, I have thought again of the transfigured second in which I realised that the rope had, miraculously, held. The fact being, I suppose, that two rather abnormally resilient anatomies at either end of a rope may introduce a confusing element into the nicest theory of strains.

At first there was nothing to do but hold on, and watch the pendulum movement of a tense cord straining over the edge and down into space. My first cautious shouts were unanswered. Then there came, from nowhere, a tranquil call to let out more rope, and to "lower away." So soon as I was convinced that, owing to the good fortune of a clear fall, he had not even been hurt, I complied. The short visible length of rope slackened, and then began to jerk along the edge of the shelf on which I stood. George had spied a line of possible holds across the face of the cliff below him. As I lowered him on the rope, he coolly hooked himself into them with his axe, and proceeded to make his way along the invisible cliff underneath me. Presently he appeared up a slanting groove, and rejoined me on the mantel-shelf, apparently entirely undisturbed. He had not even let go of his axe during the fall.

The whole incident had passed so swiftly and unemotionally —I had almost said with such decorum—that Donald, twenty feet below us, and round the corner on the north face, remained unaware that anything unusual had happened. Nor did we enlighten him at the time. Immediate action was of importance, so as to waste not one of our precious moments and to leave no time for the reaction that has sometimes as ill an effect upon a party as the crisis itself. Without waiting to alter the order, I called to both end men to look after their ropes to me—which gave me a two-fold anchor—and set to work on the north face of the tower, only vexed with myself for having allowed it to frighten me before.

Not that I liked it. The crawl up and over the baffle of the snow-fungus was an anxious performance. In angle and character of hold it was not unlike that very strenuous problem, the climb up the loose, higher part of the cut wall of a haystack. Its protrusion pushed me out of balance; and I had to try for a pick-hold at arm's-length over its crest and trust to toe-holds kicked timorously up its indurating snow face. I heard myself grunt with relief as I got a friction arm-hold over the edge, on the sloping snow-shelf above. I wriggled my chest up on to the slant of the shelf, and then swung up my legs, so that I lay along the narrow snow. A few caterpillar coilings, and then at last I found a finger-hold on the smooth rock wall behind my snow-fungus. This reduced my interest in the question of the stability of the whole jerry-built attachment. I wormed along the shelf on my chest, with finger-holds on the wall and feet kicking in air, until I could force my shoulders into the lower end of the ice-chimney between the higher organ-pipes, and so stand upright on a solid once again, and pant comfortably. A few seconds later I was up the chimney, and sitting astride of the sharp snowy neck that joined the head of our tower to the back-bone of the main ridge. If only the severe but short and well-protected effort had not been shirked a long half-hour before, what nerves and minutes we might have saved!

With our remainder of daylight and of vigour now still further diminished, we had to economize both, if we were yet to make a way down the north face before night. I determined at once to follow a course which I held to be the most suitable, theoretically, in such an emergency. Mallory was unhurt and unshaken; so was our confidence in him. The continuance of the ridge above us looked stern in the falling dusk, but seemed moderately free of snow. So, again our finest and fastest rock climber passed ahead on the rope.

He appeared, through the shadows, to float like a thistledown up the last abrupt steps: up and up, through always denser cold and closer darkness. Now and again my eye was half-caught by a splash of light like an aureole that came and went over his stir of shadow moving above me. And then I saw that this was George's long hair, roughed out by the wind and catching or losing as he climbed the level of the last sunlight lifting above the ridge. Even the austerity of the final brow, which arched smoothly and darkly upward against the summit snows and frowned sullenly out upon the evening, gave him no pause. The unmistakable feel of the wind that tells us there is nothing now between us and open skies met our faces. A short race along the icy crest, and over rock bosses that spiked like huge red horse-chestnuts out of the snow, and we stood together on the silvery tip of the highest cone.

Seven o'clock by the watch. Twelve hours since our start up the rocks of the Unterbächhorn, and with hardly a halt or longer relaxation than an occasional glance round at the promise of the weather.

The last phase of sunset seemed to have been waiting for us, and greeted our eyes across the summit with a long horizon of copper-coloured surf. The breakers of light were beating upon the far sides of the Bietschhorn and of the western Oberland peaks. They sprayed round the mountain edges and across the passes towards us in spurts of gold, and ran in a spent wash of silvery bronze up the nearer snows to our feet. Behind us, to the east, the sunward slopes of the Aletschhorn, of the Finsteraarhorn, and of their white neighbours were beginning to deflect the warm and coloured lighting from their facets in a colder order of tones; and already the pallor of alpine sleep was creeping upon their great snow faces and chilling through the ruddy reflections.

There are evenings in the Alps when the sunset pours out its

LUGANO IN THE SPRING

Photo: E. Rudeli, Lugano

ABOVE SOGLIO
(Ago di Sciora, Sciora di Dentro, Gemelli, Piz Cengalo, Piz Badile)

Photo: A. Pedrett, St. Moritz

whole colour-box on to the sky above us, but when the snow
peaks, the glaciers, and the rock walls about us will have none
of it. They remain colourless, ghostly, and unreceptive; as we
may see the forms and faces of sleepers in a dark room startled
only into outline and a resentful pallor by the passage of a
candle. And there are evenings when every corner of rock,
every snow prism, and every ripple of falling glacier, catches
fire and colour, and contributes its own varied light to the
illumination.

Our few moments of triumph on the summit were transfigured by this blaze of sympathetic celebration. The nearer
rock spires reached up towards us their late glowing torches.
The recession of snow peaks along the Oberland bore each its
dying beacon, ash-red at the heart and hurrying gold at the
edges. The uneven snow on the northern slopes descending
from our feet caught the shallow waves of retreating colour,
and threw them back lower and fainter at each instant as the
sun sank. Until the interrupting rock crests of the north ridge
hemmed the rays finally beyond our sight; and the snows about
us took shelter from the cold inrush of darkness under a uniform
monotony of steely disregard. . . .   (*On High Hills.*)

I Hold the Heights

I HAVE not lost the magic of long days;
   I live them, dream them still.
Still am I master of the starry ways,
   And freeman of the hill.
Shattered my glass, ere half the sands had run—
I hold the heights, I hold the heights I won.

Mine still the hope that hailed me from each height,
   Mine the unresting flame.
With dreams I charmed each doing to delight;
   I charm my rest the same.
Severed my skein, ere half the strands were spun—
I keep the dreams, I keep the dreams I won.

What if I live no more those kingly days?
   Their night sleeps with me still.
I dream my feet upon the starry ways;

My heart rests in the hill.
I may not grudge the little left undone;
I hold the heights, I keep the dreams I won.

(April and Rain.)

On the Mountain

HE meets me on the mountain side,
Where the white van of snow
Bursts through the sentinel grey pines
To shatter on the serried lines
Of fir-wood far below;
Or where the bastions of the fells
Surge from the clinging heather-bells
That cloak their craggy pride.

I never see him, but his tread
Sounds just before my own;
One thought designs the task of day.
One effort wins the onward way,
Dividing, yet alone;
One hope, one vigour of intent,
Swayed by one resolute consent
Of sympathy unsaid.

He waits me at the evening halt
Upon the glacier brink,
When in the hour of mountain peace
The passion and the tumult cease
As the red sun-floods sink,
And the pale lords of sovereign height
Watch the cold armies of the night
Mustering their first assault.

He shares the song-time round the fire,
The morn-break bitterness;
He revels in the sheer ascent,
And finds new worlds for wonderment
In every grim recess;
Sure foot to grip the perilous ledge,
Strong hand to grasp the rough glad edge
Of each unconquered spire.

Together on the ice-glazed wall,
Numbed by the slow snow-breath,
Oft have we heard that instant pace,
And looked intent upon the face
Of our rude comrade, death;
And our clear hearts have leapt to feel
Muscle and will brace tense as steel
To wrestle one more fall.

He opens an enchanted gate
For each untrodden ridge;
He cleaves the blue precipitate stair
Up the white domes of frozen air,
And moulds the foam-snow bridge.
How small the earth to those wide eyes,
And the near welcome of the skies
How infinitely great!

In him the sinews of man's strength
Are wrought to vibrant strings;
Echoes of movement to prolong
The secret breath of spirit-song
His hill-born fancy sings;
Health and high heart, accordant powers
To scale life's ease-enchanted towers
And wake fair truth at length.

The seamen loves too late a tide,
And greets me but from far;
The sylvan god of moor and stream
Laughs in upon my dawn of dream,
Gone with the morning star;
But on wild range and rocky crest
The soul of all that's in me best
Mounts ever at my side.

And when I grow too old to climb,
And leave him on the snow
Hastening in other form to meet
Some young self-discoverer's feet,

Mine still the joy to know
That in the years of youth and friends,
When life was fashioned for its ends,
I found him for a time.

(*Wind and Hill.*)

LORD SCHUSTER

*Lord Schuster is a past President of the Alpine Club and of the Ski Club of
Great Britain. In "The Englishman in the Alps" I have quoted at length
from an established classic of mountaineering literature, "Peaks and Pleasant
Pastures."*

*"The resolution of 1870" referred to in the second paragraph was a reso-
lution of the Alpine Club criticising guideless climbing.*

And Now What Remains?

Being the conclusion of SIR CLAUD SCHUSTER's *Valedictory Address
as President of the Alpine Club on December 10th, 1940.*

AND now what remains? Who can see clearly beyond this
"confused noise and garments rolled in blood"? It is for
old men to dream dreams and for young men to see visions.
The dreams are easy and delightful, whether they be of ridges
and peaks, high in the blue heaven, and deep green valleys
bathed in golden sun or shaded in the innumerable colours of
the morning, or, on the other hand, of fierce contests in wind
and snow and rain; of good fortune and of ill, mingling together
to make in their contrast a perfect whole; of friendships which
cannot be severed by death, and of friends who live with us
through what we have lived through together, more enduring
because they are invisible to the physical eye; of grosser
pleasures—food when we were hungry, drink when we were
thirsty, the crackle of twigs on the hearth of the hut when we
were cold, the shadow of a great rock when we had toiled in the
heat of the day; sunrise and sunset; "all sweet things." But for
the vision, that remains for those who are to come hereafter
to this chair. Only this much is sure. We hear rising through
the conflict the cries, often very discordant, of those who promise
a newer and a better world. We have in the past been told of a

war which was fought to make the world safe for democracy and to create a world fit for heroes to live in. I do not wish to speak in any despite of the aspirations of earnest and well-intentioned men and women. They have their visions. But the world can never be safe, nor is it for safety that we should aspire. We are not, nor is the common kindly race of man, heroes, nor should their aspiration be for a land, like some Mohammedan paradise, in which they should lie unmindful of mankind, of its labours, its disappointments, its toil and its dangers. Mountaineering is not life in the round, but it is a very fair emblem of life as it should be considered and as it should be lived. To aspire to and to attempt great achievement and yet to set out on the adventure after forethought, with due care and with a due adjustment of ends to means; to endure toil and fatigue, and to find the reward rather in the performance than in the accomplishment; not to court danger for her own bright eyes, but not to shrink from her unduly when she bars the path; and above all and in all to preserve a high serenity of mind. These surely are the distinguishing marks of a happy mountaineer, as of a happy warrior. Thus tempered and thus attuned, he can go on his way to whatever fate attends him.

And for the Club, now well advanced in years, beyond indeed the span of life of an ordinary man, there is this to remember. We have heard much in recent years of old and decaying institutions and of old nations sunk in sloth, as contrasted with the young and vigorous. Nations and institutions need never die while they can continually renew their youth as a mighty eagle, as the young fill their ranks and press on in their old spirit. It was apt enough that Tennyson's Ulysses should boast that though made weak by time and fate, he and his companions were yet strong in will to strive, to seek, to find and not to yield. To those who through a hundred thousand perils are now come near to evening the cry of Dante's Ulysses still to seek the knowledge of the unpeopled world beyond the setting sun sounds like a pæan. But the metaphor breaks down when it is transferred from the individual to the club or to the nation. Countries and clubs are not impersonal abstractions, but collections of those who compose them or inherit their history. To them those who came before have transmitted, as in our case, imperishable memories and indestructible traditions. While they hold fast by those memories and traditions, and yet allow them to be permeated and revivified by the continual struggle for the best, they grow not old and decayed, but stronger, tougher and more vigorous. "Past ruin'd Ilion Helen lives." The bust survives the city. The spirit of man survives physical trials and misfortunes. It lives on, using its own achievement to inspire the young who fill the ranks, as the old fall by the wayside, and march on to victory; so that in the rough and desperate gorges of the Pindus, the Greek peasant still goes forward fired by the memory of Leonidas and of Miltiades.

The Pioneers

THERE are, indeed, few more delightful partnerships than were those between the guide and his employer in the half-century before guideless climbing became rather the rule than the exception. The relationship seemed to bring out the best qualities of both. Friendships were made which were the dearer because the gulf to be bridged was wide. Each was the complement to the other. Guideless climbing has many joys; perhaps it is the highest form of the sport. But for the guided climber in the delight of coming once more home to Zermatt, one of the best moments was that of scrambling out of the train and finding one's old companion waiting on the platform, renewing old memories and planning the stuff which should make the new season as full of incident as the old.

It is the convention of the present prelude to the golden age to use words which have a definite meaning in the English language as expressing abuse or praise, as the case may be, for things and systems which they dislike or like. And some writers, though not Mr. Lunn, have chosen to describe the attitude of the older mountaineers towards their guides, and even the employment of guides, as snobbish. It is not clear how this epithet is applicable on the one hand to such a partnership as that of Mr. Young and Knubel or that of Mummery and Alexander Burgener, or on the other to the habit of elderly gentlemen who disliked carrying their own knapsacks. The word, in this connection, is unmeaning; it is very rude (though that perhaps does not trouble those who use it) and it betrays an amazing incapacity to understand the spirit of the time, indeed a failure even to attempt to do so. It is also extremely ungrateful. So far as a kind of retrospective prophecy can ever be justified, it can be said with confidence that, but for these men in whiskers, long trousers and gigantic ice-axes, climbing for Englishmen would, if it ever existed, have been long delayed. The Club is the mother of English mountaineering; perhaps the grandmother. Young men and maidens dislike apron-strings and are sometimes disrespectful to mama. But they often come to understand and to confide in grandmama; and this is a strange kind of progenitor. She likes to try the spirits, whether they be of God. She is ever ready to renew her youth. Her heart is as gay as when she was young herself and as ready for the upward path. Like Mr. Lunn himself she knows that there are many ways to heaven. But she is highly sensitive to abuse and scorn for those with whom she played when she was young. She knows impudence and irreverence when she sees it.

The giants of the Victorian age are great—the great poets, the great philosophers, the great historians, the great novelists, the men who believed greatly and those who disbelieved greatly. These were they who opened wide the doors of freedom for mankind. In many things they fell short of the adventure which they had designed for themselves. Perhaps they hardly realised that their supreme achievement lay rather in what they attempted than in any goal they reached. But we who stand where they struggled and pass securely where they strove, knowing how far more distant was their aim than their hopes pictured, have been too long silent in their praise. Hear now the Master of Trinity, speaking with the natural experience of a long life, enriched with all learning and adorned with every grace: "the higher culture of Nineteenth Century England was varied, solid and widespread over a large proportion of the community. The world is not likely to see again so fine and broad a culture for many years to come."

From this culture came the pioneers. They passed, leaving a tradition which was vigorous and yet urbane. They did not suppose that all was for the best in the best possible world. On the contrary they were dissatisfied, full of curiosity, anxious to reach the pass and to enjoy the prospect which, as they were certain, would then lie open to their view, and to go down on the other side and up the village street in the cool of the evening and so home in the gathering darkness under the cold far-distant stars to the bright light of the inn door. Their muscles, they thought, would have been well exercised and attuned to the gentle languor succeeding toil. Their minds, they thought, would be at rest, tormented as they had been through the long day with the constant effort to subdue their bodies to their wills. All through the hours of darkness through which they passed when they first set forth, through the heat of noon, through the gathering in of evening as they came down over the meadows, there had gleamed these visions, first of the peak and its attainment, and then of rest.

Rest could not come to them or to their children. The problems which they sought to solve of icefalls and routes and ridges have long ago been solved. But the eternal problem which troubled them and their generation, the perfectibility of man, remains unsolved and, perhaps, insoluble. Catastrophes, such as they never imagined, have since then fallen upon the human race and threaten to destroy it. For those sorrows and perplexities they might have been as unskilled as we are to find either cure or anodyne. But it is something more than idle fancy to suppose that, as in their quest they kept alight the spirit of bodily adventure in a generation which looked too much to mere comfort on the one hand and to pure speculation on the other, so in their deliberate yet temperate approach to conquest and to peril, they helped to make a people who can endure and conquer. Security is not enough. If the resolution of 1870 meant mere security it defeats our own tradition. But there are no short cuts to success, still less to safety. "In quietness and in confidence shall be your strength"; but it would be well to add a certain labour, for the craft is long to learn and the conquering sharp.

(*The British Ski Year Book* 1945.)

THE RT. HON. L. S. AMERY, M.P.

Mr. Amery has climbed not only in the Alps but also in the Canadian Rockies where he has some first ascents to his credit) and South Africa. He has been President not only of the Alpine Club but also of the Ski Club of Great Britain. The following passage is an extract from a speech which was made at the Alpine Club dinner in 1929 and which is reprinted in "Days of Fresh Air."

The Secret

WHAT is the secret of that worship of the high hills which bids us dedicate ourselves so eagerly to the pursuit of a sport which to the profane seems slow, toilsome, uncomfortable, and at times fraught with deadly peril? My reply would be that the secret lies in the very fact that it is a form of worship as well as a sport, that it appeals to the craving of the spirit for inward satisfaction, as well as to the need of our limbs for strenuous exercise, and of our hearts for tests of nerve and endurance. As a pure exercise or physical sport I know none more complete, none that demands a more perfect or continuous co-operation of every limb, of every nerve, of every muscle. Nor, though its normal time is slow as compared with the swifter joys, say, of ski-ing—and ski-ing is after all at its finest as a branch of mountaineering—is climbing mere plodding exertion. Rhythm and balance are as essential to good progress on rock or on moraine as in skating or dancing, and the art of effortless execution is as hard to master, and as sweet when mastered, as in any other sport. But in climbing the rhythm has for ever to be adapted to the changing conformation of our medium, and at every stage the satisfaction of physical prowess is blended with the delight of exploration and of conquest.

Every mountain is, in fact, at once a challenge to be taken up and a mystery to be unveiled. And the mystery and the challenge are in a peculiar sense personal. The great mountains are not merely elevations on the map; they have each the individual harmony of their lines, their moods, and phases—of appeal, of forbidding austerity, of sheer entrancing beauty— their tremendously real personality. They are objects of our desire, sometimes of our regret, and won or unyielding to our wooing, they become our friends for life. You at any rate who climb will understand the thrill of emotion with which I gazed, only a few weeks ago, from a summit west of Lake Maligne, across 80 miles of serried peaks at Mt. Robson towering aloft above all his neighbours, and through my glasses fixed the very spot on its stupendous eastern ice wall where after much discussion Hastings and dear old Mumm and Inderbinnen and I regretfully turned back, twenty years before to the very day.

To all these emotions of the mountain lover is added yet

another, the indefinable emotion which connects physical with moral elevation. Whether the contrast between low and high, base and lofty, humble and exalted, goes back, as General Smuts once suggested, to our whole evolution upward from creatures of the waters and the slimy marsh to dwellers in the upper air and on the high land, the contrast is one deeply rooted in all language and in all religion. The great mountain summits, from Tibetan Kailas to Thessalian Olympus, have ever been the homes of the gods, and even the more austere Hebrew mind thought of the Tables of the Law as revealed on Mt. Sinai. No one, certainly, who has once seen the snowy summit of Olympus floating aloft in the midst of a clear blue sky, or who has looked at Mr. Ruttledge's glorious photograph of Kailas now in our gallery, can deny the fitness of the choice of ancient Greece or of Vedic India. Still less can anyone who has himself reached a great summit on a cloudless day forget the sense of intoxication with the beauty of that upper world of tenuous air, of dazzling light, of pure harmonious form, or the mood of exaltation in which he felt as one with the gods. Would not most of us hope, and believe, that in its purest essence that immortal thrill of achievement and godlike content came to Mallory and Irvine before they left the summit of Everest for the Elysian fields?

These are some of the reasons why mountaineering is for us something more than a pleasant and manly sport; why it is steeped in the spirit of romance, and why it is, in short, in its highest moments, a form of worship, a communion with the innermost heart of things. It is not only for the strength and health they give us, for strenuous hours of toil and blissful moments of victorious ease, for joy of discovery and conquest, or for the sense of beauty quickened, but also for things even more intimate and sustaining, that we lift up our eyes to the everlasting hills. *(Days of Fresh Air.)*

C. F. MEADE

Mr. C. F. Meade was the first to attempt the great Himalayan peak of Kamet and to explore the neighbouring glaciers.

In 1909 Mr. Meade and the great guide Pierre Blanc set out to climb the Guglia di Brenta, a sensational pinnacle in the Brenta group of the Dolomites which resisted all attacks until 1899. Meade and Blanc, misled by two iron rings, carried through an unplanned variation which was as formidable as the most exacting climbs which the modern specialist, armed with pitons and their engineering tools, is willing to face.

An Unplanned Variation

BLANC and I might indeed have recoiled from the sinister smoothness of that forbidding precipice, had we not happened to see, several yards obliquely above us in the face of the wall that fell sheer for more than a thousand feet, a small iron ring fixed to a spike in the rock, and it seemed to beckon us on. At first sight of this place the same reflection must have occurred to both of us simultaneously: surely it could not be as bad as it looked. Obviously the ring must be an indication of the route, for we assumed it must have helped numerous climbers to overcome this very formidable-looking *mauvais pas*. Only later did it appear that this assumption was unwarranted.

Blanc, when in action, was a man of few words, and had already hitched a spare coil of the rope to a projecting rock, probably more from habit than from any confidence in the usefulness of this precaution in such a place. He then invited me to kneel down as near the vanishing point of the terrace as possible, so that by standing on my shoulders he could reach out sideways to the right, higher up the cliff, in hopes of getting a grip that would enable him to pull himself up. His new position would then be one of complete exposure on the bare face of the precipice, and from it he must attempt to reach the iron ring by continuing to crawl in an oblique direction higher and higher up the cliff. The crouching position that I now took up on the very brink, where the shelf ended, provided me with a sickeningly uninterrupted view down the thousand feet to the foot of the mountain. Every pebble that either of us dislodged fell clear, and hummed as it vanished into the depths.

Unfortunately I proved an unsatisfactory footstool. The rock above was overhanging, forcing Blanc backwards and outwards in an alarming fashion, so that he kept imploring me to lean farther out over the formidable gulf that seemed to be waiting for its prey. I must also contrive somehow to raise myself to a standing position, to enable the leader to find handholds that appeared to be desperately out of reach. All the time, while I struggled, the sound of distant shouting echoed in my head, like an incessant refrain in a nightmare, or the singing of a sick man's pulse. Eventually, after what seemed an endless struggle, I managed to raise myself to my feet, staggering under my companion's weight, and leaning as far over the edge of the abyss as I dared. Blanc, having mounted from my shoulders to my head, succeeded, after much kicking and wriggling, in launching himself on to the wall, with the result that in some miraculous way he contrived to hoist himself over the overhang. There was no sound but the scuffling of his boot-soles seeking non-existent holds, till, after a prolonged *tour-de-force*, he reached the iron ring where he could pause and cling in order to recover his breath. He called down to say that there was a second ring in sight, and that it would be necessary for him to reach it before he could be approximately secure. As for me, having no one to give me a leg-up, I should have to depend considerably on the help of the rope if I was to be able to follow; and Blanc, if he was to give any assistance at all, would be compelled to find a better position for himself still higher. But, before attempting to advance any farther, Blanc was anxious, for security's sake, to pass his rope through the ring, a laborious process; for in order to accomplish it he was obliged to untie the rope from his waist, and subsequently put it on again. He then passed quite out of sight, obliquely above my head on the right, struggling up the precipice like a fly on a wall, and in silence, so that I could only imagine what was happening. All that could be assumed from the slowness of the process, and the forbidding appearance of the cliff, was that the struggle to which we were now committed was something that exceeded all our past experience of the more formidable Dolomite expeditions. It could only be supposed that we had gone astray, with the consequence that we had now no choice but to continue forcing our way up the mountain till we reached the top or fell off.

Very slowly, with prolonged pauses that caused me the deepest anxiety, the rope uniting us slid upwards, a few inches at a time, gradually following the invisible leader above. Again there was a long and anxious delay as the leader reached the second ring; for here he was obliged for safety's sake to repeat the difficult manœuvre of threading the rope as he had done lower down.

At last he must have made himself relatively secure; for, after repeated shouting, he succeeded in making it clear that I could now advance in my turn, for the rope was securely hitched. Unfortunately, however, it had stuck somewhere, either in the lower ring or on the rocks. Moreover, Blanc was too badly placed to be able to give any help by hauling, or even by drawing in the slack, so that I had to help myself, especially at starting, by pulling myself up hand over hand on the rope. To a self-respecting mountaineer, who would in ordinary circumstances scorn to help himself by grasping the rope, this task might seem easy, not to say ignominious, but it must be remembered that the situation here was peculiar. The last man had no human ladder from which to take off, and the line of ascent, besides being perpendicular, was also oblique, a fact which greatly added to the difficulty. At the starting-place, too, there was the overhang, where hand and foot holds were practically non-existent. . . .

With a desperate effort I somehow succeeded in getting over the overhang. Providentially, too, the rope continued to adhere to the rocks, with the result that in course of time, exhausted as a fish out of water, I reached the first ring, there to cling, gasping for breath. Then followed the difficult and uncomfortable job of standing bolt upright, pressed against the cliff, with only one good foothold, untying the rope at my waist, re-tying it, and maintaining a precarious balance while doing so.

Once more it was Blanc's turn to advance. Fortunately he had reached a point where the direction, although still vertical, no longer slanted so unpleasantly across the face. Nevertheless the climbing was just as difficult. Then, as soon as Blanc could establish himself securely, I recommenced the struggle, again having to unrope and re-rope as I passed the second ring. It afterwards struck me as curious that throughout this long battle with the mountain my exclusive preoccupation had been a vivid conviction that to die in bed must be the most agreeable way of ending one's life. Moreover, the desire for such a peaceful consummation increased in intensity as every moment it seemed less likely to be realised.

How long this nightmare lasted it is difficult to say, but I well remember my astonishment and relief when the rock suddenly became easy, and I found myself stepping on to the spacious square top of the Guglia. I threw myself down beside Blanc, and we lay recovering our breath, swearing that never again would we be such fools.

After a thorough rest Blanc went to peer over the edge of the vertical western precipice, and with very little trouble discovered the orthodox route. It might be difficult, but it was certain not to be as bad as the way by which we had come, and we confirmed our suspicion that in following the south terrace we had made a mistake that might have been fatal. Presently we realised that the party which had been shouting to us was coming up the mountain. It was led by two well-known guides of Cortina, Antonio Dimai, whom Blanc usually referred to as "the king of the Dolomites," and Agostino Verzi. These two explained how local guides whom they had met at the foot of the Guglia had declared that we had deviated on to a false route and were bound to fall off; hence the attempt to communicate with us by shouting, which we had failed to understand. Dimai described the strange appearance that we presented seen from below, " human specks crawling up through the air," quite detached against the sky.

Certainly this was the most difficult rock-climb in Blanc's experience, a performance that was thoroughly up to the standards of the modern climbing of to-day, and which we had inadvertently accomplished some twenty years before its time . . .

The existence of the misleading rings requires an explanation. Certainly the man who could climb into such a position and fix two rings there can have been no ordinary mountaineer. We subsequently discovered that he was an Austrian professor of gymnastics who, with a friend, had been on the mountain only a few days earlier. They had made the attempt from the vanishing-point of the south terrace, perhaps in ignorance of the proper route. The leader had successfully climbed the overhang, and had hammered the two rings into the precipice, one after the other, while his companion was still at the taking-off place, with the joint rope of the party securely belayed to a rock. Above the second ring the leader's strength probably failed, for he lost his hold on the cliff and slipped backwards. It is not surprising that the sudden jerk of his fall snapped the rope, with the result that the unfortunate man fell a thousand feet through the air and was dashed to pieces on the rocks at the foot of the mountain. (*Approach to the Hills*.)

R. L. G. IRVING

Solvitur in Excelsis

IN an age in which men's beliefs are shaken, when the
ultimate end of life announced by mathematical philosophy
is complete annihilation, the question why we climb is likely to
be answered, and impatiently answered: "Because we like it."
There is something beyond that, however, which is worth con-
sidering, if there is any good in the pursuit of knowledge. If it
is worth while to assign true values to influences and events,
then it is not altogether a vain thing for men to weigh their
mountaineering experiences, and see what showing they make
in the balance-sheet of life. . . .

There are no moments that stand out in our long hours of
glorious experience like those in which we came to some high
point, and, as we looked out over what was before us, we knew
certainty, and doubt was impossible. Those moments are as
great rocks to which the frail tabernacle of our mind is held fast,
when the mists of doubt and the winds of fear come about it.
We cannot help being shaken or having our vision darkened,
but we know that we have had moments of clearer vision, and
that in them we had certainty. A certainty of what? It is hard
to put it into words. It was a certainty that beauty and truth
and generosity were real things, that there was something
embracing all of these that gave direction to life, and an
assurance that their reality need not be doubted when we saw
them as we generally do, as in a glass, darkly. . . .

There are two qualities in beauty more clearly revealed to me
on high mountains than in any other place. One is harmony:
the harmony of the infinitely small with the infinitely great,
where perfection of beauty in detail is found at every stage of
the building of the whole. The tiny six-pointed star that drifts
down on to your coat has beauties that multiply with every
increase in the power of the microscope. And yet these beauties
are all eclipsed for our limited vision when we see them built up
into the leaves and flowers of frost that grow under the winds of
winter on the upper rocks of British hills, the consolation
Nature awards to the smooth, hard slabs that can offer no
lodging-places to the flowers of summer. Crevasses open to let

us see translucent canopies, so delicate that a touch of the sun will shatter them, so beautiful that we forgive the inconvenience they cause thereby to our material progress. Yet we almost forget they exist as we look at the glistening draperies that fall for thousands of feet over the form of a great peak like Monte Rosa or Siniolchum. In the light that beats upon you on a snow crest, out of the deep, palpitating blue of the dome of sky, and leaps up from the tiny facets of the ice-crystals around you, the countless waves of energy seem to be moving with one purpose, a purpose in which you must have your part.

The second quality is quiet strength. There is something in the serene loveliness of a scene in the High Alps more truly spiritual and undying than in the beauty of things whose life. like our own, may be measured in hours, in seasons, or in years. The following words of Theodore Camus may help to show you what I mean. Camus was one of the many young men of Lyons who have lost their hearts to the Alps by looking at their distant snows from the hills that rise above the Saône. Not long before his death, when he knew that the illness which had attacked him must be fatal, he was talking to his sister, a nun, of his increasing detachment from things that belong to earth, and he added: "There is just one thing to which I hold as close as ever, which for me shines with a wonderful brilliance that remains undimmed though it belongs to the things of earth; I mean the High Alps at heights of three or four thousand metres. This is the loveliest thing on earth, and how few there are who know it! When I die, it is to them that I shall send one of my last good-byes, and every day I thank God, not for having created them, but for having made me know them. It is as if, in doing that, He had allowed me to have a glimpse of the infinite, through a window open only to a few privileged beings, of that infinite which cannot be described, for all descriptions are so far below the truth."

This is the beauty in mountaineering which, when we have made it ours, we can keep always with us.

There is also a beauty only seen in action, in the midst of vigorous play, when our heart is beating fast to supply our calls upon it, and our face is close up against the mountain's as we pause for breath. We struggle through the hours of a long day to make our will prevail and win the game, and all the time the mountain maintains its calm as though it knew it was its beauty

LOOKING NORTH FROM THE JUNGFRAUJOCH

that had conquered us. Nor can our idea of beauty be complete without the struggle. The Greeks are the people who have been most eager in the pursuit of beauty as an ideal, and it was in their games that it most often found expression. Nor is it only through the eye, but also through the sense of touch and other senses that beauty is gathered into our experience and helps to fashion our soul. It is no exaggeration of the fancy to claim that the climber knows the beauty of rock, its firmness, its variety of colours, form, and texture better than a mere walker. Many of the loveliest formations of ice and snow are only approachable by him, and only he knows the full fragrance of the cool air on the ridge that has cost him hours of toil on burning slopes to win.

And besides all the intimate charm that mountains reveal only to those who are not content to sit at their feet and watch, but are determined to win them, there is the beauty of artistry that is called into existence by all great sports. There is beauty in any action performed as perfectly as means permit—we may even concede that the action of a motor engine is in this sense beautiful at times. There was more than mere efficiency in the way Mallory or Franz Lochmatter would climb a slab, or in the action of a good step-cutter, where every blow is struck exactly in the right place and every ounce of effort tells in the result, while the poise of the body in the slipper steps responds to every movement of the swinging axe.

On high mountains there are never fifty thousand spectators as at a cup-tie or a test match, from whom the cry of "Beautiful! beautiful!" is drawn by a clever dribble or a glance to leg. There is only the breathless silence of two or three companions, strung out upon some narrow footholds, as they watch the series of well-co-ordinated movements that carry a leader past a protruding boss. Nevertheless it is a spontaneous tribute to this beauty of action.

Guido Rey aptly compares the man who claims to know the charm of mountains without ever risking his life upon them to a man who would claim to be a navigator without ever having left the shore, or to have known what the love of a woman can be from having sung serenades beneath her window. . . .

The great *truth* that climbing teaches us is that the physical struggle and the contemplative aim are parts of one indivisible whole. Every effort of the muscles that lifts us a little higher is giving us an assurance, absorbed unconsciously into our being, that in the right use of matter to a spiritual end we can fulfil our destiny. And, what is best of all, the enjoyment we find in so doing convinces us that the purpose that controls our destiny is a generous purpose. . . .

If there is none but a materialistic basis to mountaineering or to anything else, if the conquest of matter and the conversion of its use to material ends are the purpose of life, then my philosophy of mountaineering collapses, built though it be in part upon the rock. If you admit there is a spiritual basis to it, if there is reality in the generosity of purpose that draws us upwards to seek for truth by the gratification of our physical desires, then you will forgive me if I introduce a part of a man's being which now and then impels him to get in touch with ultimate things, the part we generally call his religion. In making this one serious attempt to justify a mountaineering faith I cannot leave out the thought that matters most of all.

If there is reality in the beauty of form, of colour, and of action that attracts us, in the truth which we climb to find and do slowly seem to find, and in the generosity which that dawning truth reveals, then we must be glad to find confirmation of our belief that mountains are indeed a true guide to these things.

One figure stands out far above all others in the understanding of these great realities, one who is acknowledged to be a supreme authority on spiritual values. I mean, of course, the Man who saw the glory of beauty in the lilies of the field, who tells us that the whole object of His life was to bear witness to the truth, and who bore witness by going about doing good.

How did He endeavour to reach the one source of these realities? How did He refresh Himself at that source? "He went up into the mountain to pray."

For men of our calibre, any form of activity which helps us to reach upwards to that source, even the mere action of climbing, may be regarded as a form of prayer. Does it diminish the pleasure or the value it has for you, so to regard it, just for a moment? "He went up into the mountain to pray, and He continued all night in prayer." Men have been led to follow His example, though it may be quite unconsciously. Follow Dr. Kugy to a bivouac in the Julian Alps, and fill in from your own experience the sketch he gives us. "Once more the sinking shadows, the distant song of waters, and infinite silence about us. So the mountain night passes in the beauty of a dream. If you have thus dwelt in the secret heart of the mountains, beholding the full glory of their revelation, as they unfold their signs and wonders from the going down of the sun to its uprising, nothing can efface the memory of such nights."

If there is indeed one great source of all reality, then all ways that lead thither must converge. That is why a mountain is such a satisfying guide; it supplies men with unity of purpose, and it demands the use of every part of their physical nature in its attainment. In the plain, or on the low hills that rise above it, there are church towers and steeples that point as unmistakably upwards in the same super-worldly direction as the mountain itself; yet men have been sorely distracted in deciding which of the appointed guides is the best to follow, so that many of them decide to remain strolling aimlessly about the plain. It is not easy when you are within the walls of one of these churches to see how your path, and that of a friend in a church some distance off, are going to come together. It becomes easy if you both follow the example of Him in whose honour both churches have been built, and "go up into the mountain to pray."

It sounds too easy; remember it is only the beginning of a solution of life's riddle. I wish our mountain philosophy had been written by a man like King Albert of Belgium; because, in these days of publicity, whatever is said by those whose names are widely known finds far more willing listeners, and because we know that this king was a great man who loved mountains as only a climber loves them.

It is my one regret for being just an ordinary man, that I bring so little credit to the mountains that have done so much for me. Only one man knows the creature I should have been without them; it is in gratitude for his escape from that existence that he has tried to add something to the knowledge and affection with which men may regard them.

(*The Romance of Mountaineering.*)

A. H. M. L.

In 1908 I founded the Oxford Mountaineering Club with my friend H. E. G. Tyndale, now Editor of "The Alpine Journal." Our little Club, with a membership of less than twenty, published in 1912 a slim volume, "Oxford

Mountaineering Essays." "The Times" referred in a kindly review to "the array of talent—all sufficiently interested in the art of writing to be qualified to tell as well as to experience." After thirty years' experience as an Editor of various climbing and ski-ing journals I know how difficult it is to find writers who can also interpret the emotions which mountains provoke in those who love them, but in 1912 I was not in the least impressed by my luck in finding in a group of twenty no less than seven young climbers, Julian and N. G. Huxley, H. E. G. Tyndale, Norman Young, Michael Sadleir, Hugh Kingsmill Lunn and Hugh Pope, who could write exactly the kind of essay which I required. I have quoted freely from this team in my earlier anthology, and I here reproduce the preface which, with its blend of gaiety and pompous solemnity ("where the talk had been unashamedly of mountains and their metaphysics"), seems to me a characteristic period piece of Edwardian Oxford.

The Oxford Mountaineering Club

OXFORD, they tell us, is the home of movements; Cambridge the home of men. Certainly the miniature movement that took shape in this little book was inspired by a Cambridge man. It was at an Oxford tea-party, where the talk had been unashamedly of mountains and their metaphysis, that Mr. G. Winthrop Young gave the first impulse to the scheme that ultimately produced this collection of essays. To Mr. Young the editor and contributors have been indebted for constant help and advice. He has heartened the despondent, and has inked cold daylight into more than one "sunset" passage.

At Oxford there are a number of Alpine clubs. The oldest and most sedate meets once a year in New College Hall. A less dignified association meets at irregular intervals on New College Hall and other hospitable roofs. Lastly, there is a genial little society which owed its beginnings to some twenty undergraduates who agreed they could spare an occasional arduous evening to the revival of their Alpine memories. One confiding member brought a lantern, and has since endeavoured—with indifferent success—to recoup himself out of spasmodic subscriptions. We shall none of us forget the first meeting. In our innocence we had hoped that a scientist might know something of electricity, and Mr. Bourdillon was in consequence entrusted with the lantern. After much hissing on the part of the machine, and of the audience, a faint glow appeared on the sheet, and enveloped in a halo of restless hues we dimly discerned the dome of Mont Blanc. A pathetic voice from behind the lantern sadly inquired whether we would "prefer Mont Blanc green and spluttering or yellow and steady." The chairman then proceeded to read a paper illustrated or rather misrepresented by lantern slides, and at the conclusion proposed a very hearty vote of thanks to himself for his interesting and entertaining lecture. The House then divided, and the motion was lost by an overwhelming majority. The minutes also record that a member moved to inhibit the secretary of the Church Union from issuing a printed prayer for "faith to remove mountains." This motion was lost, as Mr. Tyndale ably pointed out the value of a publication that might facilitate the transfer of some superfluous mountains from the Alps to the monotonous surroundings of Oxford.

(Oxford Mountaineering Essays.)

H. E. G. TYNDALE, M.B.E.

Mr. Tyndale, first President of The Oxford Mountaineering Club, is the Editor of "The Alpine Journal."

First Affections

IT is one thing, however, to arrive: it is quite another to stay the course. As August draws on and the first serious weather break heralds the coming of autumn the mountains take on a sterner aspect of challenge to our allegiance. Elsewhere there is warmth and comfort; surely after laborious days we have earned the reward of sunbathing and French cookery. And with these seductive thoughts there creeps in a doubt whether early rising and scanty provisions are really worth while, whether after all the whole thing may have been no more than mad endeavour. In such circumstances, listlessness can well win the day. I fancy Irving felt some such doubt about my attitude when one foggy morning, while Sir Prudence remained beneath blankets, he routed George and myself out of bed for a traverse of Dent Perroc and Grande Dent de Vesivi. Looking back on it, I feel we took some risk of thunderstorms, for at times the muttering grew to a grumbling, though there was always an exit from the ridge on the Ferpecle side. Despite conditions, the climb was a brilliant success as we raced over ghostly gendarmes and crazy pinnacles, and giant crags loomed up through the mist only to beetle off at our approach. We groped our way off the Grande Dent into a sea of boulders where Irving and George, refusing to halt, tripped lightly as a mountain brook, while I tripped heavily over both their ropes. That day meant more to me than barked shins. I learnt that morning mists are not a sure sign for slinking back to bed, and I gained confidence from moving in unison with my companions where doubtful weather demanded speed. But it was more than the mere winning as it were of a good conduct stripe. When at last the others condescended to unrope on a gentian-starred lawn and beneath the ragged edge of cloud a vision of rainswept valley appeared, I got a glimmer of what Godley discovered in the mists above Mattmark, that these hills can be for us the dwelling place of "truths that wake to perish never." So it is that, while other memories vanish, this day among cloud-capped towers remains clearer for me than many a sunshine holiday. Meanwhile, with the approach of thunder the grumbling grew to a mighty rumbling, and we got home soaked but triumphant for tea, where the first to congratulate us was Sir Prudence himself. Stung in conscience, he departed next morning for Zermatt with the sacrilegious sigh, "I suppose we shall have to do the Matterhorn."

It was time for us to step westward, for no season is complete without a visit to Chamonix. If the Petite Dent had been our *hors d'œuvres*, Mont Blanc was to be the *bomb glacée* of our primitive appetites. Our journey thither carried us through three countries, for in those days you could cross a frontier without attracting rifle fire, and to carry a passport was the mark of a diplomatist or an international crook. We left Arolla bound for the Valpelline by the Col de Collon, a long trudge up the easiest of glaciers,

> Till we slope to Italy at last,
> And youth, by green degrees.

There was little green about the savagery of Combe d'Oren under weeping skies, and no youth in the braised marmot of Praraye; while as for sloping to Italy, we found next day the truth of the epigram that the Valpelline runs uphill the whole way to Aosta. Wreaths of mist hung low in the wild glens to our left, fleecy washtub clouds enveloped the broad pasturages above the lower valley, and at last, turning north towards the Great St. Bernard, we entered St. Remy in a tropical downpour. As we crossed back into Switzerland by Val Ferret and Champex, where our party disbanded, the fine weather returned for good. I was led to Chamonix by the finest of all ways of access, with dawn on the Plateau de Trient, through the gateway to sunshine on the Saleinaz Glacier, and then the sudden vision in all its icy splendour of the Aiguille Verte from the Col du Chardonnet, and tea at the Patisserie des Alpes. After tea Irving, who was sadly in need of repair, vanished to the tailor's and reappeared at Coutett's hotel with an air of unwonted respectability and a French crown colour seat to his trousers.

Now Couttet's is a cradle of climbers, but in Irving's view, as he eyed me busy with Savoyard honey and rolls unrationed, it was likely to be the graveyard of training. At length he took me, grossly full of bread, by the shoulder and, pointing like Jacques Balmat in the celebrated Chamonix statue, showed me an hotel on the distant skyline of Col de Voza. There was then no railway to take you up to the snowline, and it is an almighty long way from Chamonix to the hut on the Tête Rousse. Once there, however, as you look out into the sunset over the rounded hills of Savoy, you know that there are better things than breakfast rolls in the vale of Chamonix; and when next day you pass from the icy shadows of the Aiguille du Goûter to the wide sunlit spaces of the Dome, you realise that the best is yet to be. A Mummery may scorn the treadmill of these upper snows; a Tartarain may feel that the eyes of his native Tarascon are upon him; but if you are seventeen you will step proudly on to the Calotte with every Chamonix telescope focused upon you. "Des personnes sont visibles aujourd'hui au Mont-Blanc." But you will not remain long on the summit in a tempestuous wind, surveying a thousand valleys far and wide, before running furiously down to the Vallot hut. In a very short time we were back at the First Bosse, near where Tartarain and Bompard parted company with cries of "outre" and "boufre," leaving only a severed rope to tell the tale. There was a small patch of ice here, and before I had time to say "outre" I was following

Tartarain into Italy. Irving must, I fear, have said something stronger than "boufre" as he took a flying leap into France and so arrested my descent. And this, under the nose of every spyglass in Chamonix. It was well to learn thus early at the cost of a mere knuckledusting that climbing, like matrimony, is not lightly to be undertaken, that indeed there is no such thing as an easy mountain. You may read, mark, learn all Alpine scriptures; their inward digestion is the matter of a lifetime.

From the Vallot hut we ran down the broad track towards the Grands Mulets. Braver men have turned their backs on this primrose path, but the call of Chamonix has always been too much for me. I should like to linger over the journey from plateau to plateau, with sitting glissades that made serious inroads into Irving's museum piece, and the halt for tea while the Aiguille du Midi had its final fling at us and stones whizzed past the boiler, and the descent of innumerable zigzags, till darkness overtook us as once, after the same expedition, it encompassed Moore and Almer in the lower pinewoods. But the lights of Chamonix are at hand and we are already late for dinner at Couttet's, where some Comus in a boiled shirt will bring us orient liquor in a crystal glass.

And here, amid feasting and feminine flattery, all seasons should end, were it not that for every pious novice there is one more port of call. I am thinking of the Alpine Club. In the early sixties a young climber visiting London chartered a hansom and proudly directed the driver "Alpine Club." "Alpine Club, where's that? Never heard of it!" was the crushing reply. I approached more humbly on foot, through the long couloir of Savile Row, and went up the narrow winding staircase past the menus of long digested dinners, beneath the grave portraits of former Presidents, and entered a room crowded as the Bertol hut, for it was the occasion of the December tea party. There, one of the Arolla wiseacres took pity on me and pointed out some of the great figures: here Douglas Freshfield, a golden eagle among lesser falcons; here Edward Whymper, aloof as the Matterhorn of his destiny; there Martin Conway, this time drinking tea with foresight; and I caught the rich Doric tones of that bearded apostle George Yeld, editor of the *Alpine Journal*, in converse with Farrar, our Alpine Henry of Navarre, to whom younger men never turned in vain. As I looked with awe on these paladins, the lessons of my first season lived anew in the fellowship of mountaineers who enriched and bequeathed a tradition that is indeed the fountain light of all day.

GEORGE FINCH, F.R.S.

Mr. George Finch, who was a member of the 1922 Everest expedition, describes in the following passage the first ascent of the West ridge of the Bifertenstock.

The Making of a Mountaineer

THE crest of the ridge once again became too smooth and precipitous, but close to it, on the right, a feasible route could be detected. It led up steep slabs to the foot of a crack which debouched on the very summit of the buttress. The rope was all paid out before I had gained the crack, and Forster had to make his way up towards me. But I had good standing ground on a fairly wide ledge and could hold his rope securely. He was about fifteen feet below me and just about to wrestle with the hardest part of the ascent when, in an effort to improve my footing the better to cope with a slip, I felt the greater part of the ledge, which I had hitherto looked upon as solid with the mountain, break away from under my feet, and a great mass of rock slithered down the slabs, aiming with deadly accuracy at Forster. Powerless to move out of its way, he received a glancing blow which inflicted a deep scalp wound and all but stunned him. Swept out of his holds by the impact, he was left hanging helpless in mid-air. By all that is merciful, however, sufficient had remained of the ledge to leave me with just enough footing to withstand the strain on the rope and hold Forster up. Blood was spurting freely from the wound in his head; the extent of the injury was unknown, and no time was to be lost in getting to a place of safety, where it would be possible to staunch the flow. Staggered though he was and dripping with blood, Forster still had his wits about him. As I held his rope taut, he climbed up to me and took his stand on what was left of the ledge, while I made my way up to the foot of the crack and, with all possible haste, gained the broad level platform at the top of the buttress. There he rejoined me. Inspection revealed the reassuring fact that the extent of his injuries was limited to the scalp wound, which, however, still bled freely. By means of a few sheets of paper kept firmly in position underneath a knitted silken cap, the flow was eventually stopped. Except in its purely physical result, the little drama had not adversely affected either of us. Indeed, if there had previously been any doubt as to the final conquest of the west ridge of the Bifertenstock, there could be none now. The rough handling had got our blood up, and we felt the ridge was doomed. For the present we had fulfilled the object with which we had set out, namely the reconnaissance of the first great obstacle, and it behoved us to return to the Bifertenlücke where we had deposited our kits. . . .

At 5 a.m. on September 9th we left the comfort of the hut and in little more than two hours had gained the Bifertenlücke. Then, exchanging the heavy mountain boots for rope-soled shoes, we commenced the attack upon the west ridge in real earnest. . . .

At length we stood on the ridge at the foot of the last buttress, the most formidable barrier remaining between us and success. The ridge itself and the wall to the left both overhung to such an extent that they defied attack. To the right, however, the rocks were less steep and more broken up, and for about one hundred feet we made our way across them under the great wall of the step. On attempting to strike upwards, however, we found that we had misjudged the gradient, and after a stern struggle I recoiled defeated. We then continued our traverse still further to the right across a series of smooth, precipitous slabs where, for the second time on this ridge, in spite of the great length of rope at our disposal, the utter absence of belays or suitable standing grounds forced us into a situation in which the protection afforded by the rope was nil, and a slip on the part of one of us would have involved the destruction of both. Each knowing that where one could climb the other could follow, and both confident that neither would slip, we did not dream of retreat. But had we been at the mercy of a companion who was clumsy and frequently in need of assistance, even at this advanced stage where we were so near our goal, we would have broken off the climb. Why, one may ask, not dispense with the rope altogether in such a situation where it is little more than a dangerous encumbrance? My reply is a simple statement of fact, from which each may draw his own inferences. I would prefer not to climb with the man who advocates such a policy.

Safely over the slabs, we came to the foot of a very steep, shallow gully leading to a great snow cornice on the ridge above the buttress. With much difficulty we climbed the first hundred feet and reached a broad, almost level shelf barely fifty feet below the cornice. A huge lump of the latter had fallen away, leaving a gap that gave easy access to the ridge. Between us and the gap lay a stretch of easy, broken rocks, so, once more changing footgear and donning mountain boots, we scrambled up and at last stepped out through the cornice back on to the ridge.

A north breeze, cool and bracing, met us. The snow under foot sparkled in the brilliant noonday light. The neighbouring peaks stood up bold and sharp in the clear atmosphere. The sun flooded all with warmth. It was good to be alive. A last, half-whimsical glance at the little St. Fridolin's hut, a tiny brown speck at the foot of the great four-thousand-foot wall, and we turned our steps along the snow-crested ridge towards the summit. Chipping a step here and there where the cornice forced us out on to the steep north flank, we mounted speedily. One more clamber over a pitch of easy, broken rocks, and the fight was over. At 2 p.m. we stood atop of the Bifertenstock.

(*The Making of a Mountaineer*.)

FRANK SMYTHE

Frank Smythe has climbed as high as any mountaineer on Everest. He organised the successful attack on Kamet, at that time the highest Himalayan peak to be conquered, and in company with Professor Graham Browne he made the first ascent of two magnificent routes on the Brenva face of Mont Blanc.

An Avalanche

MY lack of experience made us miss the proper route and take a line far to one side of it up the face of the Olperer. It was a very bad route. It involved the passage of a wide bergschrund by a fragile snow bridge. Next came an ice-slope slightly concave in shape, which meant that anything falling from the rocks above was certain to come in our direction. I

did not like this slope, but the absence of any debris in or near
the bergschrund at the base of it emboldened me to attempt the
ascent. Inexperience made me slow in cutting the requisite
steps and it was some time before the ice was vanquished.
Above it there was snow, but snow of the worst sort, water-
logged and resting on ice. Even to my inexperienced eye it was
obvious that it would avalanche, if not now, at all events later
when the sun was more powerful.

There was no alternative but to retreat. We were carefully
descending in our steps on the ice-slope about 100 feet above
the bergschrund and moving downwards one at a time when,
of a sudden, there was an appalling roar. Fifteen hundred feet
above us on the ridge of the Olperer an enormous mass of rock
had broken loose. The slopes were black with the avalanche.
In a few seconds the ice funnel in which we stood would be
swept from end to end. We should be erased from it like chalk
marks from a blackboard. No running, no dodging was
possible; we were standing in ice steps and the bergschrund was
below waiting to receive us. Only a miracle could save us.
The miracle occurred.

The great mass of stones suddenly vanished. Unknown to us,
there was a crevasse cutting across the slope above us. This
swallowed the avalanche. Not all of it. A few of the larger
stones had been carried by their momentum across the crevasse.
They came straight for us. Never can a man on his first
mountaineering expedition have had a more unnerving
experience. Had Munro slipped from his steps he would have
dragged me with him into the bergschrund. He did not slip.
There was nothing he or I could do save stand in our steps, and
hope for the best. The stones, there were eight or ten of them,
took a long time in coming, an interminable time it seemed.
First, they were mere dots on the white slopes above us.
Gradually they grew larger, and we could see that they were
moving at a terrific speed and in a series of great bounds.
Suddenly they were flying at us with a wicked noise.

There was one block larger than the rest, the size of a chest
of drawers. I remember watching it in a detached, calculated
sort of way—the others scarcely mattered, although each was a
potential killer. That block made a different noise from the
others, a deep, menacing drone like a gigantic bee. It seemed to
be coming straight for me. It struck the slope a few yards

above me, was deflected slightly, and passed between us, hitting the glacier below the bergschrund with a tremendous thud. So near was it that the wind of it nearly knocked me out of my steps.

The smaller fry were behind the big block. We scarcely had time to think about them before they had whirred past and buried themselves in the snow.

We resumed the descent.

A few minutes later we stood in safety on the glacier. We retraced our steps across this.

We reached the moraine. My companion breathed a sigh of relief. He had only one remark to make on the day's proceedings, "It's terra firma for me in future," he said. "Less terror and more firmer." But he was a brave man.

(Over Tyrolese Hills.)

"Though I were stricken with blindness"

THOUGH I were stricken with blindness I would still go to the mountains. I would lie on the turf of a quiet alp in the morning, when the dew is drying, and the light breezes are fragrant with flowers and moist earth. I would breathe long breaths of pine-scented airs. I would hearken to the lazy jangle of cowbells from distant pastures, the boom of glacier torrents, and the solemn roll of avalanches. And, maybe, the "Lordly Folk who dwell in the Hollow Hills" would take pity upon me: I would hear their friendly chuckles in the nearby stream, their elfin whispers in the grass, and their murmured chorus in the pine-tops.

Or I would ask to be led to some high hut and, lying on its straw-filled bunks, listen to the deep voice of the night wind, and in the early morning open the door and going forth meet the keen dawn-breath with its indefinable promise of delight.

(Climbs and Ski-Runs.)

DOROTHY PILLEY

Dorothy Pilley and her husband Ivor Richards, a populariser of Basic English and a member of the Harvard Faculty, made the first ascent in 1928 of the north ridge of the Dent Blanche, one of the last outstanding of the classic Alpine problems. The quotation is from Dorothy Pilley's "Climbing Days."

The North Ridge of the Dent Blanche

ANYTHING less encouraging than the arête as seen from this point would be hard to imagine. To begin with, the actual blade of the narrow ridge above overhangs perceptibly at several points. To the left a deep crack in its side seems to offer better chances of ascent, only to end in a much worse overhang some hundred feet higher. Above this, there flapped in the cold wind evidence of the Swiss party's descent, a frayed loop of the rope they had left behind them, flung back by the gales and hitched up among the crags. On the right is the smooth, exceedingly steep wall of the vast couloir furrowing the cliff down to the Glacier de la Dent Blanche. At one time we had talked of crossing this couloir and returning, at a higher level, to the ridge. But one glance into its bruised and stone-swept depths was now enough. There was, however, something like a remotely possible crack in its smooth wall, a crack which passed at its critical point out of sight into the unknown.

In the searching breeze we clung to the bitterly cold rocks of the pinnacle, and gazed at these crags black against the now sun-filled blaze of the sky. We were just inside their shadow, a golden touch or two showed where the angle of the ridge above eased off. Our difficulties would be over when we reached that warm and welcoming glow a hundred and fifty feet above us, but for the moment they seemed overwhelming. Whatever estimate subsequent parties may make of this passage, there is no doubt that as a daunting spectacle it will always hold high rank.

Joseph now began a series of explorations which seemed to us to touch the limiting mark of cragsmanship. He started by exploring the wall of the great couloir round the corner to the right—an anxious moment for us, since he was soon out of sight and we could easily tell by the inch by inch movement of the rope that the ground was exceedingly severe. We could do little to safeguard him as he slowly gained height. But Antoine's calm reflective confidence in his brother's skill, his quiet assumption that everything was normal, was a great reinforcement to our trust in Joseph's judgment. In such situations the amateur has a responsibility which can easily become agonising. It was with a mixture of disappointment and relief that we began to take the rope in again, ninety feet of it, and soon we were welcoming Joseph among us once more. He had been within a few feet of success but those few feet had proved insuperable.

After a pause for chilled hands to regain their strength, the second possibility was reconnoitred. This was the crack on the left, which proved both extremely hard to get into and unluckily impossible to get out of at the top. With the greatest difficulty Joseph contrived to force nearly one hundred feet of the crack. Then the problem of escaping from the overhangs which close this route came to a head. At one moment he seemed almost to be emulating a lizard on a ceiling. But human beings lack the necessary organs apparently, and we were forced to watch a series of descending movements extraordinarily reassuring in their witness to his climbing reserves. When he rejoined us on our belvedere, he told us that he had been within a few feet only of a series of holds that would have taken him up.

There remained the very nose of the ridge itself. It seemed a hopeless chance. A few sinuous, very shallow grooves wound up among its protuberant bosses, but they were mercilessly smooth and no square-cut hold showed as far as the eye could reach. There could be no rest or anchorage for the leader for at least a hundred feet. And, to begin with, the base of the nose was undercut. Its very beginning seemed inaccessible. Once on the tip the leader would be on the steepest possible rock with a clear three thousand odd feet of space under the palms of his feet. Frankly it was almost with dismay that we saw Joseph, after a thoughtful survey, turn to it.

The first step was to mount the initial overhang. There happened to be a cleft in the rock under the cave into which an axe-shaft could be fixed, leaving the rest protruding like a spring-board over nothing. We made sure that it *was* fixed, but to gain its vibrating head without assisting holds was no easy matter. From this vantage point the overhang could be breasted. The next stretch turned, it seemed to us later, upon one rather rounded hold. Hand, knee and then foot it served, while the fingers found only pressure thrusts to direct the balance. Breathlessly we watched Joseph's smooth, seemingly effortless movements. He kept up a flow of patois remarks to Antoine as he worked across and upwards. Soon he was only a shapeless silhouette against the dazzle of the sky above. It seemed impossible that he should be able to stay at all in as steep and smooth a passage, much less that he should be able to continue. After a while, as the rope still ran out, his voice grew dim with distance and we lost sight of him in the glare. Suddenly came a sharp exclamation: it sounded like "Je chouques!" Antoine, calm as ever, translated, "Il est là." The tension was over; or, rather, changed its direction altogether. Now it was our turn!

Most of the passage had to be done by the oddest series of counterpoised pressures I have ever had to manage. All on a surface too steep to allow any of the usual margin of balance. An occasional pinch-hold was a luxury. The friction of a rubber sole or the palm of the hand on some small awkwardly sloping surface had to be enough. It was with a very queer sense of unreality—as though a dream had got out of place— that I came at last to a rapturous Joseph perched on little or nothing and tied to the cliff with a network of rope by which he had supplied me with a spare handline.

The landing-place, on which I joined I. A. R., was a nook the size of a dinner-plate, with one handhold! It needs some experience for two people to stow themselves in such a place with comfort. The contortions of the human body are, for-tunately, easier to perform than to describe. For a time we were busy with the problem of how to stay there together and keep the sacks, which had been hauled up on an independent rope, from departing. There was no room to put them on again as yet. But there is an old climbing maxim about halting-places: "Where there is room for one there is room for two," which applies to cliff-faces though not to chimneys. The second man can at least stand on the first man's foot!

Joseph meanwhile was occupied with Antoine, to whom fell the job of bringing up the last axe and thus doing without it as a springboard for the overhang. Since he elected to climb the pitch in boots it has always been a mystery to me how he did it. The overhang involved him in a voluntary leap into the void. We believed him when he said it gave him "une drôle de sensation." But in time he came up the last bulge as placidly as ever, with a broad smile and an "Ah, les amoureux!" as he spied us clinging together to our joint and solitary hold. After this, what remained of the wall was only steep; its holds seemed superb in comparison with the passage below. Joseph disap-peared again, there was another pause while the sacks and axes went up; and then, suddenly, we topped a wall of rough yellow rock to a ledge and the sunshine.

We lay and basked and ate and relaxed. The ridge above promised nothing more than is normal to a great Alpine ridge. Its rough, golden rocks stood up in bold, very practicable masses, enchanting to our eye by contrast to the shadowy, frowning walls below. The plaster of ice and snow patches that decorated them would this year give no trouble. Time now was our only opponent. It was 1.30 and we had a long way still to go, so for comfort and speed we roped in twos again. From time to time, down in the recesses of the mountain below us on the right, rocks would be thawed out by the sun, slip away, slide down a snow-patch, hop, whir and vanish into the great couloir, but we were in complete safety as we clambered on our ridge. Under the clear sky the Alps basked in a heat-haze. Less than a pin's head in size the Bricolla Chalet, our starting-point, shone among its meadows.

Triumph gave us wings, and the rocks were really exhilarating, like the most sporting parts of the usual South Ridge of the mountain. Still, they were long, the day was far advanced (we had taken three hours and twenty minutes over the crucial two hundred feet), and it was five o'clock before we reached the summit. We did not pause for long, nor did we linger on the descent. In fact we raced down the southward rocks, for the sun sank with that peculiar suddenness it shows when you are sinking also. The valleys were filling with gloom as we turned down over the damp snows of the glacier. We were in no further hurry. We had only to walk, at lesiure, home to bed. Only then did fatigue descend upon me—like a black bonnet, so that I stumbled on the granulated re-frozen ice of the dry glacier, and among the tangled moraines through which the track winds its way down to Bricolla. But a current of sleepy beatitude flowed through one's veins. Not even my right foot seemed heavy, on which by accident I had been wearing one of I. A. R.'s spare boots throughout the day! A spell had been exorcized, a dream replaced by a reality which transcended it. In all the literal force of the word we were content. Once again, as I turned into bed, the candle went unextinguished and guttered itself out unheeded, so suddenly did blissful sleep descend.

(*Climbing Days.*)

MICHAEL ROBERTS

St. Gervais

COMING out of the mountains of a summer evening,
 travelling alone;
Coming out of the mountains
singing.

Coming among men, and limousines,
and elegant tall women, and hotels
with private decorative gardens,
Coming among dust,

After the distant cowbells, bringing
memory of mule-tracks, slithering snow,
wild pansies, and the sudden
loose clattering of rock,

I remembered Sunday evenings, church bells and cinemas
and clumsy trams
searching interminable streets
for quiet slums, the slums where I

remembering St. Gervais and the gorges, linger, bringing
in the worn shell of air, the pines,
the white-cloud vision of Mont Blanc, and up
beyond les Contamines the seven shrines.

HUGH KINGSMILL

The following passages are extracts from a chapter, "Childhood in Switzer-
land," in an autobiography, not yet completed, by Hugh Kingsmill Lunn.

Lucerne

SOME months passed, and we were in Switzerland again,
in a villa outside Lucerne, close to the lake. A winding
path led to a boathouse, and Uncle Holdsworth, my father's

brother, used to take Arnold and me for rows, and one day as I was returning from the boathouse alone—the other two doubtless a few yards ahead of me—Moses, a large mastiff, rushed up behind me from a dip in the lake and bowled me off the path, to my astonishment as well as fright, for I was very fond of him. The last in this cycle of memory-stimulating shocks happened in front of the villa, where there was a fountain with a wide circular basin, into which I fell one day while the sons of the house were bathing in it. Fished out by one of the boys, I was taken to my bedroom, where I stood shivering while my nurse rubbed me down. This rubbing is still prosaically distinct in the foreground of my memory; and in the background, half real, half dream-like, are the reeds in the shallow water by the shore and the cold water-lilies with their smooth flat leaves.

As the world widened round me my dreams grew worse. At the Pension Suter the mountains by the lake, of which I had been hardly conscious in the previous two summers, stood out clearly, and though in the morning sun the Rigi identified itself reassuringly with the golden honey at breakfast, it hardened forbiddingly as the day advanced. A winding path, overshadowed by chestnut trees, led up to the Pension from the river Reuss, which flowed out of the lake between narrowing banks, and swirled fiercely against the stone piers of an old wooden bridge. I was afraid of the river, and also of Lucerne Cathedral in the distance and the hill behind, which I thought concealed a land of witches. Above our Pension, in a pine wood clearing, stood a white hotel, which, in Arnold's opinion as well as mine, was inhabited by ogres, at one of whom, a Swiss peasant resting by the side of the road with a wooden milk container on his back, I very clearly remember Arnold and myself gazing from a distance of a few yards. But there were some things which tranquillised me and gave me a sense of security: the houses and cobbled streets in the old town, the smell of the sour black loaves in the bakers' shops, the little armed men in the paintings on the upper wooden bridge, and the ruined tower by the shore at Stansstad, and the whistle of the trains at night as they rushed along down in the valley.

Grindelwald

AT the west end of the valley, where the valley widened out, the mountains were not oppressive, but as we walked up the long village street, past a wash-house where the smell of soapy water mingled with the smell of lime leaves, the Mettenberg and Wetterhorn began to lose their symmetry, the great wall of the Mettenberg seeming to swell toward us and the white cone of the Wetterhorn sinking into its enormous dizzying precipices. Opposite the Wetterhorn and Mettenberg were the lower mountains of the Faulhorn range, whose starved grass slopes exuded a hopeless desolation in my dreams. The higher mountains were more terrible to dream of, but less harrowing, and the terror lasted only a few moments, drowned in a rush of water out of the blackness. There were two rivers in the valley, but the one that appeared in my dreams was nearly always the narrow discoloured torrent flowing from the upper glacier. Close under the Mettenberg was a narrow rickety bridge, where Arnold and I used to stand looking at the furious dance of the waves, splintered by the rocks in the river bed, but the waves were less frightening than the smooth sweep of the torrent over a boulder just below the bridge. The river which issued from the lower glacier had wider banks and overflowed in numberless little streams which ran between the trees of a wood in the level part of the valley. There was plenty of light in the wood, for the trees were small and scattered, and it was pleasant to hear the roar of the torrent diminish in the distance, and to look down through the clear water at the large smooth pebbles which paved the beds of the streams.

It was not till I was nearly seven, when Arnold and I began to go long walks above the valley, that I had any delight from the mountains, and then not from a sense of their beauty as external objects, but as though in a recoil from my previous fear I had become for a moment a part of the heights and distances about me, the green slopes and pine forests sweeping and sinking out of sight and the vast sides of the higher mountains reverberating the sound of torrents and falling ice.

Until I was fourteen most of our summer holidays were spent in Grindelwald. Arnold and I went up all the lesser mountains, and our parents did not interfere with our climbs, or even complain if we made them anxious by returning late. Occasionally they came with us, and I remember father jovially comparing himself to Julius Cæsar setting out to subdue a rebel chieftain as he walked up the Faulhorn to interview the keeper of the hotel at the top. But generally we went by ourselves, rising before dawn and starting off chilly and half asleep, with a glance up at the tiny hotel on the ridge of the Männlichen to see how clearly it stood out against the thinning darkness. It was our aim to get as high as we could before we came into the sun, which first touched the mountains across the valley and then, passing to the lower summits above our heads, descended the slopes towards us, and suddenly we stept into it and saw the valley far below, grey and silent. On off days we went to a wood above the west end of the village, where Arnold had discovered a rock about thirty feet high on which to practise climbing. Outside the wood the insects droned and the air was heavy with the smell of grasses, but it was cool under the pines. There we used to pick bilberries and wild strawberries, or lie and listen to the puffing of the little train across the valley as it jerked its way up the steep incline below Alpiglen. The sound died away as the train entered the wood, then some minutes later was heard again, but less laboured, for the worst was over.

Geneva

OUTSIDE Geneva, near Ferney, lived a family of wealthy Dutch Evangelicals, friends of my parents, and in the grounds of their house there was a long avenue of chestnut trees from which on clear summer evenings one could see, across the wide valley of the Rhone, Mont Blanc still glowing above the darkening lesser heights. Sometimes we went by steamer to the other end of the lake. As the Castle of Chillon came into view my father, lecturing to a party of tourists on the literary associations of Lake Geneva, used to recite Byron's *Prisoner of Chillon* in a sonorous voice; and the landscape of the poem, the blue Rhone in fullest flow and the mountains covered with the snows of a thousand years and the green isle with its three tall trees and the eagle riding the blast and the joyous fish that swam by the castle wall, blended with the real scene, the grey glacier torrent of the Rhone and one snow mountain rising above the lower hills and an island with five or six small trees and a blue windless sky and hundreds of tiny fish twinkling in the shallow water as the boat drew up by the landing stage.

BRIAN LUNN

The Journey to Switzerland

WHEN the boat train left Charing Cross Station, I felt we were really on the way, especially as the departure was usually preceded by a scare about the passes, while father searched his pocket-book feverishly. Indeed he said so often that he had lost the passes that I came to regard it as a sort of touching wood. Father never travelled with us. Once he wrote me a letter about a father mouse who was caught in a trap while his family enjoyed the cheese, but I was not quite convinced by the analogy, for he seemed to arrange his time-table pretty well as he chose, and the attitude of the boys made it clear that there were advantages in avoiding the fuss of travelling with a large family. He sometimes arrived at Grindelwald as a surprise a day or two before he was expected, and Froggy would say, "The Wappentier is here." Wappentier means heraldic beast, and she had given father this name because she said he was like the heraldic bear of the canton Bern.

The landing at Boulogne was the first big event of the journey, for now there was no more sea to divide us from Switzerland. By the low foreign railway platform the engine of our express was drawing its long sobbing breaths with a choke of delight as it mused upon its forthcoming run through the night across the plains of France. *Compagnie Internationale des Wagons Lits et des Grands Express Européens*—it was inspiring to read these words above the long compact sleeping coach, although to have travelled sleeper and gone to bed would have taken the edge off the pleasure of the night journey. Slowly the great express ambled through the streets of Boulogne, a pace-maker to flimsy carts. It was not until after Laon, when we settled down for the night, and the hood was drawn over the gas-jet, that the train acquired its authentic rhythm, of which there were two varieties, and it would pass easily from one to another as it needed a change: vv-vv-vv-vv- and then after swinging over a level crossing -vv-vv-vv-vv-vv-vv-vv-vv-vv. And underlying the rhythm all the time the roar persistent like the bagpipes' drone, the unbreathing roar of the night express traversing the plains of France.

As we rattle over points lights from signal-boxes come in through a window whose blind has slipped up, and oblong patches of white follow one another round the compartment and mother's sleeping face is lit for a moment in unearthly pallor.

When we get near the Swiss frontier, the train stops at smaller stations. Belfort, Delle, Délémont. A mysterious gong twice sounds two plaintive notes to speed the train which it cannot follow to Switzerland. I fall asleep again and the next time I wake up it is daylight. We are winding through the Jura and there directly below us is the railway line, along which we have just travelled in the opposite direction. Light mist still hangs about the pines in the valley beneath. I put my head out of the window, and the air is as keen now at the end of July as on an April morning at home. We round a bend and there is the first chalet in its close-cropped meadow. A Clouded Yellow flits across, is lost in the air and then appears again for a brief moment. Now there is a white road below. A horse is drawing a load of cut pine logs to the sawmill, and the drover in his wide hat walks beside the horse. Arnold calls Hugh into the corridor, and I join them, for we are approaching the spot from which we get our brief first glimpse of the Oberland peaks. Yes, they are there, just the same as last year. We can let them disappear, for we shall soon be right amongst them.

There are no more thrills until we reach Bern, where we have our first Swiss breakfast, coffee and rolls and cherry jam. "Breakfast at Bern is a feast of the gods"—when at the age of twelve I read that sentence in a printed essay by Arnold, it was my first experience of literature as a means of revealing one's own feelings. Now the sun is high in the heavens and the meadows on the way to Lake Thun sizzle with the chirp of a myriad grasshoppers. The train rhythm is more measured than in France and the heat seems to intensify the metallic note of the rails, while the shadows of our coaches follow one another in a crazy dance across the meadow. As we skirt the lake the whole range of the Oberland comes into view. Eiger, Mönch and Jungfrau are pleasantly magnified since we saw them from the Jura.

At Interlaken the mountain train waits with its steam engine crouching forward like a little kneeling elephant. The ticket-collector welcomes us like an old retainer, for does not Dr. Lunn bring hundreds of people to these valleys each summer? The train races across the level stretch to the mouth of the valley, the carriages swaying round the corners of the narrow-gauge railway. Then with great clanks the rack and pinion engage, and the train puffs its way up, blowing so hard that it seems as though each set of three puffs must be the last.

The boys go out of the carriage to the platform above the couplings, but I am not allowed to join them, and the savage longing to share their privileges drowns all pleasure until the Wetterhorn slides into its place at the head of the valley and the Silberhorn packs itself away behind the Eiger. Now familiar chalets come into view and the mountains finally settle into their right positions and grouping. As we walk along the village street we are greeted by confectioners and postcard sellers, lace makers and alpenstock vendors, as though we were the squire and family returning from a voyage. There is the little man in the green apron sunning himself in front of his cuckoo shop. "Here we are again," I say brightly. "All right," says the little man. *(Switchback : An Autobiography.)*

E. C. RICHARDSON

Mr. Richardson was the founder of the Ski Club of Great Britain.

Early Days

IN the winter of 1895-6 my brother C. W. R. and I thought we would like to go a-skating. We made enquiries about Holland, but were told that the skating possibilities of that country had been grossly overdrawn, and that as often as not there was no ice there at all worth bothering about. So we thought we would go to Norway, for that country, we argued, being further north, must surely be colder.

In due course we arrived in Christiania, after a good bucketing about on a small steamer in the North Sea. We asked the hotel porter, or somebody, where the skating rink was, and were directed to the University. Here, after some searching, we found a small bit of flooded ground. It was covered with stones, and small boys were sliding about on it. Was this really the skating rink? Yes, it was. Was there not any other? No, there was not, unless, indeed, the fjord was frozen, when sometimes a bit of it was cleared. What should we do? Better go up to Holmenkollen, there was a pond there, and probably there would be ice on it. So up to Holmenkollen we went. There we found the pond all right, but there was a foot of snow on the ice, and nobody was making the smallest effort to clear it away.

In the meanwhile, however, we had heard about ski, and these we saw for the first time outside the old hotel. We also saw people going about on ski, and it looked as if it was good fun. So we sent to Christiania for a complete outfit.

My education in ski-ing was kindly undertaken by a young Danish lady. I forget who it was that tackled my brother. Anyway, the young Danish lady took me for a tour. She sailed off down the road, and then went off through the woods near a place where there is now a railway station. The rest of the story will be familiar to all beginners. I was duly humbled, but from that time on, skating was not thought about any more. . . .

When I returned to Cambridge with my ski, the hall-porter thought they were some new rowing device!

Next year came another visit to Norway, with some further progress, and after that there was nothing doing till 1901-2, when I went to Davos for the first time. My brother C. W. R. joined me there. I had come in search of snow, and found lots at Davos. The first thing that happened was that we were assured that the Davos snow was, except quite late in the year, entirely unsuited to ski-ing. It was far too soft. Ski-ing could only be done on hard snow. A few people had tried it late in the year—a certain Mr. Dodgson, Mr. Collingwood, a brother of Tobias Branger (who had recently died), and possibly some others. But, it was said, ski-ing was not really at all suitable for Switzerland. This, however, we ventured to doubt, so we unearthed some ski from the shop of Mr. Branger, and began experimenting. Naturally we soon found out the truth, namely that ski-ing was every bit as good at Davos as in Norway, if not, indeed, better. It was great fun, and we felt all the satisfaction of real explorers when we discovered the "Church Slopes," and the long open run up behind the Fluella Hotel. When wending our way thither one day, we were amazed to find some ski tracks other than our own. These proved to be those of Messrs. Leaming and Fedden, who we afterwards got to know. We made some converts to the game that season, and, so far as I remember, amongst the first of these were the brothers Wroughton—though I am not quite sure whether it was this year they first came out or the next. Towards the end of the season, too, we undertook a great expedition. This was to go over the Strela Pass with Mr. Collingwood (who knew the way —so he said) to Arosa. . . . An expedition up the Brehmenbühl was about the most venturesome and foolish thing we did that year. There was a "Föhn" blowing, and we started off after new snow. Neither of us had been on a Swiss mountain of any consequence before, and we were thoroughly imbued with the idea that one could go anywhere at any time on ski. The result was that we started a small avalanche near the top. Luckily it did not go far, but my brother was buried up to the neck, and we lost important parts of our gear. So back we went to Clavadel with a wholesome respect for steep slopes and new snow, which neither of us has ever lost. We made enquiry as to the best way up when we got back, and successfully negotiated the old Brehmenbühl a few days later.

Next year we returned to Davos, and with the Wroughtons started the Davos English Ski Club. We got a lot of ski over from Norway to eke out the miserable local contraptions, and from that day to this the Club has never looked back. It is the oldest Ski Club (English) in Switzerland, for I refuse to countenance the paper things which were supposed to have had a previous existence at St. Moritz, and which for many years were in a more or less moribund condition. It is also older than the local club, which was not started till some weeks later. The boys of Davos at that time used to come out and watch us practising on the Church Slopes. From this they derived great entertainment, but it was a long time before it seemed to occur to them that they might try a hand at the game themselves. This, no doubt, was partly due to the lack of ski. Eventually, however, some of them (and these are now the cracks—or were just before the war) got ski or barrel staves or something, and joined the fun. We taught them the elements of running and jumping, got up competitions, and so on.

I am not sure whether it was this year or in 1904 that Mr.

Rickmers first came to Davos and took us all in hand. I met him first at St. Moritz. I was walking along the road there and saw somebody doing wonderful things on the steep hill opposite the Cresta. This proved to be Mr. Rickmers doing downhill stemming turns on Lilienfeld ski. I had never seen anybody swish about like this before, and I was much impressed. I tried to do likewise and failed miserably. This was partly because I did not know the knack, and partly because of my long, grooved, Norwegian ski. But Mr. Rickmers taught me those downhill turns—on Lilienfeld ski—and I have been grateful to him ever since. I have, of course, subsequently found out that short flat-bottomed ski are too high a price to pay for this extreme ease in turning, and also that one can do the turns very nearly as well—for all practical purposes quite as well—on Norwegian ski, and also that one can do downhill turns in other ways, but it was Mr. Rickmers who first put me on the track of these things. They all seem easy enough now, and there are lots of people ready to show beginners how to do them, but in those days we had to worry out all these different manoeuvres for ourselves.

In 1904 I went to the second big meet ever held in Switzerland. It was at Glarus. I expected to find everybody very expert there, but was rather surprised to hear that they were expecting the same sort of thing of me! Luckily, however, two Norwegians turned up (Leif Berg and Björnsen, I think they were) and they saved the situation, but I was here let in for trying a really big jump for the first time in my life. It was a very terrible experience, but I acquitted myself fairly well, and won third prize (or was it second?) with Herr Victor Sohm first. After we had given our little show, the Norwegians came on, and I again felt very nervous. I had been talking a bit about Norway and the wonderful runners there were there, and was afraid that these two would not come up to the mark. But I need not have worried. They jumped superbly amidst the breathless excitement of everybody.

After the winter, I embarked on literature, and wrote *Ski-running* in collaboration with Messrs. Rickmers and Crichton Somerville. This sold well, and a second edition was called for in the following year. This also was soon sold out, and then in 1909 I wrote *The Ski-runner* off my own bat. . . .

During the winters from 1904 onwards I visited most of the

Swiss ski-ing resorts of importance, as well as some in Germany and Austria. I have heard recently that these expeditions excited suspicion in the breasts of some of the Germans, and the following translation extracted from an article in the *Graz Tagespost* for 14-7-15 may perhaps amuse others besides myself:

"In the years 1905-1906, Richardson took up his head-quarters at St. Moritz in the Engadine. He lost no opportunity of attending the wintersport meetings in the Vosges, the Black Forest, and in the Swiss and French Jura, and of making a thorough study of the suitability of these places for wintersport. So far as I know, his interest did not extend any more towards the Arlberg district, but the distant Riesengebirge became so interesting to him again that Major Richardson gladly accepted the invitation of a Ski Club in Prag, and pursued his studies there. It is also known to me that Major Richardson visited the Caucasus, but I do not know whether the Carpathians offered any special attraction to him. But it would not surprise me to hear that they had done so. In view of the prevailing taste for all things English, which existed ten years ago, and of the firm faith in English superiority in all matters relating to sport, the Major was, of course, the point round which everything gravitated. E. H. Tanner, of Basle (the editor of *Alpinismus und Wintersport*), the *Deutsche Alpenzeitung*, in Munich, and others were very ready to weigh out gold in return for a few lines from Richardson. And this, whilst all the time, such is my firm belief, the Major was, even in those days, nothing better than an English spy."

This strange mixture of truth and fiction (I have never been a Major, nor have I ever visited half the places mentioned, nor did any foreign editor ever reward my humble efforts with even silver, let alone gold) seems to have gained some currency in Austria during the war. At all events, some of my Bohemian friends had a very uncomfortable time of it, owing to a visit I and some other Britishers paid to the Riesengebirge the winter before the war. I should like to take this opportunity of expressing my sincere regret for being the unwitting cause of all the trouble they went through. It must have been a most serious matter for them at the time, though no doubt they are all laughing about it now. I need hardly add that there is not a word of truth in the spying part of the story!

(*The British Ski Year Book*, vol. i, 1920-22.)

DAME KATHARINE FURSE, G.B.E.

Dame Katharine Furse, daughter of John Addington Symonds, was one of the pioneers of British ski-ing.

Tobogganing at Davos

MY own first recollection of tobogganing, as we called it (calling the "Schlittli" "toboggans," whereas they are now usually known as "luges"), was on Mother's lap, and then, as I grew older, I had a toboggan of my own, painted blue and wearing a bell, and having as its saddle a bit of the worn-out bearskin which had been used in the house as a rug and off which all the hair had been worn, part of which I also used on my wicker shield at the Uncus stage. We children spent most of our spare time tobogganing and, when races were organised for us by the grown-ups, we took the sport as seriously as any owners of racehorses or their jockeys. Toboggans were personalities to us, just as ponies are to children who are lucky enough to possess them. Perhaps scooters and bicycles and even motors are the same nowadays.

Father was quick to realise that tobogganing could provide a ground on which the Swiss and the foreigners might meet, and in 1883 he helped to found the Davos Toboggan Club, of which he was Chairman till 1889. . . .

While visitors to Davos were starting Winter Sports, St. Moritz was doing the same, as is shown in the following extract from a letter of Mother's written from the Engadiner Kulm on 17th February, 1884. The "course" she mentions was, I imagine, the original Cresta run:

"Johnnie and I with Lotta have come over to the Engadine for a few days' visit on the occasion of a tobogganing race, and are having a very happy time. This Kulm Hotel is a most curious place and well worth a winter visit; it is *immense*, all built at odd times and in various bits, so that no two sets of rooms are alike—and there is a friendly hospitable *homey* feeling in the whole place which makes it feel like paying a visit to old friends in an English country house. I know nothing like it anywhere else. We have several old friends in the house—who have lived here many winters and a large colony besides—but all are alike in being kind to us visitors. It is most delightful. The race was a queer one—it is a most breakneck course, and four of our Davos runners including two of Johnnie's natives came in *first* because they were cautious and ran for *safety*—while the Engadiners— confident in their knowledge of their own course, threw themselves out by most terrific spills. We are naturally rather triumphant because they have been despising the Davos style so long, and now we have beaten them on their own run as well as on our peaceful post-road at home. We had such a beautiful journey here, driving over the Julier in the night under the silent stars, a new sensation to us both. Johnnie is wonderfully well, and very happy I think—and we are both happier now about our two girls far away. But I don't think we can ever send them away from us again for so long."

Ladies and children were not allowed to enter for the great events, but we had our own races, and the competitive element grew fast and furious. For one blissful season I won not only the Children's Races but also the Ladies', and was very much aggrieved when told that next year if I chose to compete as a "lady" I must give up doing so as a "child." Luckily, handicaps were instituted in the adult races and as, being a child in age, I was handicapped too low I continued to win, after which I was induced to be "grown up" in so far as tobogganing was concerned. There were two very good reasons for my winning, firstly because I was very heavy and very strong, and secondly because I began to practise the moment the snow lay on the roads, while other people usually came out later.

In 1887 an upheaval took place, and it was as though a dog-fight had been let loose in the tobogganing world; needless to say, we children were like terriers, nipping at the heels of our elders, and the raging controversy is almost as fresh in my memory now as it was at the time. An American, Mr. Child, came to Davos and had built for himself, by a local carpenter, a new-shaped toboggan which he called "America"; she was long and low, built of solid wood with spring steel runners attached fore and aft. Mr. Child, who rode head first, entered "America" for the International race which led to the upheaval, because no other toboggan had a chance against her. It was finally decided that the Symonds Cup should be kept for the old type of toboggan and the Symonds Shield was instituted to cover all sorts.

Among us children there came the insuperable longing to have "Americas" of our own. I seldom had any money, and did not ask for it, having learnt to make the best of what was given to me in tips and occasional gifts. But "America" made me throw all good habits aside, and I deliberately went to the carpenter who had built her and commissioned him to make one like her. I have no recollection of analysing the position but probably just lost my head completely, as this experience has often come back to my mind when hearing of young people taking what they want and being classed as delinquent. But then I suddenly woke to facts with a bump as Madge told me that Father had received a bill from the carpenter and that he wanted an explanation of my action; terrified, I took to my bed, which was always my refuge in time of trouble, and stayed there. What happened downstairs I do not know, but can imagine the vivid sense of humour of the Symonds family coming to the rescue, for presently Madge came up to say that the trouble had blown over, and down I went and Father asked me gently for an explanation, reminding me of the unsuitability of my behaviour. Luckily my new toboggan was not only a reality but also a beauty; I christened her "Torpedo."

From 1888 onwards the sport developed fast and furiously, each new invention from "America" to bob sleigh and skeleton producing the usual outcry from the more conservative people. Quarrels grew hot in places like Davos and St. Moritz.

My "Torpedo" became a well-known personality and eventually won race after race. Mother embroidered my initials and the word "Torpedo" on a saddle made of red cloth and I inked a list of the races she had won on the board underneath. . . .

In 1895 Arthur Conan Doyle, Mr. Hugh Dobson and Mr. Stuart McLaren gave a Ladies' Bowl which "Torpedo" won. It was presented at a big party at the Belvedere, filled with pink roses, and I seem to smell the roses now, for this was one of the nights of my life. Being a considerable prude I always refused to run in any race on which sweepstakes were held; the thought of being bought or sold was repugnant. My great regret was that my parents would not let me go over the passes to race on the Cresta at St. Moritz, but they were adamant in their refusal.   (*Hearts and Pomegranates.*)

ARNOLD LUNN

The Decline and Fall of English Skating

THE contrast between the English and Continental schools of skating provides evidence in support of my thesis that sport reflects social tendencies, and I am sure that Mr. Humphrey Cobb, high-priest of the Anglican school, would be the first to insist that the decline of English skating is an outstanding example of the flight from form. The English skater keeps his unemployed leg rigidly to his side, and sweeps over the ice in long sweeping curves. Not individual display but combined skating is the ideal of the English school. The leader of a "combined" calls the required edges or turns, and the remaining members of the quartette radiate outwards, or approach each other skilfully, avoiding a collision as they reach "the centre," an orange or other object placed on the ice. It is a pity that four Englishmen skating a "combined" need more space than fifty foreigners waltzing in the degenerate Continental style.

In the days of our Imperial power, nobody dared to question the English skater's demand for *Lebensraum*. The English skated in the English style, and the great rinks at Grindelwald or St. Moritz were seldom troubled by the intrusion of the Continental heresy. But Kipling's England slowly passed away. The "lesser breeds without the law" began to murmur against the English hegemony of the ice rink, and hotel proprietors began to think in terms of square metres per skater, with the result that the English skaters suddenly discovered that they were no longer wanted. English skating vanished from the ice rinks of the Alps, and might have disappeared completely but for the fact that Morgins offered an asylum to the faithful. . . .

The English school of skating is severe, hostile to display and imbued with the team spirit. The Continental school is free, individualistic and spectacular. The English skater tries to perform a difficult turn with as little fuss as possible. To the uninitiated the most difficult of English figures looks easier than the simplest of Continental "threes."

The English skater claims that he is modest, and the Continental skater retorts that of all forms of conceit the English type is the most trying, for it is, in essence, based on the assumption that an Englishman need not do his own trumpeting, since his superiority is too obvious to require vulgar advertisement.

"Combined figure skating," said the patriarch of the English school, "appeals to me because it is English. No individual display, you know. The team spirit on the ice. I like watching good Continental skating just as I like watching ballet dancing, but I pay other people to do my ballet dancing for me."

Both schools, of course, have great merits, and meet definite needs. Combined English skating is a fine sport; figure skating in the Continental style is a fine art. And the fine artist, as we know, is often insensitive to the noble ideals of team spirit.

In skating, team spirit unfortunately is exacting in its demand on space, since fifty immodest ballet dancers on skates occupy less room than four modest gentlemen registering chaste team spirit round an orange.

Where team spirit is strong it is best to be in the team, as the stray foreigners no doubt felt who stayed at the "Bear" in the great days of English skating. These unfortunate intruders, if they skated at all, behaved rather like nervous Christians entering a mosque. But slowly things changed. The foreigners increased, and their latent opposition was fanned into open revolt by degenerate English traitors to the noble ideals of Anglican skating. They even asked for a band on the rink. On the *rink*!

The English skater of today enjoys waltzing on the ice, but Dr. Stiftone, patriarch of Anglican skating, was made of sterner stuff; he felt about ice waltzing much as his Puritan forebears felt about dancing round the maypole. It was the accursed thing.

He registered a dignified protest, and the band was vetoed. But the management had begun to think. Ice rinks cost money, and Dr. Stiftone translated into so many square metres of ice did not appear quite so desirable a guest as in the Eocene age of winter sports when the "Bear" was opened for him and his team.

The end was near.

Still the old guard hung on. Day by day they placed their orange on the rink and re-enacted the old familiar ritual:

"*Twice back and forward, turn, and inside, inward turn, off meet. . . .*"

And four Ironsiders met at the orange, miraculously avoided a collision, and once again radiated outwards on the curving spoke of a wheel whose circumference was *much* too large when worked out in francs per person.

And then the end came—on a morning in January. A band with the set faces of men going into action marched out of the "Bear" and advanced towards the rink. The ringleaders of the opposition were awaiting them. They wondered nervously whether Stiftone had noticed the band. His voice still rang out with the steely old confidence:

"*Twice back, around* TURN. . . ."

Somebody remembered that Stiftone's father had got the V.C. for a rearguard action of which he and his two privates had been the only survivors.

"Reminds me of that picture," murmured one of the conspirators nervously, "thin red line and all that. . . ."

"*Two turns, off pass, meet.* . . ."

The band struck up its first defiant notes—how thin and vulgar they sounded.

"Now for it," murmured Public Enemy Number One.

They skated nervously towards the orange. They sidled round on the circumference of the "combined." Nothing happened. Public Enemy Number One decided that the time had come to act. He skated boldly towards the orange.

"*Centre, change, turn, meet.* . . ."

Stiftone and Public Enemy Number One *met*—and Public Enemy Number One performed a figure which is included neither in the English nor in the Continental school of skating. And four dignified gentlemen of the old school continued to register the team spirit with no further interruptions from the band.

The last "combined" skated by Dr. Stiftone on the famous rink ended in the ritualistic "Dismiss." Dr. Stiftone and his team took off their skates a little sadly, and walked back to the hotel. Dr. Stiftone put his head into the bureau. "I shall not be requiring my room to-night," he remarked. "Please present my compliments to the manager and express to him my appreciation for all that the management have done to make me comfortable—in the past. I shall leave by the six o'clock train."

Such is the Lunadorned truth of the great Exodus from Grindelwald to the promised land of Morgins where only one man has been known to wave an unemployed leg on the rink and no man has been known to repeat this dreadful solecism.

(*Switzerland and the English.*)

Ski-Jumping

The jumping competition described below took place on the Olympic Schanze, St. Moritz, during the Winter Olympic Games (1928). The longest standing jump of the day was 64 metres. Today (October, 1946) the record stands at 118 metres made by a German, Behring, on the famous Planica Jump (Jugoslavia) in 1941.

WATCH a master jumper on the Olympia Schanze, and you will see something which will etch itself into the copperplate of memory. You must stand just above the jump in order to appreciate the full horror of the view which confronts the jumper just as he approaches the platform, the sense of an unplumbed void below and the far infinite distance of the valley.

A bell rings. Number 1 jumps round swiftly and darts down to the platform. He passes us crouching. Your heart bleeds for him. Swiftly, rhythmically, he uncoils. He has left the solid ground which the Creator intended for his playground, and you see him for one brief moment released like an arrow from a bow. And so he disappears from view.

And now walk down the hill and take up your station just below the platform. A sudden rush of wind and here comes No. 2. The flaps of his tightly drawn coat beat in the wind as the air pressure forces itself into every cranny of his garments. In these long jumps, the sound made by the jumper in the air is, at least, as terrifying as the sight of a man alighting from the air, a sound like an angry eagle flapping its wings before pouncing on its prey.

Watch him as he dives through the empty chambers of the sky, his body bent forward, his hands grasping as it were for the ski points. Infinite time seems to pass. Will he never land?

Smack! Nine feet of hickory have made contact with the snow, hard-beaten and polished like marble.

Will he stand? Quick as thought comes the answer. A momentary swerve, every muscle in his magnificent body fighting for control. The struggle is short, sharp and decisive.

One erring ski, seeking divorce from its fellow, is wrenched back into line. The backward tug is overcome. Erect, controlled and rejoicing, the jumper sails down the run-out, forces his ski breadthwise into the snow and swings to rest, while the Referee signals "70 metres gestanden," and a thousand voices roar their applause.

The educational effect of sport does not begin and end with the competitors. One cannot dismiss the "Publikum" as a collection of corpulent, over-fed patrons of luxurious hotels. The thrills which we witnessed at St. Moritz have a far-reaching effect upon the mind. One returns from seeing Thams jump with a new pride in the race to which one belongs, the human race. The essence of all sport is the duel between the spirit of men and the limitations of matter. A record jump stirs one like noble music. There is the same intangible sense of the finite at war with the infinite, of the unattainable towards which mankind strives, that undiscovered country whose frontier alone is dimly sighted from the Pisgah heights of high endeavour.

It is good to know that one more conquest has been registered in the struggle between man and his environment, that the mastery over mind and muscle has once again been found a beautiful and satisfying mode of expression.

Man is never satisfied, and the jumper will always strive to beat his own best performance. The struggle for the record jump will inevitably proceed, and the jumper will continue to hurl himself further and further into space undeterred by those who desire to fix a limit, "thus far and no farther."

(British Ski Year Book, 1928.)

BRIAN MEREDITH

The Oxford and Cambridge Ice Hockey Match developed out of a scratch game between Oxford and Cambridge players which I organised at Beatenberg in 1908. The first official match was played at Wengen during December 1909. Free accommodation had been offered to the teams, and the chance of a winter sports holiday evoked a sudden enthusiasm for ice hockey among the intimate friends of the gentleman who had been entrusted by a famous tourist agency with the duty of collecting a team. It did not occur to him to discover whether any Canadian players were available. The Oxford goalkeeper had never been on skates before, and had to be assisted between the goal posts at half-time. His attitude to such shots as did not actually strike his person would have qualified him for a seat on a non-intervention committee, and the shots which did strike him only failed to score when he fell forwards instead of backwards.

Before long Canadians found their way into both teams, and the annual match became an extremely skilful display. The following entertaining description of Canada's national game is taken from one of the most readable books in the literature of ski-ing, "Escape on Skis," by Brian Meredith.

Ice-hockey: Native and Imported

IT was amusing to see how we Canadians have now a new characteristic in the eyes of Europeans. For a long time they associated us with Red Indians, and we were indignant. Now they think we are all hockey players, and as their opinion of the forthright way we play hockey is not complimentary, I am not sure that we haven't cause to be equally indignant.

Europe has taken up Canadian hockey, "ice-hockey" they call it, because they play a curious game in winter when they run about a field and whack a ball like the girls' boarding-schools do in Canada, which they call hockey. But they definitely think it shouldn't be played in the style apparently peculiar to its native land.

It is too violent; this body checking can't be tolerated. The Canadian players are usually great hulking fellows and could shoulder their way through European teams if given the chance. Besides, with international susceptibilities as they are, they might start a European war. The business can't be approached with the same bloodthirsty gusto that it is at home.

So the basic game is developing in Europe with rules strictly observed; and imported Canadians are being taught to behave themselves, and to play the game like little gentlemen. Though it may be hard on them it is, in all seriousness, probably very good for the game. It makes a Canadian spectator a little homesick however; and once when in a newsreel there was a glimpse of a game in Montreal and a free-fight broke out between referees and both teams in the course of thirty seconds, I could have wept.

The spirit of the game, apart from this misunderstood element of roughness, perishes of course in being transplanted. The players may be Canadian, the play technically in England ranks close behind our best professional performances, but the electric spirit that animates the spectators is lacking. The crowds are enthusiastic enough; the sports-writer uses the right words in almost the right way; but that dynamic something that the fans put in it at home is lacking. Never, never could you reproduce the atmosphere of the Montreal Forum with ten thousand maniacs helping the Maroons and Canadians fight it out . . . never, any more than you could re-enact Lords on the University of Toronto campus.

The English, of course, are far better showmen than is generally appreciated; and in adapting hockey they have invested it with more ritual and swank than it ever possessed in Canada. "Jesus!" said one fellow-countryman fervently. "Have you seen the way they sweep the ice? Why, they do it to music, and a little page-boy in buttons opens the door for the snow every time the men come round . . . it's fantastic . . . it's like the changing of the guard of ushers in the Roxy's in New York. Eye-wash, of course . . . but it goes over. . . ."

Though suavely and within the rules, the Europeans in other sports will do things that seem curious to us, they just can't understand a little uninhibited animosity on the ice. This was brought home to a Canadian and American team playing exhibition matches in Berlin some years ago, when they decided to stage a fight with the mistaken idea that it would build up a good gate for the succeeding nights. There is nothing the fans like at home more than a little blood, and they decided to fake this properly.

But the first pass one player made at another brought down the house. And when the fight became general, the ice was littered with spectators' beer-mugs, and they had to call the game. Mobs will practically lynch players who get rough. I must admit it's a good thing, but, as I confess, I'm still enough of a savage Canadian at heart to enjoy seeing other people mix-in.   (*Escape on Skis.*)

ARNOLD LUNN

Mountaineering in winter is full of contrasts, and few contrasts could be more complete than my memories of the summit of the Finsteraarhorn (January 6th, 1909) and the summit of the Eiger (January 1st, 1912).

The Eiger was one of the first climbs which I did after shattering my right leg in a hundred-foot fall on rocks. This and the absence of crampons is a partial explanation, if not an excuse, for coming off on the summit ice-slope.

The Finsteraarhorn in January

NO sense, however, of disillusion marred the perfect and complete satisfaction of that last hour on the Finsteraarhorn, and when at last we reached the summit, six hours after leaving the hut, I felt that for once in a way the romance of accomplished fact had outdone the romance of anticipation. Once again the mildness of the atmosphere was such as one might expect on the shores of the April Ægean rather than on an Alpine peak in midwinter. Shadow and frost might still lurk in the valleys, but colour and warmth reigned supreme on those sun-kissed rocks. Adolphe went placidly to sleep. I stripped to the waist and allowed the sun to scorch my shoulders.

The Finsteraarhorn rises in the midst of a world of glaciers. It is surrounded on all sides by the aristocrats of the Oberland. The Finsteraarhorn lords it above encircling peaks and looks defiantly across a waste of minor mountains towards its peers, the hierarchy of Monte Rosa. From the Dolomites to the Dauphiny, from the Ortler to Mont Blanc, no peak with any pretensions to dignity is hidden from view. Range after range, with their attendant foothills, pass upward with a suggestion of rhythmical motion to the far limits of the visible world.

The winter atmosphere relieved from monotony this vast snowscape. Sun and shadow worked their old magic on the prevailing whiteness, subduing the glare and insinuating hints of colour into the monotone of black and white—gold where the far-off mists lay between us and the sun, dark blue or emerald green on the snows of distant ranges.

A canopy of fleecy clouds dragged themselves lazily outward to the bleak north, where Germany showed her dark forests, and broke in waves of spectral spray on the barrier of the southern Apennines. No sound and no strong movements of wind disturbed the illusion of a world frozen into immobility:

> It seemed as if the hour was one
>   Sent from beyond the skies,
> Which scattered from above the sun
>   The light of Paradise.

> (*The Mountains of Youth.*)

A Winter Storm on the Eiger

"HE shall dwell on high; his place of defence shall be the munitions of the rocks." The mountaineer can translate this verse from Isaiah into the memory of moments when the artillery of heaven and the munitions of the rocks bear witness to the majesty of One who dwells on high. No dawns are more terrible in their beauty than those in which the red and angry snows herald a day that breaks in splendour only to set in storm. No mountain memories are more enduring than those of moments when the black wings of the wind-tormented mist lift to disclose the embattlements of frost-riven rock. There is a tranquil loveliness in the slow drift of sun-tinted clouds across a summer sky, but their true glory and their might is hidden save from those who invade their mountain kingdom. No man knows the mountains until he has watched the approach of storm from high places. The puffs of mist down the gullies are the skirmishers which precede the grand assault. Slowly the last pools of light in the coppery glitter of a thunder sky are obscured by a blur of indefinite gloom. Wisps of filmy cloud gather the rocky towers into their greyness. The patter of hail or snow plays its staccato tune on the mountains, and finally all but the immediate foreground is blotted out by driving snow.

Many years ago I spent a New Year's Day struggling up through storm to the crest of the Eiger. A sudden lull tempted us up the final ice slope, but, just as we started, down from the summit a low mutter broke the silence and struck fear into our hearts. We knew what was coming, but were not prepared for the tornado which broke. The mountain quivered beneath the impact. Stones, whipped off the ice, screamed past like shells. A flood of loose snow poured down the ice and blotted out the steps which we had cut with such labour. I had left my climbing irons behind and was hurled out three times at full rope's length before I regained control. I remember a sudden vision of the valley below, but my companion's ten-pointed claws saved us. Slowly and with infinite care we crept down the ice, in which every step had to be recut; and when at last we felt beneath our feet the reassurance of rough and friendly rock we threw ourselves on the ground and lay huddled together for many minutes, indifferent to cold, intoxicated with the relief of safety, and far too weary to raise our voices above the storm.

But even that day had its moments of calm beauty. We had been climbing for thirteen hours and had seen nothing but the same drab foreground of ice-fretted rock and grey mist, and then suddenly towards evening we paused, for the blanket of grey mist seemed subtly changed, stirred by movements which destroyed its cohesion. The mist was beginning to disintegrate. Soon only a diaphanous veil separated us from the windy spaces of the sky. Then even this dissolved to reveal the dark blue waters of Thun and the distant ground-swell of the Jura. The western sun flooded the cold grey rocks with a golden light. The long hours of storm and darkness were a fitting prelude to this hour of mountain peace.

The most hackneyed of peaks provides the climber with a problem which he must solve afresh if he climbs it in bad weather. To lead in a storm up a ridge one has never climbed in fair weather is an even more stimulating test of mental and physical powers. There are moments when it is difficult to believe that one is contending with inanimate matter, for there is a human touch about the bluster of a storm and the peculiar malice of the wind. The wind will suddenly peter out when the mountaineer reaches good anchorage and make a great parade of having business in a neighbouring gully, only to leap upon him with an exultant scream as he leaves a secure ledge for the perils of an exposed slab. Cloudless skies and mountain valleys may inspire a mood of Wordsworthian pantheism, but the mountains of storm would incline one to pan-diabolism but for the queer sense of contending against something which is half friend and half foe:

Love thou the gods and withstand them lest thy fame should fail at the end,
And thou be but their thrall and bondsman who wast born for their very
friend. *(Come What May.)*

Glacier Ski-ing

WE were cautious until we had spotted the bergschrund, but then we let our ski have their heads. The summit slopes are concave, like a shallow funnel cut in two, an ideal ski-ing slope. We swept from side to side, running across the central flow, and using the banks to turn on just as a motorist

uses the banked turns of a racing track. Long, linked Christi-
anias followed swift and sure. As the ski cut round, the superficial film of soft ice fell away and rippled down the slope with
a sound like the soft splash of a glacier stream, an underlying
melody that disputed the bolder music of the wind. Near the
end of the summit slopes we set our ski for a straight run. We
crouched down, the wind sang its last song, the steepness
relented into a long unchanging gradient; the breeze died
away, four rapid swings and four breathless ski-runners faced
the slope whose swift joys they had squandered all too soon.

We threw ourselves on the snow and looked up at our pass.
We had run down nearly two thousand feet in just under five
minutes, but moments such as this cannot be measured by the
prosaic standards of time. Theirs is a music which goes on
echoing in one's heart, a music which never wholly dies away.
For many months the four of us had skied together, and sometimes one and sometimes another had skied well, but this was
one of those days when the four of us were ski-ing on the top of
our form. There is a subtle joy in doing something delightful
not as an individual, but as a member of a team, a pleasure
which is nowhere greater than in ski-ing, especially when you
know your friend's ski-ing as thoroughly as you know his jokes,
his best swing as well as you know your virtues, and his weak
turns as completely as he knows your vices. Solos have their
charm, but there is a ski-ing joy known only to a quartette of
friends, all of whom are moving well together, placing their
swings at the right point, and neither over-running the leader
nor impeding those that follow.

Glacier running has its own peculiar charm. On these long,
unchanging gradients the sense of personal motion often dies
away. It is the foreground that rushes up to meet you, and
your ski seem a narrow skiff anchored in midstream, a slender
boat that sways gently as the river sweeps round the bows. In
late spring the illusion is emphasised when you reach the limits
of the snow kingdom, where the sun has cut wrinkles in the
ageing forehead of winter, and where the snow is furrowed and
moulded like waves of a ground swell. As the speed dies the
hills adopt a sedater measure. The magic network of dancing
shadow and fugitive light sobers into separate and successive
ridges. The wind that thunders in one's heart melts into a fitful
breeze. The snow in front of the ski hunches itself together, and

thrusts the ski backwards. Suddenly the world gives a little jerk, the mountains stop moving, and you know that you are a creeping thing once more. (*The Mountains of Youth.*)

The Alpine Spring

IT is an interesting experience to see the year through in one of the loftier of the Alpine villages. One gains a deeper knowledge of the mountains when one has watched their changing dress through the procession of the seasons, and I am very sure that nobody can welcome the spring with more passionate joy than those who have lived through the six months of an Alpine winter and have watched with ever-growing impatience the slow rout of the tenacious snows. "He comforteth the earth with the south wind" had less meaning for the man who could only remember the mild winters of Palestine than for those who have been numbed by the unending winter of the Alps and have at last seen the Foehn strip the southern slopes in a few brief hours, and restore in a few short days to the hungry soil the grateful solace of the sun.

The first tentative experiments of the Alpine spring possess a shy and timid charm which one misses among the prodigal loveliness of May. The first plucky soldanella which fights its way through the edge of the snow has all the pathetic beauty of a forlorn hope. And the June meadow, rich in gentians and anemones, makes a less instant appeal than the first few vivid blades of young grass which struggle through the old and withered herbage, the husks of dead pastures.

I remember, early in March, following the course of a new-born stream which had just contrived to fret away the smother of snow from a scanty plot of marshy ground. In the edge of the damp lush grass which bordered the stream a brave little cluster of marsh marigolds showed up—a defiant splash of colour in a world of whiteness unredeemed.

The Alpine spring has to fight for its place in the sun, for winter puts up a stout resistance. March may close in a blaze of sunshine and, just as you are wondering if the winter has spent its force, you will waken to a sky sullen with falling flakes. For days the storm will rage as it only can in April.

But the transition from winter to spring is often gloriously abrupt. In England the few sparse snowfalls have ceased long before the leisurely advance of the spring has begun. Slowly the days lengthen, "blossom by blossom the spring begins." But in the Alps it is otherwise. The persistent snowfalls of April suddenly cease. The clouds lift and a world appears in which no unruly rebel challenges the despotism of winter. Even the lakes are edged with snow. And then the sun sweeps imperiously into his kingdom and settles down in real earnest to reduce the winter to submission. Snow is stripped off the southern slopes, and flowers pierce through the white palimpsest. Music returns with colour to the world. The valley river, which has crept among the stone, a poor, dispirited, listless thing, takes heart again. The hills once more are full of music, the happy litanies of streams no longer muted by the forest. The mountains turn in their sleep. They awaken from their long winter trance and shake their shoulders free from the draperies of snow. Their pulse beats higher. The time for introspection is at an end. Every busy little torrent seems anxious to make up for wasted hours and to resume with redoubled energy its appointed task of levelling the high places of the earth and carrying down its wreckage to the distant seas.

Winter may still fire a few Parthian shots, but nothing can arrest the advance of the spring, and nothing can resist the alchemy of the sun that continues day by day to trace

> Under the common thing the hidden grace,
> And conjure wonder out of emptiness,
> Till mean things put on beauty like a dress,
> And all the world seems an enchanted place.

In England spring advances like a shy girl, with gentle tread, but in the Alps colour and life are not so easily delivered from the womb of winter. The mountain sides are torn and riven before the child is born. Even valleys carpeted with the delicate loveliness of May bear witness to the unending struggle —life at grip with death. Among meadows rich in beauty, the avalanches still lie, black with trees and earth uprooted from the mountainside, strewn with rocks and boulders which have been torn from the slopes.   (*The Mountains of Youth.*)

During those long war winters, my wife and I always escaped from Mürren in April for a few days beside the lakes. I remember leaving Mürren after an exceptionally severe winter. As the funicular from Grütsch started its slow descent to Lauterbrunnen, the weary senile snow, pitted and lined and wrinkled, faded out into grey and dirty drifts beneath the shadow of the pines. As we came out of the station at Lauterbrunnen the spring welcomed us. The renascent Staubbach, which in winter is a pitiful trickle oozing down through fluted icicles, was a falling foam of triumphant water. The meadows were splashed with colour, and the air was fragrant with growing things. At Interlaken, where we lunched, there were violets in the woods, and there were gentians on the Brünig, and at Alpnach we could see the triple-crested Wetterhorn showing through a tracery of apple blossom.

The blossom falls, the violet fades, and even the mountains themselves will cease to be. And yet among the things that pass there are some which bear witness to the thing that remains. In the loveliness of the lakes in April there is something which is not wholly of this world. There have been moments beside the shores of Lucerne or Leman when I have seen quite plain in the beauty which dies the hope and promise of a beauty unshadowed by the doom which is the fate of all mortal things.

On the earth the broken arc, in the heaven a perfect round.

(*Mountain Jubilee.*)

GERALD SELIGMAN

Gerald Seligman is recognised today as the leading scientific expert on the structure of snow. His book "Snow Structure and Ski Fields" has no rival in any language.

The Treasures of the Snow

MY DEAR ARNOLD,
You have asked me whether my researches into the natural history of snow and ice have stimulated or dulled my appreciation of the beautiful in mountain scenery.

You and I can call to mind many occasions on which we have skied by moonlight. One such moonlight run which stands out sharply in my memory dates from the period when the Parsenn

Hut was still the focal point of Grisons skiers. The conditions
have remained imprinted on my mind as being about as near
perfection as is allowed us. At four o'clock on a late winter
morning we set out to see the sunrise from the Weissfluh. No
flicker of wind stirred. No cloud could be seen. No track
broke the surface of the snow. But it was not the purity of the
snowfields which thrilled us most; it was the myriads of gems
with which they were studded, some showing pin-points of
white light, others the many-coloured fires of diamonds,
constantly changing as we moved so that the snow seemed alive
with the scintillations. This, as you know, was due to the
shapes in which snow crystals form themselves. They had
grown to unusual size, shielded from the sun's destructive rays
by the extreme cold of the past few days. They had become
sharp-cornered magnifications of their former selves, some tiny
prisms, breaking up the moonlight into tiny spectra, others
little mirrors and reflecting it. I think you will agree that this
rather obvious explanation of a very simple phenomenon can
only have the effect of enhancing its beauty.

I shall never forget my first apparatus for watching and
photographing snowflakes as they fell—a crude, artificially
cooled plate in the field of an old microscope. I had read
of their countless permutations, and had studied some two
thousand photographs of their symmetrical shapes, but to
collect them myself and to see them in actuality in their dozens
was unforgettable. From those early days of apprenticeship I
have seen nothing but beauty, and this has impressed itself on
me if anything more as my work has grown in complexity. Not
the least fascinating part of this microscope work was the
tracing of the transformation of the fragile snowflake stage by
stage into solid glacier ice. Is it possible to imagine that these
microcosms, magnified many millionfold in the wild scenery of
the Alpine highlands, do not add to its beauty for those who are
lucky enough to be able to look beneath the surface?

Men who can carry out serious work amidst conditions of
romance and beauty are very fortunate. I have in mind the
naturalist collecting specimens of animal life in some Brazilian
forest or off some tropical shore, the geologist in some mountain
massif or the archæologist working in some lovely spot giving
back the atmosphere of bygone heroic or savage days. But I
have sometimes thought it well-nigh indecent to describe

myself as "working" in some of the conditions in which I have had to work. A solitary exploration of the tongue of the Gorner Glacier above Furri on a cloudless spring morning comes to mind. The high hills were my laboratory. The absolute silence stimulated my thoughts. The sun provided my comfort. Good substitutes these for the venerable architecture, the peaceful atmosphere and the sense of well-being in some ancient university. Or perhaps there would be an observation to be made on the Upper Mönchjoch, with five minutes' bliss to finish up with, the ski sliding through the new snow on the run back to the Jungfraujoch for breakfast. How can one speak of work in such conditions? Once, during a long stay at this spot, we dug a tunnel deep into the ice frozen to the ridge of the Sphinx. In some places we reached the living rock; the ice frozen to that rock must have been there unaltered for tens of thousands of years. In that winding gallery some fifty or more yards in length, you could study both glaciology and geology and in the deathly silence, save for the occasional groan of the overweighted ice, there was a snug feeling of remoteness from the jarring, warring world outside, that I would be glad to recapture today. Our laboratory was a chamber hewn out of the solid ice, and fitted with good scientific apparatus and machines and sufficiently lit to reveal the wonderful ice growths that hung from walls and roof. In this sanctuary we could study and calculate and theorise uninterrupted by the howl of storms outside even though on some days, in order to reach its shelter, we had literally to cleave our way through the blizzard tearing through the narrow Joch.

I think that even in the study of avalanches there was something beautiful. In one sense there are few things more hideous or grating than to see masses of snow lying untidily strewn on the hillside; perhaps there is the added discordance of human tragedy. Yet there is also something sublime—some awe-inspired beauty, the great masses of snow, the evidence of gigantic power, the fascination of witnessing conformity to theory or law. Is there not the analogy of the pathologist who may see a kind of indefinable beauty in the segregated bacilli of some horrible disease?

Some of the most exciting of my Alpine experiences have been the explorations of crevasses which we carried out over a period of two years in the late 'thirties. Crevasses give valuable data of the cross-section through a glacier so that you may trace its history for many years back. Access to some crevasses is gained by easy climbing, or sometimes even by walking. Others need the use of a rope ladder. When the icy wall overhangs, the ladder often has to be pegged to it and you may find yourself in the most unnatural and uncomfortable reverse positions. Some crevasses are wide and brilliantly sunlit, others are so narrow that your body can scarcely squeeze between the two cold, hard walls, and there is twilight or even complete darkness in the depths. Especially when the crevasse is part of an icefall —a mass of snow or ice with little design—there is practically no end to the weird shapes of corridors, chambers, trenches and shelves that spread in wild disorder in all directions. Here you could wander for hours or days without retracing your steps. Throughout our crevasse wanderings I often felt as if I were reliving a Jules Verne or Ballantyne novel. But wherever we went there was wild, unbelievable beauty.

From the moment you lower yourself over the crevasse lip you become conscious of the most fantastic decoration nature can fashion. Here there are rows upon rows of icicles; there part of the crevasse side has peeled off, like a vast strip of neglected wallpaper, to form a curtain perhaps twenty yards in vertical and horizontal extent, but only a few inches thick, convoluted into the most graceful folds and bends and imprison-ing between it and the crevasse wall a seagreen half light. Looking upwards, you may see the underside of a thin snow-bridge, forming a roof over your head. A snowbridge, though barely presenting an incident on the snow surface when seen from above, shows translucently some of the most delicate tracery that even snow or ice can shape. Its underside is often twisted and whorled into the most wonderful designs by the wind which originally built it, and brings to mind the delicacy and design of some ancient cathedral roof. We explored these crevasses and worked in some of them day after day to obtain data for our work, and it would indeed be a prosaic student who could enter their depths without finding his æsthetic feelings deeply roused.

Another means we devised of exploring the inside of a glacier was the sinking of a shaft deep into the firn. As we dug, the glacier's history would reveal itself stage by stage—this layer being formed in a dry and dusty summer—that in a winter of

PARSENN (DAVOS)

Photo: Caspar, Davos

unusually prolific snowfall. As we descended in an improvised "cage" operated by a decrepit machine brought up from the valley, we lost all touch with the outside world. Voices did not reach us owing to the blanketing effect of the snow and only signals could pass—isolation more perfect than even the mountain tops can give.

But I think perhaps the most vivid and satisfying of all my experiences occurred during a night spent in 1939 at the Concordia Hut during a pleasure tour. I was fresh from a long research in which my colleagues had been able, I think, to make a final contribution to the 150-year-old controversy on the mechanism of glacier flow. Ice appears to be an unyielding body, yet a glacier flows down conforming to the inclination and bends of its bed as easily as a river. There had been many theories to account for this.

It was late spring. After supper we went out for a little fresh air on to the platform overlooking the Great Aletsch Glacier. The lower crags of the Drieeckhorn opposite glowered black and threatening but everything else was brilliantly lit by a full moon. It was as still and windless as on the night I described in my opening words, but there was a creaking and groaning, a rubbing and scraping, below us, never ceasing but ever varying. And suddenly I realised that *I knew* what these noises were, exactly what caused them and exactly how the ice grains were shifting and adjusting themselves to the sweeps and bends as the great frozen stream flowed over its rocky bed. Who can doubt that this knowledge added the splendour of completeness to that already impressive scene? Does not this single experience almost by itself answer your question?

As always,
GERALD SELIGMAN.

(*British Ski Year Book*, 1943.)

AIR CHIEF MARSHAL LORD DOWDING, G.C.B.

Lord Dowding is an ex-President of the Ski Club of Great Britain. The following contribution to the British Ski Year Book is characteristic of his sardonic humour and will, I believe, be read with appreciation not only by ski-runners but by those who served under him in the battle that saved the world.

14

Monte Leone in May

AT 10 a.m. on Monday, May 15th, Knubel arrived at Brig, and at 10.45 we left to walk up to the Simplon.

About 200 yards from the hotel we encountered a nice funeral; I wish we had stopped to watch it, and subsequently camped out in the cemetery; it would have been quite as amusing as what we actually did, no more uncomfortable, and much less trouble.

Another hour or so sufficed for K. to say all that was in his heart to the various friends whom he met in the streets. . . .

After Berisal it began to rain, and continued to do so, with a few minor pauses, for three days. At about 1,600 metres we struck the slush-line, and found the wheeled diligence waiting the return of the sledge upon which the upper half of the journey was still being done. We could have saved much labour by taking the dilly, but it started at 7 a.m. and K. could not get to Brig in time. At about 4.30 p.m. we reached Refuge Five (marked Ref. V. on the map, about 1,950 m.).

It was a forbidding-looking hovel, and my heart sank when K. announced that this was our destination.

I murmured something about the Hospice, where monks "with fat capon lined" might be encountered, and where I hoped we might acquire a similar lining. I also expected that if they did not specialise in the production of some curious liqueur, they would at least have brandy in little wooden kegs for the refection of slush-bound travellers.

Knubel, however, was adamant; or at any rate, I gathered that he was adamant. Our only means of communication consisted of a mixture of Dumb Crambo and the French language, with which latter we were both imperfectly acquainted.

I daresay that the Hospice is really anything but what my fancy painted it; but whatever it is like, I can confidently recommend it in preference to Ref. V.

Ref. V. was clean inside, contained good beds. The inhabitants (consisting of a man, his wife and boy, and his great grandmother) were kindly and civil, but the commissariat was limited in the extreme. It consisted of bread, tea, goat's milk and goat's cheese. I am not a connoisseur of the products of the goat, so I subsisted for the first day on the two former commodities. By superhuman efforts some eggs and black ham were later produced. I gathered that they had to send to Zurich for them.

The small boy was extraordinarily well behaved, a phenomenon which was explained by a birch rod hung in a conspicuous position on the guest-room wall.

The goat's cheese was full of small holes containing poison gas, and was the nearest thing I saw during my tour to the "Perforated Crust" with which students of Mr. Lunn's works will be familiar.

On the morning of the 16th it was still raining, so we waited till 10 a.m., when we started for a little exercise on the west of the Simplon Pass, where the clouds appeared to be least dense.

We climbed to the Inn Nanzlucke (2,605 m.) just south of the Straffelgrat and about four kilometres west of the Simplon Pass. The climb took us 2½ hours from the Pass, including a halt for lunch. After lunch an improvement took place in the weather, the rain turning to sleet; the condition of the slush, however, was not affected. From the top we had a magnificent view of the inside of a cloud, and after a short halt we walked and punted ourselves down again in our climbing tracks, reaching home in a regular deluge of rain.

This would be quite a nice little run on snow (if there is ever any there), and it might be worth while to climb the Schienhorn which lies to the north of our route. A very fine view would be obtainable from its summit in the absence of cloud (if it is ever absent).

The last 200 or 300 feet would probably have to be done on foot.

The next day (May 17th) at 4 a.m. we discovered to our surprise that it was raining, so we returned to our beds to acquire additional vigour for our attack on Monte Leone.

At 9.30 a.m. it cleared a little, and I received a postcard from my eagerly awaited travelling companion, saying that he had bought a yoke of oxen and went to prove them, wherefore he prayed me have him excused. Cheered by this intelligence we started for the aptly named Kaltwasser Pass at 10.5, intending to go on up Monte Leone if the weather gave us a chance. We left the road just south of Wasser Gallerie. From the road to the bottom of the ice face the climb is rather steep, being about 35 degrees in places, and inclined to avalanche in certain slush conditions; we reached the bottom of the icefall at 11.20, and after that the climbing was easier, and we reached the Kaltwasser Pass at 12.5.

We were now on the frontier of Italy, and to the east we enjoyed a magnificent internal view of an Italian cloud, which bore a curious resemblance to the interior of the Swiss cloud which met our gaze in the opposite direction.

Near the pass (about 200 feet to the north-west) there is a Swiss military hut, not marked on the map. Here we lunched in shelter from the sleet which was falling drearily.

After lunch the visibility became low, one's ski-tips looming vaguely out of the mist.

My compass and Knubel had a difference of opinion as to the direction of Monte Leone, and, as we were not really enjoying ourselves vastly, we decided to descend in our tracks and catch the afternoon dilly. The first part of the descent was laboriously effected by walking and punting; but below the icefall on the steep slopes we struck some of the best Telemark slush which it has been my good fortune to encounter.

It was possible at times to attain a speed of fifteen miles an hour, and the spray splashed merrily as the ski-tips surged through the water.

Merry peals of laughter arose when one or other of us (principally myself) fell with a resounding squelch beneath the surface; we were both strong swimmers, and had ample opportunity of testing Caulfeild's rudder action theory.

The descent occupied twenty-two minutes, and is probably a good run in winter.

I have no idea what Monte Leone is like, or what the difficulties of the final ascent may be, because I never caught even a glimpse of it; but under reasonable weather conditions one would be assured of a first-class run from the top of the Kaltwasser Glacier.

We duly caught the dilly, and descended without further fatigue to the valley.

Here I parted from the inestimable Knubel, who, apart from his supreme efficiency, possesses the faculty of maintaining an undisturbed serenity in all circumstances. After this I shook off the slush of Switzerland from my feet with as little delay as possible.

Well, my dear Lunn, that's that. Mind you print it all in the *Year Book*.   (*The British Ski Year Book*, vol. i.)

LORD SCHUSTER, G.C.B.

Recollections of a Derby Dog

WE all felt refreshed as we left Wolfgang. My skins seemed disposed to stick to my skis, the sky was blue, the air was keen, the pace was judicious. Even the appearance of the other parties bent on the same errand at first caused me no anxiety, though I ought to have taken warning by the fact that one traveller was dragging behind him a wooden construction which was something between a sledge and a toboggan and which could only be intended for the carriage of an injured man. We had, indeed, passed beyond the steep path which skirts the first bluff and were in the long trench beyond, when there went by us, at a speed which I thought indecent, a youngish gentleman bearing on his back a bundle of flags. By that time I needed my breath for purposes other than idle conversation and postponed inquiries until the hut. There, as we sat in the full sunshine and ate and basked and fed the birds which hopped on to our knees and ate from our hands, we learnt the full significance of these omens. We had chosen the least appropriate day of all the year. Two hundred competitors, representing universities from all over Europe, were to race from the pass to Conters and we were to enact the part of Derby dogs.

As it turned out this, for me at least, was not the worst blow from fortune. So well had my skins been secured that the wax which secured them would neither come off nor rub into my skis; or, to be accurate, one ski was free and slippery, and one black with some detestable compound and sticky. Thus while one foot set out gallantly towards the valley, one dragged itself reluctantly through the snow. The human frame cannot conveniently be carried thus and the natural consequences followed. I fell, and struggled up, and tried to scrape the offending surface, and became all flustered as I saw my companions already waiting at the first gathering place, and so did not make a job of it and began again, and again endured the same humiliation and went through the same vain endeavour. To increase my grief the snow itself, hard-beaten as it seemed, was slightly sticky with an oncoming thaw. It was a day when the strong man cried out on the slowness of the conditions and the weaker brother or sister felt that anything might be taken straight; and there was I, staggering and crashing and panting like an aged cab-horse, trying to stride down the course after a string of thoroughbreds.

The most unpleasant moments pass if friction and gravitation do their acceptable work. Somehow I came, uninjured save in spirit, to where the line swings left-handed along the hillside, and found that my ski had worked itself free, and so at last to Schwendi, where it is the custom to count the labour over and to drink. By then I had forgotten about the race. But, as we stood or sat there, I heard a sound as of a great rushing wind, and there whizzed past us a living creature. It was crouched over its skis, giving a terrifying sense of movement and intensity. It uttered no sound, but its garments rustled like the silk of a jockey's jacket, and, as its skis shot between the two cottages which all but block the path, they rattled on the pitted frozen ground. It was time for us to be going if we were to make any way towards the valley before the full rush should be upon us.

I have a distorted nightmare vision of what followed. Where the way goes over open hillside or through wide glades we went as best we could, casting from time to time a fearful glance behind us and to either hand. But at times the glades contract, or the hill must be skirted on a path where one man cannot pass another, with sharp corners and sudden deep descents. At the entrance to each of these perilous places we paused, huddled together like a flock of sheep, to let some adventurer speed on his course, and then to dash after him in feverish haste to escape him who should be next on our heels. In one thing the fates were kind. The unexpected thaw had softened paths which would otherwise have been icy and the going was very easy. Still, the fear remained. On the open fields one heard the approach, swung this way or that as the lump of animated muscle swept by, and found oneself in the path of his pursuer and wondered vaguely what would happen if he fell upon one and lost the glory for which he strove. And many fell that day and there was much glory.

(*Men, Women and Mountains.*)

A. H. D'EGVILLE

In replying to a toast Mr. A. H. D'Egville remarked: "I have been referred to as 'the well-known cartoonist.' That means that I am not *a 'well-known cartoonist.' Nobody talks about 'George the well-known King.'"* It is therefore only for those who are not skiers that these few words of introduction are necessary. "Deggers" was one of the founders of the Kandahar, the inventor of its badge, and the most famous of all Stimmung providers at ski-ing dinners.

No contrast could be greater than the contrast between the friendly, informal, care-free atmosphere of the "Inferno" and the intense strain of World Championships upon the results of which might depend the future career of a successful Nazi or Fascist skier. Many a time when refereeing or organising World Championship races, with all their paraphernalia of electrical time, Press reporters, cinemas, and broadcasting commentaries, my mind has travelled back to the first "Inferno," which was everything that a race should be, friendly, informal, impromptu.

Nostalgic memories of the "Inferno" haunted me while I was refereeing the Slalom race at the 1936 Olympics in Garmisch. At the end of the race I was invited to broadcast my impressions and I was expected to compliment the Nazis on their organisation and on their double victory (in the men's race and in the women's race). But I wept when I remembered thee, O Inferno, and my broadcast had only one virtue, brevity. "Gentlemen, there are still some people who ski for fun."

One of the most significant facts about D'Egville's account of the race is that he was so preoccupied with describing what tremendous fun the race had been that he forgot to mention who won. Let me supply this comparatively unimportant detail. The race was won by Harold Mitchell, now Colonel Sir Harold Mitchell, Bart.

The contrast to which Lord Schuster draws attention between "the somewhat serious attitude of the older mountaineers" and the "gay and care-free" attitude of the ski-racers is very apparent in D'Egville's account of this race. "True to Club traditions, we carried no rucksacks, maps, compasses or theodolites." The only competitor who was not a member of the Kandahar carried a vast rucksack and seemed slightly disedified by the fact that the competitors carried their lunch "in the roomy pockets with which all right-minded ski-runners are provided." The gentleman with the rucksack finished last.

The Inferno Race

COURSE. — Schilthorn (9,817 ft.) to Lauterbrunnen (2,615 ft.) Aggregate vertical descent about 7,500 feet. The course included three short climbs and three flat sections, totalling about seven to eight kilometres.

Weather.—Fine. Cold sharp wind at summit.

Snow.—Touched by the wind and inclined to be crusty on the top part, breakable crust in the lower fields.

Remarks.—The descent from Grütsch to Lauterbrunnen (2,500 feet) was very steep and difficult.

Such is the cold, bleak description on the official "Race Result Form" sent to the Secretary of the S.C.G.B., of the longest Downhill race ever held.

The idea of this race originated with Messrs. Ford, Harold Mitchell, "Patsy" Richardson, Pelham Maitland and Lord Knebworth. The Cup takes its name from the torments endured by competitors on the most gruelling course ever set for a Downhill race. Quite apart from its length, the section from Grutsch to Lauterbrunnen contained the most difficult ground that has ever been raced over. A few years ago nobody would have thought of ski-ing, much less racing, beside the Grutsch-Lauterbrunnen funicular.

The betting was that not more than six people would be persuaded to enter, of whom, of course, none would be women. Lunn and I naturally refused to have anything to do with such a ghastly race.

Gradually, however, the list of entries increased, and seventeen competitors entered, of whom four were ladies. Here is the full list of competitors: Mrs. Harvey, Miss Doreen Elliott, Miss Sale-Barker, Miss D. Crewdson, Messrs. Mitchell, Maitland, Ryder, Allinson, Arnold Lunn, d'Egville, Humphreys, Harbidge, Eaton, Pembroke, Cadbury, Heaton, and Captain Brierly. Lunn and I, having done our best to discourage other people from entering, were at the start on January 29th.

When Lunn and I are racing against each other, I look for a certain amount of trouble. If the race involves an ascent, I anticipate a certain amount of discomfort and agony. The reader will soon see that I was justified. Lunn lost no time.

During the first hour or so of our ascent from the Allmendhübel, there was little to be done in the way of demoralising the competitors, so he contented himself with humming something, which he alleged to be the Club Song, but which was generally believed to be the Dead March in a wrong key. True to Club traditions, we carried no rucksacks, maps, compasses or theodolites. Lunch was stored in the roomy pockets with which all right-minded ski-runners are provided. Feuz and Amacher came along to carry sticks, and to stand by and to follow the party down on the descent.

Lunn selected the worst possible place for lunch, under a wind-swept rock, the seating accommodation consisting of several hundred small, sharp-pointed stones. During lunch, Lunn suggested that the race should start, not from the Col between the Gross and Klein Schilthorn, but from the actual summit.

Now the donors of the Cup had expressly ordained that the race should be started by a simultaneous (geschmozzle) start from the Col between the two Schilthorn peaks. But the moment Lunn gets above 8,000 feet he sees red. In spite of opposition, he insisted that the Inferno Race should be as infernal as possible, and that the race should start from the Spitz itself.

Moreover, he had old scores to pay off. Earlier in the season it was alleged that Lunn's nerves were beginning to fail. As the man responsible for most of the big races, he is the natural victim of the Mothers' Trades Union. He had shifted the Roberts of Kandahar Race from the Schiltgrat to a shorter course for the quite insufficient reason that a heavy snowfall had rendered the traditional course unsafe. Nay more, he had tried to enforce the Hindmarsh start dead against the sacred traditions of the Roberts of Kandahar Race. He had been overborne. The "Tough Guys" trades union had fairly trodden him in. Eighteen competitors duly started together from a narrow ledge just above a nice narrow gully, with the excellent result that the opening stages of the greatest of all ski races closely resembled the opening stages of the greatest of all horse races, the Grand National. The "Tough Guys" had won.

"It's all very well," remarked Lunn, "being a 'Tough Guy' if you are a mere competitor without any responsibility. In this race I am a competitor and I intend to enjoy myself, and

I appeal to the 'Tough Guys' to start the race not from the Col but from the Spitz."

Harold Mitchell, who was one of the donors of the Cup, had taken a prominent part in the "Tough Guy" campaign in connection with the Roberts of Kandahar Race. He was therefore at a disadvantage and weakly yielded. Mitchell, Lunn, Allinson, Ryder, and one or two others went on to the Spitz, while the rest of us stayed on the Col. Lunn explained that they would start when they were ready, and that we could join in as they swept gaily past.

We removed our ski, started to wax and to fold up our skins. I got out my camera, intending to photograph the competitors before the start. The wind, which had quieted down for a few moments, suddenly burst upon us with renewed vigour, driving the snow into our faces. It was at this particular moment, when many of us were ski-less, that Lunn, his eyes protruding like poached eggs, and a devilishly idiotic grin on his face, suddenly appeared and yelled, "Come on, we're off!" I could hardly believe my eyes, but Maitland yelled, "Come on, they're off!" and I yelled to my ski, "Come on, you're off!" and by the time I had fastened my ski, closed and pocketed my camera and fastened up my Lapp bindings with frost-bitten digits, Lunn and his satellites were specks down the slope.

Down the first slope of the Schilthorn the snow was tricky, with a thick, heavy, breakable crust which prevented any of us taking it straight. There was somewhat of a scramble to get on to the "Lunch Traverse" first, and my teeth ground continuously when I thought of Lunn there first holding up the whole show.

At the end of "Lunch Traverse" came a short climb to the top of the "Happy Valley." A ski-runner who is not racing runs straight down to "Happy Valley," but this loses a little time, and the racer prefers to avoid the short climb from the bottom of the "Happy Valley" by means of a traverse. On this traverse I had the pleasure of overhauling most of the "Tough Guy" brigade who had started from the top. I did not see Harold Mitchell. Indeed, I never saw him throughout the race, and therefore cannot pass any hostile or critical comments on his style of running.

The gods are just. Lunn had used Sohm skins on the ascent. It had been too cold on the summit to spend much time, and so he had omitted to rub in the remnant of his Sohm wax, with

the result that his ski were sticking. He lost a great deal of
time—notably on the railway—dauerlaufing where others were
sliding. This traverse, of course, counted as a Langlauf section.
In other words, a competitor who was being overtaken had to
stand out of the track on hearing the warning cry of "Tracks"
from the man behind. As I reached Lunn, there was a note of
vindictive pleasure in my hoarse cry of "Tracks." If I could
have spiked him with my ski stick as I passed, I daresay I
should have done so.

The traverse ended on "Castle Ridge," the ridge which
divides the "Happy Valley" from the Engethal. It is a castle-
shaped ridge leading up to the queer-shaped rock known as the
Mutthorn. The slopes from "Castle Ridge" down to "Charon's
Gully" are a joy to the heart. There is a wide choice of line, so
much so that I lost sight of all my fellow competitors until we
converged again near the gully.

Charon's Gully leads on to "Inferno Slopes," as we have
re-christened the steep slopes visible from the Allmendhübel.
The snow here was very tricky, but not too tricky to prevent
stemming turns. Half-way down "Kandahar Gully" I heard an
angry shout of " Tracks," and turned just in time to avoid
having my eyes spiked out by the tip of Lunn's ski. He had
selected the steepest part of the gully in which to lift a pretty
Stem. As he passed me he quoted in full the British Ski Racing
Rule which, he declared, justified his assault on my person.

From the bottom of "Shotton Slopes" there is a steepish
climb to the top of "Hindmarsh Gully." . . .

From "Hindmarsh Gully" we ran down the usual route to
"Halfway House." Thence we raced full out along the railway,
more or less level, but with a slight downhill tendency to
Grütsch, a distance of about two miles.

Just before Grütsch, we turned sharply down to the right to
tackle the most gruelling slopes that have ever been set for a
Downhill race.

Three hundred feet of open running on snow which was just
beginning to crust badly, led to a dense wood. A two hundred
foot drop through the wood, the average gradient of the slope
being about twenty-five degrees, brought us to a path, too steep
to take straight and too narrow to stem. Some steep open
slopes, another short icy path, and we emerged just above the
wood shute.

The wood shute, as its name implies, is intended for shooting wood (not competitors) down into the valley.

This subtle distinction was made clear during the course of the race.

The tree trunks which thunder down the wood shute soon transform the snow into something remarkably like ice. The shute at its steepest point is about forty-five degrees in gradient.

The racing track crosses the shute by a gentle terrace, and the wilier competitors treated this section with care, and made haste to escape back again from the shute into the wood on the right.

Even on the comparatively gentle parts of the shute the snow was hard, and I hoped to gain time by side-slipping briskly before turning right. Unfortunately, I overdid my part, and found myself approaching a blind edge which conveyed very little idea of what lay beyond. I threw myself down, but too late. I began to slide over that blind edge. At first I did not fully realise my danger, but suddenly I had a vision of Lauter-brunnen roofs far below. I grabbed at a small bushy shrub, which came away in my hands, and I at once developed a speed which, if it could only have been maintained, would have won any ski race in the world. I fell mostly head first, and I can still hear the rattle of my ski on the hard ice surface, a distressing sound. I missed several rocks by inches, and expected every moment a final and decisive crash.

It is curious that, when you fall, you experience a kind of angry resentment against those who are not falling too, and who appear to make no attempt to stop you, and always there is the feeling that someone will do something. Surely they will not stand by and see you killed? Why the devil doesn't old So-and-So do something?—he is just ahead. It can't be true that you are going to be smashed up without anyone trying to save you? As if they could do anything!

It was all over in a few seconds. With a mighty "Wump" I bounced off the track, over a rock, and fell with a thud on some softer snow at the side. It took a minute or two to wake up. I looked—I felt—nothing broken—not even a ski—and yet I had turned head over heels fifty times. Both my ski sticks were grasped firmly in my left hand and my left ski was off, but still hanging by the Lapp. Nothing worse than a skinned right arm and left shin.

Both Ryder and Miss Elliott must have lost much valuable time calling out to me to see if I were all right. I was just refixing my ski, preparing to get up when, to my horror, I heard a call behind me, and there was Miss Sale-Barker falling down the same path. I remember weakly calling to her, "You're all right. I've just fallen there myself."

She followed identically the same course, but fell much harder. I tried to stop her and she carried me several yards. She was badly shaken and had clearly broken a rib.

On seeing this, Miss Elliott climbed back to attend to Miss Sale-Barker. I think we must have been there eight to ten minutes at least, so that Miss Elliott's place at fourth is all the more remarkable and creditable.

Rather dazed, I gave Miss Sale-Barker my brandy flask. More dazed, she passed me hers.

We could never find her sticks again, and so after a little rest, we started off again with one apiece. Truly an Inferno course.

The bottom part of the course provides about 1,500 feet of steep but open running, very good fun in good snow. The snow, however, was soft breakable crust through which it was just possible to force a Telemark if one were not feeling too tired— but one was.

Here I was caught up by Lunn. His game leg was hurting him, and he took a nasty toss over an icy bank and struck something solid with the more sensitive part of his game leg. I thought for the moment he had fainted, but he started on again. I was feeling done in, as my fall had taken all my strength, so we agreed to call it a tie as far as we were concerned. There was nobody immediately behind us, but perhaps we did not trust each other, for I do not remember going very much slower. A few minutes later we passed the last fence, and reached the road from the Steinbock Hotel to the Funicular Station. Here finishing flags had been placed. "Patsy" Richardson, one of the founders of the race and one of the donors of the Cup, was at the finish. He had strained his ankle badly in the race against Wengen, and was unable to compete, thus depriving the race of much of its interest, for "Patsy" Richardson is one of the most gallant racers I know, and my ideal indeed of the "joyous ski-runner."

We were glad to see him. His staff work was admirable. In

the neighbouring inn he had prepared for us a fine confused
assortment of wurst, dunkles, coffee and grog.

> Drink we Dunkles, drink we Dunkles,
> If the worst comes to the Wurst.
> Gott sei dank—we are alive still,
> Gott sei dank—we've got a thirst.*

(*British Ski Year Book*, 1928.)

ANTHONY VISCOUNT KNEBWORTH
(1903-1933)

*Anthony Knebworth was a period piece. His light-hearted gaiety lingers in
memory as a symbol of the Golden Age of British Ski-ing. Anthony was a true
amateur in the proper sense of that much-abused word. He skied for the love of
ski-ing, and he always gave the impression that he was enjoying himself even
in World Championships. He died before the dawn of ideological ski-ing,
before the Nazis had ruined international meetings. Many a time as I have
watched the tense expressions on the faces of Nazi competitors my mind has
travelled back to the first Anglo-Swiss, Anthony roaring with laughter as he
flashed past to finish second. He will be remembered not only for a consistent
record of successes in the Anglo-Swiss, World and British Championships, but
still more for his contribution to the Anglo-Swiss parties, some of which have
acquired a legendary fame.*

*A few weeks before he died he visited Sweden as the result of an invitation
extended to the Ski Club of Great Britain. The Swedes were the first of the
northern nations to take a sympathetic interest in Alpine Ski-ing and in the
British campaign for the recognition of downhill racing (see pages* xvi, xvii).
My book "The Complete Ski-runner" was translated into Swedish in 1934.

*Anthony's allusion to "using the downhill bits 'to rest'" will, I suppose, be
unintelligible to most modern skiers. It is an allusion to a memorandum which
I drafted in* 1927 *and which was sent to all continental associations in support
of our campaign for the recognition of downhill racing.*

*"Downhill ski-ing," I wrote, "only gets a passing reference (in the
Norwegian pamphlet on 'Langlauf'). 'When going downhill one should
regain breath and rest as much as possible. Avoid falling, as it both fatigues
and lowers the spirits.'"*

An Atheist in Heaven

THE atheist does not believe in the existence of God, but
when his time is come, he will find out, like the rest of us. A
certain member of the Kandahar Ski Club did not believe in

the existence of ski-ing in Sweden. In April, 1933, his time was come.

Storlien is described by the Swedish as a very sporting place. This only means that there is no brass band, no bobsleighing, curling or skating and no extensive casino. The Swedish love their countryside as no other people, and at Easter, 1933, Storlien was full. The station platform was literally hidden by ski. The hotels—three of them—were packed; and in the siding were about eight or ten sleeping coaches with every bunk occupied. Incidentally the organisation in the hotel for feeding these hundreds was beyond praise.

I arrived in a snowstorm at midday, and having lunched, said I would like to ski. The country had been impossible to see from the train owing to the snow clouds, but I had noticed no indication of hills and was afraid that my broad racing ski would be inappropriate. So the first thing was to consult about that and the hire of langlauf ski. The guide who was going to take me out inspected them, brass edges, feldstramen spring bindings and all, and pronounced that they were just the thing. So we set out. The guide had an instinct about these things which I subsequently found was peculiar to him. He talked Amstutz and slalom in a language which must belong to skiers alone, since we could neither of us speak any common European tongue. We climbed leisurely and comfortably through the snow at the back of the hotel, and I began to think that perhaps after all there was a God. After about half an hour we bore to the left and stood at the top of a birch-covered slope about as steep as the bottom of "Martha's Meadow." The guide pointed down it and uttered the monumental word "slalom." I felt that something was expected, and so lifted a peaceful stem round one of the birch trees and then, as the guide shot past me, followed him into the mist. After about ten seconds of gentle slope, we came to a broadish bank about twice the length and three-quarters the steepness of " Claudé's· Gully." And that was that. I said it was delightful and so we walked up and slid down again twice. He kept on asking me to do a turn and was enchanted when I tried a *Geländesprung* and fell into a bush. I subsequently discovered (1) that this was the slalom ground of Storlien, (2) that it was scorned by the proper skiers, (3) that, though looking upon this kind of thing as a kindergarten amusement, the great men had a sneaking admiration for it and

thought it slightly dangerous, and (4) that the guide reported
on me as something of a phenomenon.

The next day was perfect—blue sky, bright sun and not more
than ten miles an hour of wind. I looked out over an enormous
undulating plain, more like the lowlands of Scotland (without
the valleys) than anything else to which I can compare it.
They took me out for a proper run and I learnt more than a
little. We went to an hotel on a ridge called Blohammar. It
was 18 kilometres away and 500 metres higher than Storlien.
I took 3½ hours to get there and noticed small children and their
mothers darting past me with an ease and nonchalance which
was more than humiliating. The patience of my companions
was absolutely beyond description, and no one has ever wanted
or enjoyed food so much as I wanted it and enjoyed it after
the last three kilometres up that slope. Heavy brass-edged ski
and feldstramen bindings are not the thing for Swedish ski-ing,
even if you have the technique and the natural ease of movement which is apparently born in all Scandinavians. I haven't.

On the way up I saw in the distance quite a fine snow-covered
sugar-loaf hill. I was told it was Arescutan, and as I was going
to Åre, hope rose in the heart. They said: "It is an interesting
and beautiful trip to go right round Arescutan, keeping always
at about 800 metres. It is 15 kilometres round." Hope sank.

Having eaten enormously and drunk a certain amount of
beer and been sympathised with by the exquisite and (for the
Swedes) rather frail girls, it was decided that we would not go
on, but straight "down." So "down" we started. That took
three hours and, if I was tired at the end, I was at heart
pleased with my 36 kilometres on the first day. My guide, a
Captain in the Swedish army and a very charming man, told
me that his usual time there and back would be about three
hours—less than half. That's all.

Next day again we wandered among the hills on the other
side of the hotel. Hill is perhaps not quite the word. We
wandered over the countryside. But by now they had got my
number and "wandered" is the word, the wandering being
accompanied with delightful compliments on the speed with
which I had mastered the proper technique! There was one
hill with a decent face and a cornice. I could not resist a little
interlude and climbed it only to slide down. They watched
with mild disgust and, I think, a concealed envy. They ex-

plained that in Sweden they did not practise that kind of thing
and so must be excused if they refrained from accompanying
me. But they hoped, too, that I wouldn't kill myself. By the
end of that day I had learnt what is meant by using the downhill bits "to rest." How few they were! How hard I had to
push! But how I blessed them!

But now a word on Swedish ski-ing. First of all it is not ski-
ing and has nothing to do with ski-ing as we understand the
term. It is hiking. But it is hiking with considerable ability.
The day before I arrived two Swedes had set off with a tent to
cover 1,500 kilometres. They would be away six weeks. That
is the ideal. The Swedish go out for runs in groups of twenty
or thirty with a leader, and the countryside is crowded with
parties moving in a long line which, as one of my companions
put it, are soon absorbed by the forest. The best of them go
along in step, and no one who has not seen them has any idea
of what *langlauf* movement can be. It is not a technique, as
often described, and it has very little, if anything, to do with
stick technique. It is just a natural way of walking on ski
which, incidentally, uses muscles that I found I hadn't even got.
(I found that next day.) Some of them walk along with their
sticks under their arms and without the least effort, talking and
gazing round the landscape. But I could not keep pace with
them by any means known to me, or with any degree of
effort. . . .   (*Kandahar Review*, 1933.)

KENNETH D. FOSTER

Casting Rosemary on the Graves

EACH spring since the outbreak of war I have had a brisk
battle with Hobart Place on the subject of cancelled
banker's orders, and so the sight of the familiar blue envelope
with a ridiculous starfish on the flap caused me no misgivings.
I took it to be the opening shot fired across my bows.

When I opened it, however, I discovered that it was from
Arnold, and that he was demanding padding for the *Year Book*.
The depression induced by this communication was somewhat
lightened by the fact that his secretary (who is probably a Gold

K) could not bring herself to soil her typewriter with the word "Wengen" and had therefore transposed his request into one for "some tender, nostalgic memories of *Mürren*"! My reply to Arnold was that to address such a request to a confirmed Wengenite was rather like asking Dr. Benes for some tender memories of Berchtesgaden.

. As it happens this simile is quite an apt one because, in the nineteen-twenties, we used to view the "K" symbol with much the same apprehensive interest that the smaller nationalities took in the swastika. In our case the menace was even closer. We had only to glance across the valley to see the local Berchtesgaden, where sat the Führer planning for *Lebensraum* and despatching hordes of Fifth Columnists to invade us every Sunday on the pretext that they wanted to do the Männlichen run.

We even had our Hess incident, when John Joannides deserted Mürren for Wengen. Had parachutes been in more general use at that time I have no doubt whatever that he would have used one; as it was he made a more unspectacular arrival on the 9.40 from Lauterbrunnen.

To return to the Führer, there was one memorable year when we managed something that the small nationalities never got around to—we handed the *Wehrmacht* a nasty crack. In an earlier article I told how, aided by a certain amount of luck, we managed to defeat a "K" Task Force that was sent into Wengen and how we followed this up with a victorious invasion of the enemy's own territory. To do this we had to throw in our Heavy Armour (Tom Fox) and the full weight of our Mobile Artillery (C. J. White and Donald Dalrymple).

As I was in the tail of this team I hastened to borrow a copy of Arnold's *History of Ski-ing* as soon as it was published. I felt sure that even the most humble member of a team that had defeated the Kandahar was bound to be mentioned. Sure enough, I saw "Foster, K." in the index. Turning feverishly to the page indicated I found that—as usual—the last word was with Arnold:

"K. Foster swings a pretty stick when slaloming," was all it said.

It was after our victory at Mürren that I was guilty of a sin which I still recollect with horrified remorse. One of the trophies we had won was the Bernese Oberland Challenge

Shield. Delivery was made on the spot and for some reason I was entrusted with the base—a very heavy circular affair—to carry home.

Late that evening I left the Palace, and when I got under the archway I found that my ski, my sticks, my rucksack and the circular base combined to make a very awkward and uncomfortable load. The road ahead sloped down to the station and the Bernese Oberland base was, as I have said, circular. I regret to admit that the temptation to avail myself of the law of mechanics connecting circular objects and inclined planes proved too strong to resist. I placed the Bernese Oberland base edgewise in the snow and (God forgive me) gave it a gentle shove. It disappeared instantly into the night at an incredible speed, the silver shields round its edge flashing bravely in the light reflected from the hotel windows. Never shall I forget the agonising quarter of an hour spent in searching the backyards of the chalets below, expecting every moment to find Arnold standing over me.

I started these reminiscences out of sympathy for Arnold, having been an editor myself (I edited the D.H.O.* Journal until the Swiss blew up their frontiers and cancelled their advertising), but I am finding it a very pleasant form of escapism and the difficulty now will be to stop me.

Going back to my first day in Wengen, in January, 1921 (stick it out, boys, grandpa will be taking his teeth out and going to bed soon), I caught the train on the first morning, tastefully attired in my ex-Army breeches with lots of woollen sundries above—an *ensemble* giving the general impression of a ratcatcher who felt the cold—and eventually arrived at Wengernalp. As I noticed that all the best types remained seated I decided to follow their example, being careful to keep a mental air plot to make sure of finding Wengen again.

When we reached Scheidegg I climbed out with the rest and rescued my ski from the truck. Kneeling down by the railway track I lashed them on to my feet according to the instructions given me the previous day by Mr. Molitor and then had a morning's healthy exercise attempting to climb over the bank of snow heaped up alongside the railway.

About one o'clock I knocked off for lunch, which I ate in the station restaurant. There was no Bellevue Hotel in those days.

* Downhill Only Club, a famous racing club.

Whatever it was that I had for lunch stimulated my brain cells to such an extent that when I resumed operations in the afternoon I had the bright idea of walking round to the other side of the embankment before I put on my ski.

This manœuvre enabled me to point myself in the general direction of Wengen, and I started on my return journey.

Of what happened then the less said the better. I do not believe that any visitor to Switzerland has ever been wetter, stiffer or more bruised than I was when I eventually arrived at the bottom.

The beginner of those days was almost permanently wet, thanks to a combination of woollen clothing, untracked snow and no organised tuition. Nowadays the beginner negligently flicks a little powder off the seat of his serge pants, whereas his prototype went around looking as though he needed putting through the mangle.

This moisturisation of skiers (to coin a word in the modern manner) was particularly noticeable in the train returning round the valley from Grindelwald. In those days, of course, the line back to Scheidegg was not open in winter, and the hardy spirits who had bounced their way down to Grindelwald were compelled to undertake the return journey by rail under conditions that made Scott's Arctic Expedition look like a week-end jaunt to Brighton.

When I started to comply with Arnold's request for material for the *Year Book* I hesitated between drawing on these memories of the past or compiling an anthology of place names in Wengen, and I still think that there would be scope for the latter.

Most of the geographical features in Wengen were christened in the early 'twenties. The name of the sadistic humourist who christened Slip-Cartilage Corner has not, as far as I am aware, passed into history, but Fisken and Donald Dalrymple were responsible for many of the other names. As gunners, they disliked loose references to "the three rocks near to the fourth chalet," and since the woolly-minded civilians declined to tackle any system of map references they were compelled to invent place names.

As my sister skied a good deal with Fisken she is associated with several of the names he coined. For example, the pink hut on the line above Scheidegg was known, with rather odd formality, as "Miss Foster's Hut" right up to the time when the Jungfrau Bahn dug it out and revealed it proudly as a real railway station. This name even appears on many of the local ski maps.

Fisken seems to have become less formal as he got higher, because "Oh God!" derives its name from my sister's involuntary (and unladylike) exclamation the first time she found herself looking down it.

Eighteen consecutive seasons in Switzerland would provide material for many articles of this kind, but youth soon becomes impatient of the ancient voice quavering out of a shrubbery of white whiskers. During the final years winter sports facilities, amenities and tuition improved out of all recognition, but the ancients cling to the idea that they had a lot of fun the new generation misses. In fact we echo the sentiments of the Old Man of Southwold, of whom the poet (probably Wordsworth) wrote. He said, it will be recollected, that the youth of to-day, he was told, are so used to the nude that they don't think it lewd—My God! but it's nice to be old!

(*The British Ski Year Book*, 1943.)

G. R. DE BEER, F.R.S.

The Parsenn

IT is difficult to do justice to the richness of the joys of the Parsenn. We always began with a run to Küblis, to greet Herr Flütsch at the old Conterser Schwendi inn and Frau Durl and her beautiful niece Franzi at the terminus at Küblis. I would exchange no hunger or thirst in the world for that produced by a good run to Küblis, and no banquet on earth for such a well-earned lunch at Küblis, consisting of filet bifteck garniert with lashings of Haldengut beer, raw onions and cheese. People may ask how it is possible to get any enjoyment out of a smooth-tracked tramline run like that to Küblis. My reply is that every time (even twice a day), and whatever the conditions, I enjoy every inch of its ten miles. The fact that so many other people like it, too, is insufficient to mar my pleasure. Arnold Lunn has spoken of the litany of lovely names: "Calais Delle Berne Spiez Interlaken" which he longs to hear recited again. I also have such a litany, the Stations of Joy on the route to Küblis, and it runs as follows: Gents' Tee or Ladies' Tee, First, Second and Third Shoot, Ladies' Delight, Crossroads where the beautiful view of the Tödi, the distant Finsteraarhorn and the Rhätikon opens out, Derby Shoot or Elbow, Amphitheatre, Telemark Hill, Hole, Traverse, Gaudergrat, Outer Bumps, Alpine Garden, Inner Bumps, Devil's Staircase, Conterser Schwendi, Shambles Corner, Devil's Bridge, Path, Upper Meadows, Sheep's Gate, Lower Meadows, Conters Valley, Conters, the Terraces, First and Second Galleries, Brunnen, Third Gallery, and Oh God before the final run down to the river and the happy tramp through the streets of Küblis. I am firm friends with them all, and like friends in changing moods we frequently had our little rows. But the feel of their shapes beneath my ski gives me an indescribable pleasure.

One of the reasons why the Küblis run is so satisfying is that it has a balanced form and composition: it is in fact a symphony on ski, and a work of art. Like a symphony it is made up of a number of movements. Those who do not know the Küblis run will pardon me if I explain this. The first movement, *allegro vivace*, typifies the freedom of action enjoyed on the higher open slopes, and, again, like a symphony, it is composed of cyclically recurring subjects. The first subject, the sweeping curve of the Gents' Tee, is developed and repeated through the successive Shoots, until the movement winds up to the climax of the Derby Shoot and comes to an end at the Hole. The second movement, *andante espressivo*, depicts with syncopated treatment the progress from the beginning of the tree-line, and begins at the Gaudergrat. Its first subject, the Outer Bumps, is followed by the lyrical second subject of the Alpine Garden. The first subject is then taken up again by the Inner Bumps, and, next, the element of difficulty overcome is introduced at the Devil's Staircase. This is developed with variations such as Shambles Corner and the Devil's Bridge, and the movement comes delicately to an end with Path. The third movement is the *scherzo*, and it begins with the lovely joke that is the Upper Meadows. The difficulty motif is then introduced in unobtrusive form at the Sheep's Gate, and this is again followed by the first subject in the Lower Meadows. The scherzo then winds up with the arrival at Conters. The fourth and last movement, *allegro maestoso*, is, as it should be, a recapitulation of the previously presented subjects. The Terraces reflect the broad sweeps of the first movement, tempered by the lyrical theme of the second, and a new subject is introduced with the Galleries. This subject is then developed with increasing passion until, after the Third Gallery, Oh God and the final run down provide a *coda* which resumes in a few brief seconds the glories of the higher sweeps.

Such is my analysis of the Küblis run. It is not just one damn thing after another, but a sequence of harmonious experiences. The snow provides the score; your ski are the orchestra, and you are the conductor. Who is the composer?

(*The British Ski Year Book*, 1945.)

EVELINE AMSTUTZ

Mrs. Amstutz is the wife of Walter Amstutz, a famous Swiss mountaineer and skier. I quoted her poem on Murten (Morat) in a book of mine, and a reader was so impressed by the poem that she wrote to me:

"In your book you mention a little town called Murten or Morat which greatly took my fancy. After the war I hope to go to Switzerland and would love to stay in this town. Where is it, please? Is it difficult to get at and are there possible lodgings for a limited income? Would it be possible to buy a tiny cottage there for a small sum? Do the people speak French or German, or have they any English?"

This letter was an unconscious tribute to Mrs. Amstutz's success in recapturing the atmosphere of Murten.

Murten

THE sober citizens of Berne, what could they do but stare,
When I came back from Murten with poppies in my hair,
When looking in my eyes they saw the gay contentment there?

For Murten is a little town where quiet laughter lies,
Where shopmen deal in simple jokes with everyone who buys,
And even all the fat old dogs have twinkles in their eyes.

Half-open doors grin broadly at the sunshine in the street:
The dark arcades are laughing with the sound of children's
    feet,
And sweet contentment lingers in the eyes of all you meet.

The streets are very, very wide, and always very bare,
No cars go dashing through them, and the dust lies thickly
    there,
And aged dames, with shrivelled hands, walk out to take the
    air.

For Murten is an old town, and men can well recall
The history of the passing years within its city wall.
But no one comes and no one goes, and no one minds at all!

An Englishwoman Writes from Switzerland

SOME time ago I read *Mountain Jubilee* by Arnold Lunn in which his nostalgia for Switzerland and the mountains and snows of Switzerland flows out on almost every page. This is all very flattering for Switzerland, but I wonder how many people who have been privileged to "see the war through" in England realise the nostalgia for England which people—chiefly women like myself—have endured all these years. Nostalgia, not just to be home, but to be able to pull our weight with all the others in England.

I use the word "privileged" advisedly because I feel that it *has* been a privilege to witness at close quarters the resurrection of England, of English tradition, of all that made the English what they have been and what they will always be. It looked, to many of us who saw the view from the distance and who did not live in it, as if England was losing something, and we yearned over our country and clung fast to our belief that it couldn't really be happening.

And then the war came and all our beliefs were justified, for England showed herself to be what she has always been— superb! We who have made our homes in other countries have—at least, I have—longed to be home during this resurrection and to do something! I don't mean that I longed for honour and glory, at least not the bombed out of house and home kind of honour and glory, but just to feel that I was doing my share with all the other women of England. I felt I wouldn't mind coping with food shortage, difficulties of transport, danger, lack of fuel, national work, anything, if I knew that whatever the discomfort was I was putting up with it quietly and as a matter

of course—for England! Letters I had from England did not
help. There were things waiting for me to do there, I was
wanted. One letter ran: "Why aren't you here now? We need
women like you."

However, I am still here, and I found things to do, later.
None of them the least heroic or important, but I am still
doing them. There was "Digging for Victory" to be done,
which has played, and which is still playing, such an important
rôle in Switzerland. Every corner, every sloping bank, every
inch of land must be made to produce. I could dig, and I dug
with a will, joining the big cultivation plan put into action
throughout the country. Public parks became vegetable
gardens, potatoes adorned the squares in our towns and corn
waved where corn had never waved before. There were the
refugees, civil and military, pouring into the country. No
public body could cope with them all at once and it was up to
private people to do what they could. In my letter of last year
I may have told what happened when I started to beg for the
French soldiers in Mürren. Within ten days I was able to fit
out two hundred and fifty men with clothes, thanks to the
Swiss! That's the way the Swiss give. Everyone I asked, asked
someone else, and things came pouring into the house till it
looked like an old clothes shop. One woman in the village took
two shirts off her washing line and gave them to me, saying:
"I must just wash a little oftener."

The Red Cross is always needing help and getting it;
organisations which provide clothes, food, parcels, comforts for
prisoners of war, exist in every town. We sew, collect books,
anything and everything, and since the capitulation of Italy,
has come another influx of refugees, English and American
soldiers and Italians, civil, military and political refugees, from
the highest in the land to the poorest and meanest. They all
have to be cared for. In the beginning many Italians came in
with permission from the Swiss government, but the only way
open to them now is the "black" route, slipping between
German guards, braving the mountains or the dangers of being
smuggled in somehow by Italian partisans. I have just come
back from a little place on the Italian-Swiss frontier, where I
was in touch with these brave men and women, and knew as
much of their activities as their trust in me allowed them to
tell. Their lives are in their hands every moment of the day and

night and they are still bringing Italians, British and American soldiers over the frontier at an incredible rate. They brought 27 British officers up to within sight of the frontier whilst I was there, but when these men decided to join up with their own forces instead of crossing into internment in Switzerland, the partisans took them all south and handed them safely over in an amazingly short space of time. Many of the tales I should like to tell must wait till after the war, because quite a few of these Italian partisans are living in Switzerland as respectable citizens, and those of us who know anything—just don't know anything at all!

We women who have our relatives in England are in constant anxiety, often without news and with no hope of reunion till after the war. True, we, our husbands and children are safe and that is a great deal for which to be thankful. Life is complicated, housekeeping is difficult, little food can be bought without coupons, and clothes and footwear are rationed. We have all we *need* if not all we want, and when one remembers that we are feeding and clothing eighty thousand refugees as well as ourselves, it is a miracle of organisation that we *are* all fed and clothed, particularly when one looks at the map and studies the position of Switzerland for a moment!

For the last ten months I have had two Italian children in my home, and they will remain for the duration of the war. The extra coupons I have had given me for them has enabled me to see that they have had not only all they need, but all they *want*. And the first to give was a village woman who slipped coupons into my hand, saying: "We don't need it. Give it to the little ones, they need feeding up." Strict as the rationing is, everyone can spare something where they see refugees.

Difficult times bring out character, and I have seen many surprising things in this country. I have seen true heroism in the little, irritating affairs of everyday life and I have seen a lot of sad exploitation of circumstances. I have heard grumbling from people whose position certainly does not entitle them to grumble and I have seen stoicism where I least expected it. Generosity and open-heartedness have come from people whom I never suspected of possessing either and mean behaviour from people I had believed to be made of different stuff.

We have had our alarms and excursions, of course. How could it be otherwise, situated as we are? Our men are mobilised, our frontiers fortified and manned. But inside those frontiers, no matter what happens outside them, is Switzerland, safe, her people pursuing their normal lives as far as possible, eating their daily bread in confidence and trust, the children secure, homes undamaged and the future—we hope and trust— assured. And in this hope and trust we can look proudly at the three flags which fly side by side over Swiss soil. Three flags very much alike in shape and form, since all are crosses. The cross of Christianity, oldest of them all, which has never been torn down to make room for any other emblem; the white cross on the red ground, our national flag which has flown over free Switzerland since the Middle Ages; and the red cross on the white ground which Henri Dunant, Swiss founder of the Society of the Red Cross, made by reversing the flag of his country. As long as we can keep these in our hearts, I think we need little else, the cross of Christ for faith, the cross of Switzerland for hope, and the red cross of charity, the charity which out of our own security we give with both hands in thankfulness that we have it to give.

(*The British Ski Year Book*, 1944.)

EUGENE BAGGER

In Praise of Switzerland

IN September 1937 my wife and I drove up to Lake Leman, and for the next fifteen months Switzerland was our base. The first twelve we spent at a hotel at Glion, a hamlet situated on a cliff rising sheer two thousand feet above the lake, and accessible from Montreux by a narrow corkscrew road, the gradient of which rises to one in five for the last kilometre. And I wish now that I had yet another chapter or two to go before this book comes to an end; for I should need at least as much space to tell what I feel should be told about Switzerland. It was before the war the most-publicised country in Europe, and one of the least-known; for all that publicity was purely commercial, aiming to attract moneyed people to the winter sports and other touristic amenities which were Switzerland's chief source of income. There is nothing wrong with that; to sell holiday facilities to people who want them is as legitimate as

selling automobiles or harvesting machinery. But the trouble
with the sort of publicity which was so brilliantly organised by
the Swiss was that it put a false façade on their country,
encouraging the idea that Switzerland was nothing but an
agglomerate of ski-ing *hôtels de luxe,* and that the Swiss regarded it as their historic mission to act as head porters and
mountain guides to wealthy and less wealthy Anglo-Saxons.

Now Switzerland is not, and the Swiss are not, like that at all,
once you have come to know them. I cannot speak of and for
the German-speaking cantons, as I do not know them; but I
did learn something of *la Suisse romande,* as the French-speaking
states of the Confederacy are called. Most of their population
are Calvinists, and the Calvinist temperament and mode of life
are alien to me; but in those fifteen months I conceived not
merely admiration, but also affection, for those Swiss Protestants. They possess to an eminent degree two of the finest
qualities of civilised men, and these happen to be qualities
which I particularly prize: a sense of order, based not on a
mere external observance, but on a genuine penetration of the
meaning of the Law; and a sense of reality. The French-
speaking Swiss are realists in the best sense of the word; not in
the confused sense of everyday parlance, which applies it
indiscriminately to the hard-boiled materialistic and cynic, to
the gangster of *Realpolitik,* international or private, and to the
low time-serving opportunist. The realist, according to the
proper signification of the term, is one who is able, and keen, to
distinguish the real from the apparent, the true from the false,
the genuine from the sham; one who does not believe that we
can create facts by hoping for them, and remove facts by
wishing them out of the way; one who does not believe that we
can change things by changing their names; one who, to put it
as briefly as possible, refuses to be taken in by words. Now the
Swiss are a people of realists in this very sense; and I shall give
two instances of their realism. They know that in a world like
ours, a world teeming with evil, the way to maintain democracy
and individual liberty is not to make, and listen to, speeches
about democracy, but to practise sharpshooting; and beside
being the truest democracy in the world, the Swiss are also a
people of enthusiastic trained soldiers. And, true lovers of
liberty, they know that to grant unrestricted freedom to
freedom's enemies is to invite its destruction. So the Swiss were

not taken in by the fashionable bunkum about the Communists being the champions of democracy, and being entitled anyway to the privileges that the democratic commonwealth vouchsafes to its citizens; to the noisy claims of their Communists to freedom of speech and association they retorted by inquiring just how much freedom of speech and association is granted to non-Communists in Soviet Russia.

In those fifteen months I came to regard Switzerland as the finest democracy in the world, a democracy based on the effort of hard thinking, on the dignity of hard work, on the beauty of self-imposed discipline. It was the one democracy in Europe that was, on the one hand, truly democratic, and that, on the other hand, *worked;* and this was because, of all European democracies, it had remained most faithful to the Christian origins of our civilisation. It was the most advanced of European nations because it was the most conservative.

(*For the Heathen are Wrong.*)

PETER LUNN, R.A.

Through a Glass Darkly

Peter Lunn raced in eight and captained five (including the Olympic) British ski teams. He has won events for which there was a crack international entry and has often finished high up among the Aces in World Championships, known among skiers as the FIS races, the word "FIS" being formed from the initial letters of the International Ski Federation.

IT was May 1942. In April they had dropped 6,800 tons on the island, and they were still keeping up the pressure. Day after day the bombers swept in from Sicily: one by one the towns of Malta were being devastated. Stoically, the Maltese watched their churches and homes drift out to sea in great clouds of grey dust.

Our fighter protection had been worn down. Twice Spitfire reinforcements reached Malta, only to be bombed on the ground or, hopelessly outnumbered, shot out of the sky. The A.A. ammunition was running short, and the gunners were rationed. After the raids we watched German reconnaissance planes cruising unmolested about the sky; that belonged to them, though we still held the ground we stood on.

On May 9th fresh Spitfires reached Malta, this time in greater numbers than ever before. The people of Malta watched them flying in low over the roof tops and hardened their hearts with hope. Everything had been done to prepare for the Spitfires, to give the pilots every chance against the enemy. The infantry had been called in to assist the R.A.F. in servicing them, so that damaged planes might be returned to the battle as soon as possible and avoid the ever-present danger of being bombed on the ground. As we went to bed that night we did not care to think how much would depend upon what those pilots could do the next day. It was more than our fates in the war. If the Axis could succeed in blasting Malta into submission, then our planes and submarines would cease to harass Rommel's lines of communication; he would be able to reinforce his desert armies unhindered, and then . . .?

Early the next morning pilots waited for the signal to scramble. One of them made a last minute entry in his diary under the heading, "DAWN, MAY 10TH." He wrote, "To-day will be one of the great days of history." They had not long to wait before news came of German fighters flying towards Malta.

At breakfast we could hear the sharp rat-a-tat-tat of invisible planes duelling in the morning sunshine. We knew that our fate was being decided up there, thousands of feet above us. Later the bombers came over, and we saw at once that the gunners had orders not to ration their ammunition; the barrage was heavier than it had ever been before. We looked round for our fighters, wondering with sick fear how many of them had been knocked out by the Messerschmitts earlier in the morning. Then we caught sight of them, more of them that we had ever seen, flying into battle. One by one, with incredible heroism, they roared into our own barrage, pursuing the German planes with unquenchable determination. I saw one of our own planes crumpled like matchwood by an A.A. burst. But though we had losses, the enemy suffered far worse; bomber after bomber crumpled and fell slowly on to Malta or into the sea.

The sirens wailed many times that day, but each time they presaged another victory for our Spitfires. The toll of Axis planes destroyed, and probably destroyed, mounted rapidly. During the past months the population of Malta had spent the raids in the safe rock shelters. Few, who had no cause to do so, stayed above ground to watch the familiar, dismal spectacle of bombs devastating their native island. But the news of our victories spread and brought the people crowding out of their shelters on to the roofs. As one Axis plane after another crashed to earth, or limped feebly out to sea, so the cheering swelled, echoing from roof top to roof top across the tiny barren island.

The final wave of enemy bombers came over in the clear light of evening. My wife brought our two small children on to the roof, and they saw the last planes shot down to burn defeated upon the island they had striven so long to subdue.

A great weight had been lifted from the minds of the people. Now as they stood upon their roofs, they went crazy with relief and happiness, cheering and waving flags. A handful of pilots, who had won, as the Prime Minister was to announce later, a great victory, flew backwards and forwards across the island, low over their heads.

"Vat I vant," the Editor wrote to me, his incorrigible mistyping lending on this occasion an oddly Semitic touch to his letter, "is something which will give the spirit of (a) the FIS races, (b) the odds we were up against, and (c) what it felt like to be a tiny handful competing against these toughs."

This, it seemed to me, was an impossible assignment. Success in the FIS races had seemed incredibly important at the time, worth working for and worth writing about. But it was very different to look back on those races now through the dark glass of my Malta experiences. I did not see how any man, who had watched the gallantry of our pilots facing incredible odds, could then have the egoistic vanity to sit down and solemnly write about the petty thrills of pre-war racing.

I thought there were only two attitudes which one could take towards one's ski-ing memories. One was to argue the value of ski-ing on the grounds that it developed dash and quick-thinking, which are so essential in war. But this attitude I hated. However proud I might be when fellow-members of the Kandahar distinguished themselves (for to me the Kandahar is what the old school is to so many Englishmen), I thought it the most complete humbug to justify our love for the sport by arguing its hypothetical value as a training for modern war.

If that is the excuse for ski-ing, then we shall have to abolish the
Kandahar at the next disarmament conference.

And if ski-ing could not be justified as part of a rearmament
programme, then we could only look back upon it with frank
and unapologising hedonism. Ski-ing and racing were worth
while, simply because we found pleasure in the thrill of speed,
in mountain scenery, and, certainly as far as I was concerned, in
friendship with the Swiss. This alternative attitude seemed to
me a reasonable one. And I thought, looking back, that we
had attached a quite disproportionate and, in the light of later
events, rather undignified importance to the principal races.

So, when I got the Editor's letter, I determined to write an
article, ignoring the FIS races, about the thrill of speed, the
beauty of the mountains and my affection for the Swiss. I
remembered how once in Malta the Swiss nanny of some friends
of mine walked into the room. She had never met me and knew
nothing about me. When I was introduced, I spoke in Swiss-
German. A look of startled happiness came over her face and
Malta faded away as we talked in that lovely dialect about the
mountains.

Before I started to write the article, my copy of *Mountain
Jubilee* reached Malta. The first effect of this book was to
undermine my wife's last beliefs in Lunn respectability. "We
were married," my father writes, "on December 10th, 1914."
Now I was born on November 15th of the same year. However,
I convinced her (my wife) that it was the Lunn typewriter
that had lapsed.

The second effect of *Mountain Jubilee* was to make me realise
that my rather superior attitude to racing memories was false.
We may all have attached undue importance to international
racing, but I realised suddenly how much poorer my life would
have been if I had never known the thrill of competing in the
British team against the teams of other countries. Those
experiences were exciting and good; they remain exciting and
good, even though the safe and unimportant rivalry of sport
has now to be compared with grim and fateful struggles. A
thing which is good remains good, even when it is dwarfed in
comparison with other good things. There is no need to be
like the man in the cartoon, who turned his back on the
Matterhorn because he had seen Mount Everest.

"The road of memories" is a common phrase, but memories

are not really like a road you wander along, but more like flowers in a garden, which you wander among. For memories do not come back in chronological sequence; sometimes the things of childhood stand out more sharply, and return to the memory more persistently than those of later years. One of my own most vivid memories is sitting as a small boy in the old Number 4, where Joannides was turning over some papers. Suddenly Joann said to me, "I suppose you think ski-ing the most important thing in life?" I told him I certainly did. "You'll grow out of that," Joann said. I did not argue, though I was certain he was wrong. But it worried me a lot that someone as sensible as Joann—and on that score I had no doubts—should think I would outgrow the one enthusiasm which made life worth while. If I grew to care less for ski-ing, what, I wondered, could there be left to live for? My heroes then were those who had their names engraved on the big boards which recorded the winners of the Roberts of Kandahar and Alpine Ski Challenge Cups. I remember the anxiety with which I used to watch Christopher Mackintosh racing brilliantly, but haphazardly, among the slalom flags in the Anglo-Swiss and the care with which I would select my own ideal ski team to represent Great Britain. I remember, too, failing dismally in the Mürren elementary test at the age of six; I ran into a snow-drift and had to be extricated by my nurse.

Few things are more interesting to oneself, and few things more boring to other people, than childhood memories. Though I repeat this excellent maxim to myself, I find it difficult to stop writing about those early Mürren days and start writing about the FIS. Pre-FIS Mürren, Mürren between 1920 and 1931, was the cradle, or rather the nursery, of downhill racing and British ski-ing. It was the spring-time of those movements, and in spring there is an expectancy which autumn fruits do not fulfil. We love spring because it is the season of hope, and hope is the one earthly emotion which we humans enjoy pure and pristine, for it is the only emotion that, by its very nature, is untinged by disappointment.

Hope is essentially the emotion of youth, the youth of people and movements. An old man, however fully he may have achieved the ambitions he cherished in his youth, will still look back with wistful longing on his early days of struggle, penury and hope. And the pre-FIS Mürren must inevitably have that

16

appeal for those who knew it. In those days ski-ing was an almost unknown sport to our compatriots in Britain, and down-hill racing was regarded as a joke by our fellow skiers on the Continent. Those who frequented the pre-FIS Mürren were united by a great enthusiasm to raise the standard of British ski-ing and the prestige of downhill racing. They dreamed that one day a British team would compete without disgracing itself in a World Downhill Racing Championship recognised as such by the International Ski Federation; and I personally dreamed that I should be a member of that team. 1931 saw the realisa-tion of our dreams, and perhaps there the story should end, as the fairy stories end: "And they raced happily ever after." But this is a record of facts, not a fairy story, and it does not end with the first FIS. The spring of downhill ski-ing was followed by the leaden days of summer, when the glare of a great popularity shone upon our favourite sport.

I write away from records, and the aspect of the FIS's which I find most difficult to recall is the final results. I remember outstanding successes like Muffie Mackinnon's victory in 1931, and Evie Pinching's in 1936, but little else. I cannot even remember who won the men's event, or where I finished myself, every year. The reader may think that I am trying to be *blasé*, to pretend that I have a mind above such mundane considera-tions. The more uncharitable may suggest that I am indeed wise to have forgotten the results of races in which I never did particularly well. However, believing that truth, if not the best policy, is certainly the most interesting, I can only say that the one thing which seemed to me all-important at the time is now the most blurred in my memory.

Kind friends always prophesied that one's sense of values would alter in just this way. When we got very worked up about our chances in the FIS, they used to soothe us, or try to soothe us, by saying, "Never mind, it will all be the same in a hundred years' time." I never really believed them; at any rate it never stopped me worrying a great deal about how I should do in the race. Now I find that the kindly prophets were indeed right, and that one's rating in the FIS has ceased to matter, even to oneself, after only seven years' time. But the FIS races themselves do still matter a lot to me, and I owe to them many of my most thrilling, most interesting and happiest experiences. Similarly we find great interest in reading about the ancient Olympic Games, their organisation, the spirit they evoked, and the religious and political cross-currents which permeated them. But nobody now cares who won the different events, though this must have seemed of primary importance at the time.

Looking back on international racing, and trying to analyse the memories it has left me, I realise one thing with great clearness and considerable surprise. It is that I cannot think of a single international racer whom I disliked. There were blazing rows, and I can remember being right in the middle of at least one of them; on several occasions competitors did contest the decisions of officials in a disgraceful manner. But I cannot recall a single instance of two racers quarrelling with each other. From what I saw of the figure-skating and ice-hockey at the Olympic Games, ski-racing is an exceptional sport in this particular. And I think the reason is that the ski-racers were united by having to solve a common problem. We all met practising over the course, and we all had to face the same difficulties and dangers; it was only natural that we should exchange ideas as to the correct racing line. Of course, the Nazis tried to discipline their team into an attitude of unsporting egoism, which allowed no contact with other competitors. But even after the Nazis came into power, I can remember practising with Rudi and Christl Cranz, who were racing for Germany, and discussing the course with them just as frankly as I would have done with British competitors. And it was an Austrian, Hans Nöbl, who broke his leg in the 1935 FIS and yet, though in considerable pain, shouted advice to me as I came past a few moments later. He had crashed because he took a particular line too fast. As I came down the same line he yelled that I would never hold it unless I checked. His advice came too late, as I was already committed to the line I had chosen, and I fell heavily shortly afterwards. I did not injure myself, as he had done, but I wasted valuable seconds.

The main rows between competitors and officials nearly always arose from the competitors' conviction that the course was unnecessarily dangerous. This belief, that they were being asked to face pointless risks, would always unite the racers in frenzied indignation. I signed only one protest in my life, and that was when there was delay in flagging a particular FIS course, which was full of concealed rocks. I can remember no racing captain who did not join in this protest; it was signed by the male and female captains representing the organising country.

There is, of course, a big difference between saying that the competitors of all the different countries got on well together, and saying that international ski-ing promoted international friendship. It did no such thing. One is not more likely to condone German foreign policy because one remembers with affection German skiers. The Germans, as everybody knows, did their best to introduce political dissensions into ski-ing. Though they succeeded well enough with the officials, they failed with the racers, who were far too interested in discussing the fastest safe line to argue about their respective foreign policies. It was harder for the officials to steer clear of politics, because it was their thankless task to ensure that their racers got fair play; and that necessitated arguments with the Nazi representatives.

Perhaps the most exciting FIS days were those spent practising over the course before the race. There would probably be one slope of outstanding difficulty, and here all the racers would congregate. I will try to describe a typical scene, a scene which is a composite of memories rather than the recollection of any particular incident. The British team are climbing up the most difficult slope on the course for the first time; we climb slowly, examining every bump and frequently turning round so as to familiarise ourselves with the line from above. At the top of the slope a small group is huddled together, obviously discussing the best line, for periodically one of them points down the slope with his stick. We strain our eyes upwards and recognise the Swiss team. Suddenly one of them starts down the slope; perhaps it is Zogg, or Furrer, or one of the Steuris. All the other competitors on the slope stand still and watch him. Perhaps he takes a very dangerous line and then our nerves tauten as we watch. If the racer falls, there will be seconds of suspense while one wonders whether he has injured himself. Then, as he picks himself up, one's weaker self will start arguing that that line at any rate is impossible and that there is no need to make certain by trying it oneself. But if he holds that dangerous line, which perhaps means racing past rocks and tree-stumps at high speed, one will feel suddenly weak because one knows that one will have to follow the same line oneself several times, on the day of the race itself and in the days of practice beforehand.

Later one stands at the top of the slope and knows, as one starts down, that all the other competitors are turning to watch. If one tackles the slope well, they will be asking each other who one is and what country one represents. On these occasions, perhaps as much as on any other, a racer felt the thrill of carrying his country's colours. For the competitors up and down the slope would all be in national groups, and it was a wonderful experience for any racer who could impress them with what his countrymen could do. In the race itself one skied in front of a large crowd, the majority of whom were quite incapable of appreciating the finer points of technique. But in practice the racer was watched by the most intelligent ski-ing audience in the world, his fellow competitors: the judgment of his peers. We competitors saw little of one another in the race, and those days of practice were our unique opportunity of watching the best ski-ing in the world. And good ski-ing is a wonderful thing, even when it is the ski-ing of one's most dangerous rivals from other countries. As a racer showed some unexpected brilliancy, the thrill of appreciation and excitement would, for a second or two at any rate, be untinged by any thought of rivalry or any feeling that one would now have to attempt the same brilliancy oneself. Once, when one of the Ruud brothers showed real genius in tackling a certain hazard, the other competitors burst into spontaneous applause.

On the day of the race itself I would climb to the start in a condition of appalling nervousness, wondering why on earth I endured such misery and wishing never to race again. I do not think that this nervousness can be described as stage fright, because everybody seemed to suffer from it before the straight race but nobody did before the slalom, even though in an important slalom one had to compete solo in front of a very large crowd. The conclusion from which is that a very large part of one's nervousness before the straight race was simply due to physical fear. The racer had made up his mind to follow a particular line, and that line inevitably entailed certain risks. It is true that the racer had almost certainly taken exactly the same line in practice, but then he had been able to choose his own moment and brace himself for the effort. But in the race he had to start at the exact moment the starter told him.

He was no longer a free agent, but was caught in the toils of a remorseless organisation.

I was never one of those who found that all nervousness departed as soon as the starter has said "Los." I was always uneasy on the top slopes, in fact I was always uneasy until I had faced the worst slope of the course. This normally came about half-way down and could be considered the crisis of the race. If I held my line there, I was filled with such confidence and happiness that all subsequent hazards seemed easy. Suddenly I would find a tremendous exhilaration in my ski-ing, and would leap into every slope with a passionate desire to master its difficulties.

And it was difficult to lose one's nervousness on the top slopes for another reason: because they were so bleak. They made one realise that ski-racing is an intensely individualistic sport. The racer never sees another competitor except on the rare occasions when he overhauls somebody else, or is himself overhauled. There is no team spirit possible, for each racer must face alone and unaided the hazards of the course. A race is like a struggle against nature rather than a competition against one's fellow men. The top slopes of the course are always empty of spectators, and this accentuates the racer's feelings of a lonely contest with something inhuman. He feels isolated in the vast landscape and rather helpless; he does not feel that he can ever master the course's hazards, but instead that these will conquer him and buffet him mercilessly. But on the bottom slopes the racer skies between serried ranks of spectators and he feels somehow that they are his allies against nature. Sometimes the spectators cheered, and there are few things more exhilarating than being cheered when one is doing something difficult and slightly dangerous. It is quite different from being cheered in cold blood at a prize-giving: that is very nice, but it is in no way exhilarating. But to race between ranks of cheering spectators and to hear the applause swelling as one approaches, that is wonderful. It happened to me once or twice because in the old days, before the group draw, I started immediately behind bad racers and passed them on the lower stages. The public would seldom realise that there is nothing commendable in gaining a minute on a bad racer, or one who has met misfortune on the way down, and would thrill to the sight of a lower number overhauling a higher. It is perhaps not very praiseworthy that one should enjoy being cheered under patently false pretences, but I can only say that I did enjoy it very much indeed and am sorry to think that it will never happen to me again.

I am very conscious that I have not succeeded in explaining why ski-racing means so much to me, or in recording satisfactorily the wonderful memories it has left me. Indeed, my comments about the unimportance of results may at first seem ungrateful to those who spent so much time, trouble and money in managing the British team and raising the standard of British racing. Such ingratitude is very far from my real feelings. Though I find it very difficult to recall individual results, I remember with intense pride—and always shall—the part which British skiers have played in international racing. Britain is a non-snow country and we have one skier for every hundred Swiss, French, German or Italian. But in spite of this the Ski Club of Great Britain entered the FIS races with teams, which competed without disgracing themselves, against the finest racers in the world. The glory of British ski-racing lies in the general results achieved rather than in any individual effort. For an isolated British skier might enjoy, as I certainly did, all the advantages of the Continental racers. I had those advantages, far more than any other British racer, and there is therefore nothing very praisewothy in my getting into the first half of a FIS race. Such individual results are not particularly commendable. What is commendable is the high general standard achieved by the British racers, and this was very largely due not to the racers themselves, but the organisers who worked unselfishly behind the scenes. It is thanks to them that British ski-ing, in overcoming the odds it did, achieved something really exceptional in the annals of sport.

I skied for the last time on my honeymoon in May, 1939. Before then the winter used to mean ski-ing to me as surely as the summer meant warm weather. Five snowless years have followed, but ski-ing is still part of my life and perhaps I value it more than I ever did. I know that when my daughter was born I found it only fitting that she should be christened Mary Blanche in dedication to Our Lady of the Snows, and I felt then that there was some tenuous link between the gaunt Maltese church and the race courses I have loved. For a man's recreations, the things he does because he loves them, often

mean more to him than the sterner things in his life. Though I
am not an ambitious father, nor one imbued with a strong sense
of family tradition, I hope that my children will one day thrill
as I have thrilled to the imperative words of the starter and the
sliding of ski downhill. To me a Lunn who does not ski is rather
like the Great Auk, now extinct, a bird that does not fly.

(*The British Ski Year Book*, 1944.)

Parachuting and Ski-ing

BUT the similarity between ski-ing and parachuting is to be
found in the emotions they evoke as well as the technique
they require. The parachutist jumps from the aeroplane into
a slipstream of roughly 100 miles per hour. The wind is so
violent that he has to grasp his trouser legs to prevent his arms
being flung outwards. During the few seconds between the
exit from the plane and the opening of the parachute, I used
to get a tremendous sensation of speed, very similar to that
experienced during a fast schuss. I found that I enjoyed this
thrill of speed more with each succeeding jump, as I became
accustomed to the novelty of it all and my bewilderment
lessened. On my first jump I enjoyed no pleasing thrills. I
made a bad exit from the plane and did, what is quite common,
a somersault. I found myself hurtled through the air, seeing
first the ground below me and then my parachute, before it had
opened, above me. I remember thinking it a most unpleasant
experience and being reminded of the bewildering and slightly
nauseating moment when one awakes from an anæsthetic. I
was not frightened, though I had certainly been scared up to
the moment of leaving the plane.

But the real quality which ski-ing and parachuting share is
the conquest of fear. In an article on *The Thrill of Ski-ing* I once
described fast schussing as " a medley of sensations, but the
most essential of these, that from which the others take their
life, is the agony of indecision and fear one undergoes before
pointing one's ski downhill." Exactly the same words could be
used to describe parachuting, as could also these sentences—
from the same article—in which I tried to describe the skier's
emotions as he successfully completed a schuss and ran out on
to the easier slopes below. "Your heart leaps with relief and

triumph; relief because you have escaped danger, triumph because you have forced yourself to do something from which your whole body instinctively shrank. Mind and will have conquered matter."

Mind and will have conquered matter. That is the real thrill of parachuting, a thrill which you never seem to lose however many times you have jumped. I have been told by instructors, some of whom had done over 100 jumps, that they still experienced—it was described in different ways—an attack of nerves, a definite uneasiness, a leaden feeling in the pit of the stomach, every time they parachuted. For though parachuting is not a brave thing to do, it is a very unnatural one. You sit in the aeroplane, battling against every normal instinct you possess. As the moment approaches and you get into position beside the aperture, you feel in your limbs a clumsy torpidity, an unwillingness to obey the orders from your brain. And then, suddenly, almost before you realise what is happening, you are out of the plane into the tremendous blast of the slipstream. You feel a great wind roaring in your ears, clutching at your arms, lifting your feet till they are almost horizontal with your head, blowing you irresistibly before it. The wind dies, there comes a great peace, and you look up to see the parachute open above your head, billowing slightly in the breeze. You hang there, going, it seems, neither up nor down. You have a view like that seen from a hill, but there, down below your feet, is nothing except the far-away earth and the insignificant figures who are your fellow men. You float thus, supported by nothing except the pliant, rustling silk of the canopy. You feel a great freedom, a great independence, there, between heaven and earth, as though you were some being whom the Lords of either world had overlooked and left free to live in this spacious No-Man's-Land.

But all this is an ideal rather than actual description of your feelings. The parachutist, especially the inexperienced one, is too busy, and perhaps too apprehensive, to abandon himself to these heady sensations. You have to get any twists out of your rigging lines, prevent your parachute oscillating, look to see in which direction you are drifting, and generally get ready for the landing. As you hang in the approved position you begin to realise that, though you have seemed stationary before, you are really dropping fast towards the earth. The speed of your descent seems to increase violently as you get lower and lower, till suddenly you touch down with your feet and roll with a thud on to your back and shoulders. Then you collapse your parachute and undo the harness.

You look up and realise that you have done the seemingly impossible: you have jumped out of the aeroplane which you can, perhaps, still see flying remote and other-worldly in the sky. You have had a strange and tremendous experience. I remember picking myself up after my first jump and realising that parachuting is one of those things which you either have experienced or you haven't. It is indescribable simply because it is unique. There is no other experience to which you can compare it; you cannot say it is like this or that, only much more wonderful. For this reason you cannot really evoke its sensations in those who have never experienced them.

After a parachute jump you feel a tremendous elation and self-confidence; they spring, not so much from the strange and tremendous experience you have had, as from the conquest of body and emotion by mind and will, from the fact that you have forced yourself to do something from which you instinctively shrank. And this elation and self-confidence are, perhaps, more complete after a parachute jump than after a schuss. This is partly because jumping from aeroplanes is more frightening than schussing, and partly because there are in parachuting no further dangers and difficulties to which you can aspire. Your elation after a schuss is always tinged by the thought that there are steeper slopes which you have never taken straight, slopes which, perhaps, you might have schussed if only you had had a little more courage. But it is not so with parachuting; each jump from an aeroplane is a complete and final act. You cannot increase your dangers and difficulties by flying higher, only by flying so low that the parachute has insufficient time to open, and that would obviously be a senseless thing to do. With parachuting it is all or nothing; either you jump out of the aeroplane or you don't. You are not haunted by the thought, which you get ski-ing, that you might have taken a steeper and more difficult schuss. When you land from a parachute jump you are free to wallow unreservedly in your self-satisfaction and your memories.

Your memories: they will remain. Later you will have to evoke them, but for some hours after a jump they will flash

vividly and unbidden across your mind, so that, as you are
engaged once more upon your humdrum daily tasks, you feel
the fear as you waited in the plane, the sudden rush of the
slipstream, the freedom as you floated so delicately in the sky.
Your jump, from the moment you left the plane till you reached
the ground, lasted less than a minute, but they were seconds
of packed emotion. It is the same with ski-ing. An expert
gets perhaps five minutes of downhill ski-ing in his day; it must
seem to many that they cost him a quite disproportionate
amount of his time, energies and money. But the skier does
not calculate his thrills by the time they endure, for he knows,
as the parachutist knows, that a few seconds' intense excitement
and struggle will colour his whole life and vitalise, by their
memories, many long days of drab monotony.

(*The British Ski Year Book*, 1945.)

MARY ROSE FITZGIBBON

*Mary FitzGibbon is one of the most experienced of our lady mountaineers.
She made the fifth ascent of Ryan's route on the Plan, and the third ascent
of Finzi's route on the Wetterhorn, two extremely severe expeditions.*

Rainbow Mountains

RAINBOW Mountains; they have been that for nearly six
years now, snowy Alps seen across a rainbow bridge of
memories between the old world and the new. But it is good to
know that in all the turmoil of the present the Wetterhorn still
sweeps up towards eternity from the meadows of Grindelwald
and that up on the Croix de Fer, above the Chalets of Chara-
millon in sight of the snows of Mont Blanc, the great trumpet
gentians will be blooming again this June, spreading their
carpet so thick that even a mountain goat could scarcely put
his foot between them. We have such vivid memories of our
Alpine holidays, we can go over them day by day almost hour
by hour. So let us get away from what Homer called the wide
mouth of bitter war for a while into the past; into a world of hot
sun and crystalline air, of green lakes fringed with red-roofed
chalets and flower-strewn pastures set against tall alpine trees.
Then high and far and incredibly beautiful the snow mountains

piling up to heaven peak upon peak and range upon range, filling us with an unbearable longing to be up there among the snows and the rocks, to know again the splendour of dawn and sunset high above the world, to live once more through all the wonder of an Alpine day.

It seems almost unbelievable now that we ever strolled down the Continental platform at Victoria to catch the four-thirty with half an hour to spare. A leisured journey with a breath of sea air to give you an appetite for dinner on the French train. Then there were the familiar landmarks of the journey. The Battersea Bridge Power Station, which to me—possibly quite wrongly—always seemed to be a poem in brick. The orchards of Kent. The delightful tangled mass of steel that the French call a railway engine. Then across the flat golden cornfields of Somme and Aisne, slipping past dark woods and little osier bordered streams, all covered with that gentle mystery which at morning and evening pervades the land of France. Somewhere in the night the train wheezes to a stop. It is Chalons or Chaumont. If you have the window shut it is too hot. If you have it open it is too cold. You try to sleep, but always you are thinking "To-morrow I shall see the snows."

Again there were those days on the way to the Alps. Days in Berne or Bâle or Grenoble. On one of them in Paris we started from André Wahl's bookshop through the dim glory of Notre-Dame across the Seine to look into the trays of old books along the Quais. Then to Fischbachers to add to our collection of guide books and maps of the Alps, and down the Rue St. Jacques browsing in the windows of the old shops. I know I have always regretted a set of what appeared to be First Empire fire-irons, and my friend who is given to having strange things about the house regrets a dog-kennel, or was it a bee-hive? It was a large rounded object painted in the Imperial Yellow of the Ming Emperors, adorned with Chinese motifs in a clear blue. The only place it could possibly have looked at home would have been Pillnitz, that fascinating Chinese-Baroque Schloss near Dresden, built when the Germans must have had some sense of humour.

Then those Swiss hotel rooms; the bare scrubbed floors, the blissfully comfortable bed, the inevitable table which you immediately cover with coils of climbing rope, spirit cookers, aluminium egg boxes, fat candles, glacier lanterns, all the necessary paraphernalia of the climber. In through the open window steals the scent of pines hot in the sun, and down from the pasture rings a carillon of cow-bells.

Ella Maillart says ". . . Happiness is the intoxication produced by the moment of poise between a satisfactory past and an immediate future rich with promise. . . ." If this is not an altogether satisfactory definition of that elusive state known as Happiness, it nevertheless describes very well one's feelings on an Alpine day.

In the Alps the day is bounded only by the old measures of time, sunrise, noon and sunset. Free as the birds from hours, you eat when you are hungry and towards evening you come down from the mountains. The artist cannot tell how his finished picture will turn out, neither can the poet his poem. To the mountaineer each day is a blank canvas to be filled with light and shade and colour, with laughter and friends and beauty and all the other things that the mountains have given him, the finished picture remaining always in his memory. It is not always a large canvas, nor yet the view from a high peak. More often it seems to be a joyous little vignette, or some human contact which is the central theme of the picture. You are so conscious everywhere of the exuberant life of the summer Alps. Even on the summit of a high peak there is no silence. The wind is singing in the rocks, or there are avalanches falling somewhere. The *choucas* intrude noisily after crusts or the luscious remains of sardine tins. It is all so alive you feel that like the glaciers the mountains are moving. On the glacier water is dripping, a piece of ice falls into the cool green depths with a hollow tinkling crash. Down on the pastures there is the sound of the torrent, the wind in the pines, a jangling of cow-bells.

But there is so much to remember. You can crowd so much living into a short Alpine day. Perhaps we have spent a day idling up to a hut, stopping under the last larch trees to make tea and to pick wild strawberries. We have greeted the cows on the pastures and crossed an Alpine lawn starred with the vivid beauty of tiny flowers and finally plodded up a steep dusty moraine to the hut near the edge of the snow. Between the making of tea and soup we go outside to look at the evening. It is already night in the valley far below but here the last light lingers on over the mountains. . . . Then comes the intangible pause of twilight, that moment between dusk and dark when the Earth seems to stand still, silently waiting for something— then slips suddenly into darkness.

And the morning. In the soft velvet of the Alpine night slowly we follow the lantern up the gravel of the moraine path. We go slowly because it is the hour at which life is at its lowest ebb, but presently we see grey shadows over the snow, the light grows quickly and our mountain looms ahead. Dawn amidst great peaks is not like a slow English dawn where the mists hang sleepily over the water meadows until the bird chorus awakens the sun. But high among the snows above the birds and the mists and the slow sounds of Earth, as the dark rim of the world turns swiftly into the sun, the morning bursts over the mountains in a shower of light and sparkle. The universe awakes to a new day and the amazing vitality of the Alps takes hold of us again.

All through the heat of the day we climb. We know the joy of sunbaked rocks hot to our touch, of the scrape of bootnails on granite slabs, the narrow snow arête and the feeling of achievement on reaching the summit of our peak. Then we go down to the welcome longer shadows of the afternoon, leaving the hot glacier for the flowers and the fresh coolness of the meadows, to descend to the valley through the tangle of the cow-bells and to the music of the grasshopper's singing.

And so at the far end of our rainbow bridge we see again the snows, faint on the horizon like summer clouds at evening; we see the surge of cornices cloud-curled, the beauty of the gleaming snow wind driven and frost riven, moulded, fluted, curved, hammered, beaten to an alchemy of wonder. There is a fairy tale which tells us that if we can only reach the foot of the rainbow there we will find a crock of gold, and so we cross our bridge of golden memories to find our mountains again, even though they may be cloud mountains, only seen in dreams.

ARNOLD LUNN

Farewell to Switzerland

I SLEPT that night at Brigue. It was May 13th, a turning point of the war, for it was on May 13th that the Germans broke through the extension of the Maginot line near Sedan.

On May 14th the French military attaché at Berne said to his British colleague, "We've lost the war." From dawn until sunset the Germans were massing troops and artillery along the Swiss frontier, in order to keep as many French divisions as possible on the Franco-Swiss frontier. On the night of May 13th-14th the German agents in Switzerland spread rumours to the effect that the Germans had already crossed the frontier, hoping to trap the French into an invasion which would provide the Germans with a pretext for "assisting" the Swiss to repel the French.

The Swiss were not deceived. On the contrary, they moved troops from the French to the German and Italian frontiers. I woke early to hear the rumble of army lorries on their way to the Simplon Pass. It was a glorious morning, and I left the hotel while the day was still young, and wandered up the village street to the great Benedictine church, and joined the worshippers at an early Mass, and prayed for England, and for my son John who was having his baptism of fire on the plains of Flanders.

I lunched at the Hotel du Lac Interlaken with Walter Hofmann. Walter loves England and his faith in victory had not been eroded by Nazi victories in Poland and Norway. But, like many people in Switzerland, he had not been to bed during the long and anxious night when an invasion was hourly expected. The strain had told, and he was feeling rather despondent. "If the Nazis come," he said, "I shall stay here and hope to be shot. I have been a free man all my life and it is too late to form new habits."

I left Walter after lunch and went for a last walk through Interlaken. I found a quiet corner and sat down. The Jungfrau was veiled but not hidden by transparent mist. There were still a few streaks of snow on "Plum Pudding Hill," and I knew that there would be gentians in Wengen and soldanella in the Blumental. The green meadows were powdered by snow-white blossom, but the scented manuscript of Spring and the chorus of mountain torrents in the fullness of their triumphant release from the prison of frost had lost their magic. I looked at the beloved Jungfrau showing through a dust of silver, and felt a stab of fear. If France collapsed, could England save Europe? And I knew that if Europe went down into the pit of Nazi slavery, and if Gauleiters were installed in Grindelwald and

Mürren and Interlaken, May torrents might still make music for the Germans, but not for me.

> Three parts of Spring's delightful things
> —Aye and for me the fourth part too—

would perish, if Switzerland died.

Walter came with me to the station. I climbed into a carriage labelled *Interlaken-Spiez-Thun-Bern-Basel*, and wondered whether I should ever find myself in a carriage labelled *Basel-Bern-Thun-Spiez-Interlaken*.

My last memory of Interlaken Ost is of Walter's disconsolate figure on the platform.

I was to spend my last night in Switzerland with Tony Torr at Berne. We were dining late at the Legation, and towards sunset I wandered along to the Terrace, from which I had so often greeted the Oberland on my arrival, and said good-bye to the mountains on leaving Switzerland. In the 'nineties there were no through trains to Interlaken, and we breakfasted at Berne on the outward and dined at Berne on the homeward journey. The ritual of the Terrace was never omitted from the Alpine *introit* or from the *De Profundis* of departure.

In those days the sorrow of parting was blunted by the knowledge that we should return, but no such consoling certitudes cheered me on May 14th, 1940. I was going back to a country which might be invaded, and to a London suburb which would almost certainly be bombed. I looked across the roofs and spires of Berne to the noble company of the Oberland, and realised that I might be seeing them for the last time.

In one's youth one thinks of death as something which happens to other people, and long after youth had faded into middle age I continued to plan my life on the tacit assumption that I should return to the Alps every winter as inevitably as the swallows go south. And as I looked at the Wetterhorn I reminded myself that even though I should, in all probability, survive the war and return to share the rejoicings of a liberated Switzerland, yet this poignant moment of parting was a salutary rehearsal of death, a foretaste of the ultimate and inescapable separation from the mountains, which I have loved this side of idolatry.

The setting sun worked its wonders on the distant snows, but there was no tranquillity in this hour of mountain peace. It was

THE WETTERHORN FROM ABOVE GRINDELWALD

Photo: R. Schudel, Grindelwald

THE VANGUARD OF FLOWERS
(Mürren in April. Eiger in the background)

Photo: Franz Roth, Interlaken

impossible to forget that the guns were thundering through
the gap near ill-fated Sedan. Thousands had died that Europe
might not die, but had they died in vain? Had the death rattle
of France begun?

The rose of sunset withered; the snows paled and colour
ebbed from the sky.

> Lo, thy great Empire chaos is restored-
> Light dies before thy uncreating word.
> Thy hand, dread Anarch, lets the curtain fall,
> And universal darkness buries all.

(Mountain Jubilee.)

Return from Exile

OF all approaches to Switzerland I love best the Les
Verrières approach. The gentle plain between folds of the
Jura and the long narrow limestone ravine are a fitting introduction to the moment when the train swings out on to the
curves above Neuchâtel, "and then . . . and then . . . beyond the
blue dominion of the lake and the green hills uncrested with
snow the power and the glory of the undiminished and im-
mutable heights." I remember thumping out those words on
my typewriter—the last of a book—in a merchant ship that was
battling its way across the Atlantic in a December gale. How
remote seemed the colour and calm beauty of the Alps from the
storm and fury of those submarine-infested seas! No Victorian
mountaineer, for whom the irreversible routine of the return to
Riffelalp or Grindelwald was as inevitable as the cycle of the
seasons, ever experienced our rapture of Paradise regained, for
the supreme felicities must be paid for in the currency of suffering. As indeed the Psalmist knew. "*For Thou, O God, hast proved
us: Thou hast tried us as silver is tried*," at Dunkirk. "*Thou
broughtest us into the net: Thou laidst affliction upon our loins*," when
France fell. "*Thou hast caused men to ride over our heads*" in
bombers. "*We went through fire*" in the Battle of London, "*and
through water*" in the Battle of the Atlantic, "*but Thou broughtest
us out into a wealthy place.*"

I hung out of the window awaiting the great moment—and
then it came. My eyes sought the horizon. The Oberland was
veiled in mist, but the long line of the limestone alps of Fribourg
carried the eye southwards to the Dent du Midi, the last snow-

17

covered peak which I saw in 1940, the first to welcome me back in 1945, and immediately below was a sweep of untroubled water, a mosaic of darker and lighter blues flecked by white sails. . . .

Neuchâtel—and never was the neat and orderly assurance of a Swiss town more striking than to eyes accustomed to the unpainted streets and bombed houses of heroic, battered London.

An hour later I sat down to my first dinner on Swiss soil, a dinner washed down by half a litre of Fendant, and at that moment I would not have bartered the authentic flavour of glacier and granite and snow-fed torrent, bottled and preserved in every honest bottle of Swiss wine, for the choicest vintages of Burgundy and Champagne.

On May 14th, 1940, I said good-bye to the Wetterhorn from the Terrace at Berne. The Germans were thundering through the gap at Sedan, and I wondered whether the Swiss flag would still be flying from the Bundeshaus if and when I returned to Switzerland.

The light mists which had veiled the Oberland peaks as the train swept out of the ravines of the Jura had thickened as we approached Berne, but though I had no hope of seeing the great peaks I decided to visit the Terrace before turning in for the night.

Many and many a time during the dragging years of exile I have wondered what context of place and time the fates would ordain for the first vision of the recovered Alps. Would I see them first from the curves above Neuchâtel? Or from the Terrace at Berne? Or would I arrive in rain and awaken next morning to see through the open windows the gleam of unclouded snows?

But I never foresaw that I should walk sadly towards the Terrace, expecting to see nothing but clouds beyond the roofs of Berne, only to be overwhelmed by the impact of unexpected revelation. . . .

Blümlisalp, Eiger, Mönch and Jungfrau, the peaks of terror and the peak of the dark Aar, and dearest of all dear mountains, the Wetterhorn.

The same and yet not the same as the mountains from which I had parted on May 14th, 1940, for it was difficult to believe that these phantom peaks, faint and spectral in the dissolving veils of diaphanous mist, were the same as those whose granite one had grasped and whose powdery snow one had furrowed with one's ski. I felt as if I were in the presence of the heavenly archetypes of the mountains we have known on earth, the divine originals which we shall see when we rejoin those friends who loved Switzerland and who died in those battles which saved these mountains from Nazi desecration.

Against the ebbing twilight I saw them, secure and untroubled. There they stood, serene and detached, untainted by the cruel and evil things against which we have been fighting, uncontaminated by the infection which still poisons the life of Europe. The hills stand round Jerusalem and the great Alps still tower above the tormented plains, and in their unshrinking splendour still bear witness to the eternal loveliness which man cannot mar and which time cannot corrupt.

"These the great Alps seen thus," writes Hilaire Belloc in *The Path to Rome*, "link one in some way to one's immortality. . . . Let me put it thus: that from the height of the Weissenstein I saw as it were my religion. . . . Since I could now see such a wonder and it could work such things in my mind, therefore some day I should be part of it. That is what I felt."

I SLEPT at the Belmont and left the hotel next morning at six, and climbed the wood path to the Prämisegg, and sat down on a little bench near the chalets. The plain-chant of the valley river, subdued and softened by distance, floated up through the thin air and mocked the flux of time. The ancient beauty of the mountains—*pulchritudo tam antiqua et tam nova*—"so old and yet so new" had suffered no corruption. I remembered battered London, and the fury of her war-tormented skies, and the friends who had fallen. No rumour of the glory and tragedy of war had troubled the serene quietude of the Jungfrau.

I do not know why one should instinctively expect the places which one loves to reflect one's own experiences, or why one should faintly resent their obstinate immutability, but there are many passages in literature in which this irrational emotion finds expression, as for instance in Mary Shelley's account of her return to the place where the Shelleys and Byron had spent a memorable summer beside the shores of Lake Geneva. Shelley was dead and Byron was dead, but there stood the Villa Chapuis, and the old boathouse, and the blue waters of the lake reflected no gleam from the light of past happiness and no shadow from the clouds of past sorrow.

The sound of cowbells disturbed this reverie. I turned to see five cows moving in stately procession across the crest of the "Nose-dive."

Man has lived on this little shelf above the Lauterbrunnen Valley for many centuries. Generation after generation has followed the ancient routine, seedtime and harvest, the ascent of the cows to the alps in June, the return to the lower levels in October. The true peasant, as Spengler somewhere says, has no history. During all these centuries the little shelf above the valley was untroubled by wars or rumours of wars. Mürren knew nothing of the outside world and the outside world knew nothing of Mürren. Clio, the Muse of history, passed Mürren by.

Clio, the Muse, first heard of Mürren when the mid-Victorians discovered this queer shelf suspended above the Lauterbrunnen Valley. First came Frederic Harrison, who worshipped humanity, and Addington Symonds, who worshipped the mountains, and Tennyson, who tried hard to worship God and who only succeeded in worshipping Tennyson. And the Alpine Clubmen began to climb the peaks and cross the passes in the great wall of rock and ice which towers above Mürren, and thereby endowed these chance irregularities of the earth's surface with a kind of shadowy personality, and the dead bones of granite and limestone "stood up, an exceeding great army," because the spirit of man had breathed upon this inanimate matter and exploited it for great adventure.

But the grassy humps across which the cows were passing meant nothing to Tennyson and nothing to Leslie Stephen. Even those visitors to Mürren who did not climb could probably have made from memory a recognisable sketch of the Eiger as seen from Mürren, but not one of them, I am very sure, could, on his return to England, have begun to trace on paper the outlines of "Nose-dive" and "Känelegg" and "Schiltgrat." Then came the skiers, a lighthearted company, very different from the serious-minded Victorian mountaineers, and the obscure hump, across which the cows had just ambled, emerged from the mists of anonymity and became famous as the "Nose-dive," first of a family which includes a "Nose-dive" in the Appalachians, five thousand miles from Mürren. And Clio, the

Muse, who is a bit of a snob, and who had resented the necessity to admit mountaineering achievements to the realm of history, began to suspect that she might yet be forced to recognise the existence of the skier, and Romance, which the mountaineer had wooed among the remote rocks, Romance which only deigned

to walk
With Death and Morning on the silver horns

came down "from yonder mountain height," and the obscure kingdom of the peaceful cow became the arena of ardent adventure. Of the famous peaks which I could see from the Prämisegg there was none which I had not climbed, but on the keyboard of memory these grassy slopes which witnessed the birth of downhill racing strike notes as dear to me as those of Jungfrau and Eiger.

I could just see Halfway House and the little path which leads from Shrub Slope to the station. And I thought of all those whom I have seen rattling down that little icy track to catch the train, Roger and David and Will and Carlow, and many others, a ghostly procession,

Who carry back straight to the coiner the mintage of Man,
The lads who will die in their glory and never be old.

"Our only consolation in 1940," writes a Swiss friend Herr Felix Meyer, "was to know that there were men who continued to fight for ultimate values, and that these fighters were Englishmen who risked their lives not only for their freedom but also for ours."

May God grant eternal rest to all those who will never return to the Switzerland which they loved and helped to save. *Requiem æternam dona eis, Domine, et lux perpetua luceat eis.*

(*The British Ski Year Book,* 1945.)

INDEX OF AUTHORS